W9-ALV-130

SCIENCE LESSONS

SCIENCE LESSONS

What the Business of Biotech Taught Me About Management

Gordon Binder

Philip Bashe

HARVARD BUSINESS PRESS

BOSTON, MASSACHUSETTS

Copyright 2008 Gordon Binder
All rights reserved
Printed in the United States of America
12 11 10 09 08 5 4 3 2 1

No part of this publication may be reproduced, stored in or introduced into a retrieval system, or transmitted, in any form, or by any means (electronic, mechanical, photocopying, recording, or otherwise), without the prior permission of the publisher. Requests for permission should be directed to permissions@hbsp.harvard.edu, or mailed to Permissions, Harvard Business School Publishing, 60 Harvard Way, Boston, Massachusetts 02163.

Library of Congress Cataloging-in-Publication Data
Binder, Gordon M., 1935–
   Science lessons : what the business of biotech taught me about
management / Gordon Binder, Philip Bashe.
      p. ; cm.
   ISBN 978-1-59139-861-5 (alk. paper)
   1. Binder, Gordon M., 1935– 2. Amgen Inc.—Management. 3.
Biotechnology industries—United States—Management. 4. Chief executive
officers—United States—Biography. I. Bashe, Philip. II. Title.
   [DNLM: 1. Binder, Gordon M., 1935– 2. Amgen Inc. 3.
Biotechnology—economics—Personal Narratives. 4.
Biotechnology—history—Personal Narratives. 5. History, 20th
Century—Personal Narratives. 6. Industry—Personal Narratives.
HD9999.B442 B612s 2008]
   HD9999.B444A443 2008
   338.7'6151092—dc22
   [B]   2007038583

The paper used in this publication meets the minimum requirements of the American National Standard for Information Sciences—Permanence of Paper for Printed Library Materials, ANSI Z39.48-1992.

Dedicated to my wife, Adele

—Gordon Binder

Contents

Introduction

HERE'S WHAT *NOT* TO say when a senior partner of San Francisco's most prominent law firm calls to recommend that you interview for the chief financial officer position at a fledgling outfit called Amgen.

"Amgen? What's Amgen?"

"It's a biotechnology company. We represent them."

I nearly blurted, "What's biotechnology?"—not an unreasonable question in 1982. The biotech industry, barely a decade old, had yet to market a single drug. My twenty years in the business world had been spent almost exclusively at major corporations like Litton Industries and Ford Motor Company. The comparatively small System Development Corporation (SDC), where I served as vice president of finance for ten years, supported a workforce of roughly four thousand.

Now, at age forty-six, did I really want to get involved in a start-up operation with only a few dozen employees and no products even remotely on the horizon? Probably not.

Except that I was newly unemployed, again, having had a company sold out from under me for the second time in twelve months.

In 1980 the board of directors of SDC's principal owner, a foundation, decided to unload the firm, which designed information technology and computer systems primarily for the U.S. military. The board's plan was to donate the proceeds to various universities and other worthy institutions and then shut down the foundation. As CFO, it fell to me to find a buyer and arrange the sale—rather like being asked to conduct your own funeral.

I wound up negotiating a deal with Burroughs Corporation for $100 million cash, one-third more than the board had projected. But I had no interest in staying and being downscaled to a Burroughs division controller. Nor were my wife, Adele, and I eager to uproot our two young sons and move from Los Angeles to Detroit, the business machine giant's headquarters. We'd lived there during the first five years of our marriage, when I was a unit controller at Ford. We had nothing against Michigan, but it wasn't for us, a couple of native Southwesterners. Thus, by closing the transaction with Burroughs—handshakes all around—I was in effect laying myself off.

Then United Geophysical Corporation (UGC), the world's leading oil-exploration company, promptly hired me. Its parent company, Bendix, had recently tried to sell the division but couldn't find anyone willing to meet its price. Then investment firm Lehman Brothers stepped in to propose taking UGC public. Bendix, a manufacturer of automotive and aircraft parts, agreed.

There was no better news as far as I was concerned. Finally I would have the opportunity to realize a goal I'd set when I was a graduate student at Harvard Business School: to be chief financial officer of a company listed on the New York Stock Exchange. In short order, a board of directors was assembled and a preliminary draft of the public-offering prospectus was written.

However, news of our impending initial public offering (IPO) rekindled interest from one of the prospective suitors that had come courting only months before. Suddenly the company doubled its bid, matching Lehman's IPO price. You can probably guess the rest: Bendix took the money, and once more I found myself out of work.

But not for long. Unbeknown to me, Ed Huddleson, of Amgen's primary law firm, heard about what had happened. Huddleson, a former trustee of the foundation that had owned System Development Corporation, apparently had been impressed by my handling of the sale to Burroughs. He took it upon himself to play matchmaker by pitching me to Amgen's chief executive officer, George Rathmann, who was seeking to hire his first CFO. I knew next to nothing about the young biotech firm, but I greatly respected Huddleson's opinion. If he thought that Amgen and I would prove a comfortable fit, that was good enough for me.

I drove out for an interview at company headquarters in Thousand Oaks, California, about an hour west of Los Angeles. Nestled in the scenic Conejo Valley, the developing city had to be one of the prettiest in the state. It still is, its sparkling wide streets lined with stately oak trees and rimmed by rolling foothills and rugged mountains.

In contrast, Amgen's offices on Oak Terrace Lane were, to be kind, on the plain side: eight thousand square feet of space in a lonely single-story concrete building set in a mostly barren industrial park just off the Ventura Freeway. There were three other tenants, one of them the Continental Ministries traveling evangelical choir. I noticed their road-weary bus convalescing out front.

George Rathmann, a PhD in physical chemistry, exuded almost a ministerial zeal as he talked animatedly about biotechnology's vast potential to create revolutionary new drugs. I'd read up on the nascent field in preparation for the interview, so I was already intrigued. But when George offered me the position following a second meeting, I explained that I needed to discuss the matter with my wife before I could give him an answer.

A stall tactic for negotiating a higher salary? Only in part. Adele and I had been married since almost the beginning of my career, and

I had relied heavily on her advice many times. This was a decision that needed to be made jointly.

The two of us talked it over after dinner. The salary represented a sizable cut from what I had been earning. We were comfortable enough, though, to ride out the reduction in pay. Much of the compensation would take the form of stock options, a standard practice for a promising but risky new venture. Those shares might one day turn into the proverbial pot of gold at the end of the rainbow. Or we could be left clutching a worthless piece of paper—as countless starry-eyed victims of the dot-com collapse of the 2000s know well.

After we volleyed the pros and cons back and forth, Adele said, "Gordon, I think you should do it. If it goes belly up, you can always look for a new job."

"And who knows?" she added. "Maybe it will turn into something really big."

REALLY, REALLY BIG

That it did, by any standard, albeit at the glacial pace typical of biotech success stories. Nine years—no, that's not a typo—passed before Amgen brought its first therapeutic product to market: epoetin alfa, sold under the brand name Epogen.

EPO, as it's called for short, is a genetically engineered version of the hormone erythropoietin (pronounced *ee-rith-row-poy-i-tin*). I explain genetic engineering in depth later. (I know: you signed on for a book about business practices, not science. You can relax. These concepts aren't difficult to understand, even if you dozed through high school biology.) But for now, genetic engineering is a process for creating and mass-producing copies of natural substances that activate or suppress certain biological functions. Hormones, for instance, travel the bloodstream, bearing chemical messages for various organs.

A healthy person's kidneys release erythropoietin into the circulation for delivery to the spongy bone marrow inside our long bones.

Marrow is the factory for the three primary components of blood: red cells, white cells, and platelet cells. Erythropoietin stimulates the production of red cells, which carry out the vital task of transporting oxygen from the lungs to every cell. Your body depends on oxygen for energy.

More than four hundred thousand men, women, and children in the United States suffer from irreversible kidney failure, or end-stage renal disease (ESRD). Their damaged kidneys cannot manufacture enough erythropoietin. Until the introduction of Epogen in 1989, ESRD patients regularly experienced debilitating exhaustion from severe chronic anemia: a deficiency of red cells and consequently of oxygen. The condition often closed the door on their ability to work or to be as active as they'd once been.

Epoetin alfa returns anemics' red-cell levels to a nearly normal range within a matter of weeks. It is no exaggeration to say that the drug has given millions of folks back their lives and livelihoods.

By the time EPO received approval from the U.S. Food and Drug Administration (FDA), the government agency charged with regulating all medicines, George Rathmann had retired and I was in my first year as Amgen's CEO. The company finished fiscal 1988 $8.1 million in the red. But with Epogen's much-anticipated arrival, we netted $19.1 million in 1989 and $34.3 million the next year, on total revenues of $199.1 million and $381.2 million, respectively.

In 1991 Amgen launched its second human therapeutic: filgrastim (Neupogen), EPO's biologic cousin. Neupogen, too, exerts a stimulatory effect on bone marrow, stepping up its output of a type of white blood cell called neutrophils (*noo-trow-fills*). For cancer patients undergoing chemotherapy, this can spell the difference between life and death. The toxic anticancer drugs destroy malignant cells, but one of their adverse side effects is to decimate the population of healthy neutrophils, the immune system's foot soldiers against infection.

Should the blood's concentration of neutrophils fall perilously low, chemo may have to be postponed or the dose reduced. While the patient, her family, and her doctor wait anxiously for the white count to rebound, the delay affords cancer cells lurking in the body an opportunity to proliferate unchallenged. What's more, men and women whose immunity is compromised are susceptible to potentially fatal bacteria. By stabilizing neutrophil levels, Neupogen enables cancer patients to receive the most effective dose of tumor-killing medicine, on schedule.

Nearly two decades later, Epogen and Neupogen remain the best-selling biologic agents in history. Each has earned additional applications, known as *indications* in FDA parlance. EPO is now used to treat anemia triggered by the human immunodeficiency virus (HIV), cancer, chemo, or surgery, and Neupogen's patient population has expanded to encompass people with HIV, myelodysplastic syndrome (MDS), and low neutrophil counts brought about by certain medications.

Between 1988 and 2000, the year I retired, Amgen grew into the largest and most successful biotechnology company in the world, far outdistancing all but a handful of competitors. Our financials ascended so sharply that you could strain your neck trying to follow the trajectory on a line graph. Accordingly, I've confined them to table I-1. Putting these figures in perspective, bear in mind that in my final full year as CEO and chairman, when Amgen earned $1.1 billion in net income and $3.6 billion in total revenues, the biotech industry as a whole *lost* $5 billion, a reflection of the approximately $500 million it costs to deliver a single biologic drug to patients.

Such consistent growth enabled Amgen to establish itself as one of Wall Street's top performers of the 1990s. The company debuted on the NASDAQ stock exchange on June 17, 1983. Considering that Amgen didn't have any products at the time, going public seemed premature to some observers. And it was; an IPO wasn't in the original timetable at all. But our other sources of capital had shriveled up like foliage during Southern California's dry season, leaving an initial public offering our only option.

TABLE I-1

Amgen financials, 1988–2000

Year	Profit/Loss	Revenue
1988	- $8.1 million	$19.1 million
1989	+ $19.1 million	$199.1 million
1990	+ $34.3 million	$381.2 million
1991	+ $97.9 million	$682 million
1992	+ $357.6 million	$1.1 billion
1993	+ $383.3 million	$1.4 billion
1994	+ $319.7 million	$1.6 billion
1995	+ $537.7 million	$1.9 billion
1996	+ $679.8 million	$2.2 billion
1997	+ $644.3 million	$2.4 billion
1998	+ $863.2 million	$2.7 billion
1999	+ $1.1 billion	$3.3 billion
2000	+ $1.1 billion	$3.6 billion

The IPO tossed us a $43 million life preserver, enough to keep Amgen afloat until our medical research started producing results. If you'd purchased one hundred shares that day, at $18 per, by 2000 your original $1,800 investment would have been worth eighty times that, roughly $150,000.

Twenty-five years have passed since I first pulled up to that nondescript white building on Oak Terrace Lane. It's still there, by the way, but now it's dwarfed by more than forty other structures on Amgen's sprawling 100-acre campus. The staff, in Thousand Oaks and at nearly sixty other facilities in the United States and overseas, numbers close to seventeen thousand.

Naturally it's a tremendous source of pride to have had a hand in nurturing the first *Fortune* 500 company to emerge from an industry that, like Amgen, was in its infancy. More than 300 million people have benefited from the roughly 130 genetically engineered drugs and vaccines licensed thus far for public use. But because the gestation period for new biotech medicines is long—it takes nine to twelve years, on average, to run the gauntlet of scientifically rigorous tests that must be passed in order to win FDA licensing—only now is this revolution in health care coming of age. Currently, there are seven hundred drugs at various stages of development, or "in the pipeline." Fully half the candidates are descendants of biotechnology. All told, they target more than two hundred medical conditions, including many that have proved resistant to conventional pharmaceuticals.

WHAT THIS BOOK IS—AND ISN'T

Writing a memoir seems to be as expected of retired CEOs as perpetual rounds of golf. (It might seem heretical, but for the record, I don't play golf; I'm a tennis buff.) I wasn't interested in adding to the clutter of books in which former corporate executives declaim one boardroom epic after another, as if regaling colleagues over a glass of sherry at the hunt club. I've read only a few titles from the genre, usually when I'm stranded in an airport or on a long flight. But I generally come away with the impression that little effort is made to clarify for readers lessons they can extrapolate and integrate into their own businesses, divisions, or departments, however large or small.

Science Lessons is not primarily a company history, nor is it my life story. My purpose in taking you behind the scenes is to highlight real-life examples of the guiding principles and management techniques that contributed greatly to Amgen's success. Amgen was and is a unique place. We did things differently from most businesses, beginning with our decision to let research and development lead the way. The strongest science determined which products we pursued, as opposed to the conventional method of targeting a desirable market—say, diabetics or people disabled by painful rheumatoid arthritis—and then trying to come up with a drug or device that might benefit them. You can be fairly successful that way, but will your company establish itself as a true innovator? Probably not.

Although the story is set in the pioneering days of biotechnology, I'm confident that you'll find the advice in these pages to be both practical and universal, helping you sharpen your managerial and leadership skills no matter what field you're in.

AMGEN'S SECRET WEAPON

From the beginning, Amgen was a magnet for gifted, innovative men and women. How does an organization attract outstanding employees? Not to sound glib, but it does that by being a place where good people want to work. Five years in a row, magazines such as *Fortune, Working Mother,* and *Industry Week* named Amgen one of America's best companies to work for.

Certainly we offered attractive salaries and benefits, and the stock options made available to every Amgen employee no doubt induced some folks to stay who otherwise might have sought opportunities elsewhere. As numerous studies have established, however, pay and perks aren't what foster long-term employee loyalty. It's something more profound, something that speaks to the very soul of a company.

In 1994, as Amgen approached its fifteenth anniversary, we set out to put into words the qualities that made it special. For years our people had contended that much of the organization's success could be attributed to its culture. Because a company's culture emerges from its values, we interviewed hundreds of staff members in all areas of Amgen to learn which values they believed constituted the core of that culture.

Today it seems that every company under the sun (or under a cloud) has a values statement. Some are written by the CEO, and others are concocted by the public relations or human resource department. Sometimes they're written by consultants who don't even work there. More often than not, the statement doesn't truly reflect the organization's values; it's either a wish list of what the company aspires to be or a PR tool for impressing customers, suppliers, and investors.

Our project was as simple as it was unusual: define Amgen by defining the values that had shaped it over the past decade and a half. Personally, I'd hoped that we would end up with five values on the list. Why five? No particular reason, other than it just seemed like a number that would be easy to remember. In the end, there were exactly eight. Many people, both inside and outside the company, considered the Amgen values our secret weapon (see "Amgen Values").

As you will see throughout this book, operating on the basis of clearly understood and accepted values has many advantages. When these concepts permeate all levels of the company—helping guide personal behavior, decision making, and daily interactions with colleagues—your people are better equipped to manage themselves, with less need for supervision. In a crisis, they're more likely to know instinctively the right thing to do, as compared with people workng for a company whose values have not been articulated or are not universally shared.

Here's an example of what I mean: people suffering from end-stage renal disease must have their blood cleansed through an outpatient procedure called hemodialysis three times a week. A dialysis machine filters out waste products and other toxins and then returns the blood to the patient by way of a tube inserted into a vein in the arm. Without these treatments, the poisons build up in the circulation, eventually bringing about mass organ failure and death. For most men and women on hemodialysis who use Epogen, the drug is injected into the tube.

In the 1990s, a hurricane demolished a kidney dialysis center in Florida. Most of its clients were elderly people, who would now have to travel to other dialysis centers. The local Amgen representative, hearing that many roads were impassable because of flooding and downed trees, took it upon himself to hastily charter a bus. He called the head of the center and told him to notify everyone to report for dialysis as scheduled. Amgen would take them to and from treatment

Amgen Values

Following are the eight Amgen values, together with a brief clarification of each, extracted verbatim from a pamphlet we gave to all employees.

Be Science Based

Our success depends on superior scientific innovation, integrity, and continuous improvement in all aspects of our business through the application of the scientific method. We see the scientific method as a multistep process that includes designing the right experiment, collecting and analyzing data, and rational decision making. It is not subjective or emotional but rather a logical, open, and rational process. Applying the scientific method in all parts of the organization is expected and highly valued.

Compete Intensely and Win

We compete against time, past performance, and industry rivals to rapidly achieve high-quality results. Winning requires taking risks. We cannot be lulled into complacency by previous achievements. Though we compete intensely, we maintain high ethical standards and demand integrity in our dealings with competitors, customers, partners, and each other.

Create Value for Patients, Staff, and Stockholders

We provide value by focusing on the needs of patients. Amgen creates a work environment that provides opportunities for staff members to reach their full potential. We strive to provide stockholders with superior long-term returns while balancing the needs of patients, staff, and stockholders.

Work in Teams

Our teams work quickly to move scientific breakthroughs from the lab through the clinic to the marketplace and to support other aspects of our business. Diverse teams working together generate the best decisions for patients, staff, and stockholders. Our team structure provides opportunities for Amgen staff to impact the direction of the organization, to gain a broader perspective about other functions within Amgen, and to reach their full potential.

Collaborate, Communicate, and Build Consensus

Leaders at Amgen seek input and involve key stakeholders in important decisions. In gathering input, strong leaders will welcome diverse opinions, conflicting views, and open dialogue for serious consideration. They will clearly communicate decisions and rationale openly and in a timely manner. Once a decision is made, the leader and members of the team will all be accountable for the results and for implementing the decision rapidly.

Trust and Respect One Another

Every job at Amgen is important, and every Amgen staff member is important. We attract diverse, capable, and committed people and provide an environment that fosters inclusion, respect, and individual responsibility and that values diversity. Trust is strengthened through personal initiative and by obtaining quality results rapidly.

Ensure Quality

Quality is a cornerstone of all of our activities. We seek the highest-quality information, decisions, and people. We produce high-quality products and services. Quality is woven into the fabric of everything we do.

Be Ethical

We are relentless in applying the highest ethical standards to our products, services, and communications.

A number of principles evolved naturally from the eight values. Among the most important of these are the following:

- Employees must have the freedom to make mistakes.

- A manager's primary function is to help staff members do their jobs; it is not a staff member's primary function to help the boss do his or her job.

- The people who do the work should help plan the work.

- Every rule, policy, and procedure has exceptions.

- Have fun! (Most of the time.)

at no cost. Only after he'd made all the arrangements did the rep have time to tell his supervisor about the situation and his response. Under the circumstances, there was no need for him to obtain permission in advance; the Amgen values made the appropriate decision obvious.

An executive who was fairly new to the company heard the story and remarked to me, aghast, "Boy, Amgen is really out of control! Can you imagine a guy doing something like that without first getting his boss's approval? A sales rep has no authority to charter buses!"

I replied, "I can't imagine anybody *not* chartering the bus first."

He gave me a dumbfounded look. Then the light bulb flickered on. He realized that Amgen was a different kind of place. Hewlett-Packard, IBM, and a few other outstanding companies ran this way, but they were a minority. Given the benefits—superior management, lower cost—it's a mystery to me why more organizations don't adopt a values-driven approach.

Given an expanding global economy, faster communication, and an endless parade of technological advances, the business climate is increasingly subject to volatility. Companies must keep watch on the horizon and respond quickly and intelligently, or else they will fall behind their competitors. It's difficult to compete if your organization is so intricately structured that it lumbers along even in its highest gear.

As Amgen grew exponentially, we constantly wrestled with the same quandary that confronts most flourishing companies at some point: how to remain nimble when you're no longer a small start-up. You do it by decentralizing power, of course, but also by establishing an entrepreneurial culture that embraces change and encourages innovation. For that to happen, management must empower its people and then support them 100 percent, because staffers do not offer ideas freely if they secretly believe they will be hung out to dry should their promising project flop. In an industry such as biotechnology, failures abound. Had Amgen not lived its principle "Employees must have the freedom to make mistakes," we would not have survived.

Although I'm not a fan of the New York Yankees, they epitomize an organization self-governed in part by values. When I was growing up in Alamogordo, New Mexico, the franchise was often compared to industrial colossi like U.S. Steel and General Motors for the way its members carried themselves, not to mention the businesslike manner in which the team dismantled opponents. From 1949 through 1964, only twice did the Bronx Bombers fail to take center stage in the World Series.

Yankees managers, then and now, have rarely had to assume the role of strict disciplinarians. It wasn't that the players didn't enjoy the nightlife, as young professional athletes are prone to do. But if someone's carousing got out of hand to the point that it adversely affected his performance, his teammates could be counted on to confront him and growl, "Don't mess with my World Series money!" This was before athletes commanded higher salaries than most CEOs, so the extra thousands in their Series checks were a windfall. Rarely did the skipper have to intervene.

I've always been fascinated by the inner workings of companies. When you think about it, a business is much like a living, breathing entity, experiencing constant change. How are some corporations able to achieve success year after year? Does the company mold its personnel, or is it the other way around? I say it's a bit of both.

When hiring, an organization with consistent internal values selects candidates that possess similar traits. However, it can also afford to take chances now and then on gifted people who may not be completely compatible with the corporation's values. Returning to baseball for a moment, look at the Yankees of the late 1990s and the early 2000s. Why was it that they were able to sign stars saddled with reputations as troublemakers, egotists, malingerers—you name it—and yet almost from the start they adapted and became model citizens? It was the combination of a proud tradition as the sport's preeminent franchise, continued excellence on the field, the quiet but firm dugout presence of manager Joe Torre, and the self-discipline that came from a teamwide desire to be part of a winner.

I'd like to think of Amgen as being the New York Yankees of its field—although if using that analogy means casting me as Yankees' owner George Steinbrenner, I will have to reconsider.

1

The Start of a Start-Up

IF I ASKED YOU to reel off the names of the most successful executives of the past twenty years and describe their individual traits, probably no two profiles would be exactly alike. The extroverted and the introverted, the micromanager and the delegator, the personable and the borderline misanthropic—any one of them can be ideally suited to run a particular company or department. The success of executives depends largely on external factors, such as the caliber of the people around them and the stage of the organization's development. As the old saying goes, horses for courses.

In the setting of a start-up operation, I can think of no one better qualified than my predecessor, George Rathmann, first CEO of Amgen. The group of venture capitalists and scientists who decided to enter the biotechnology sweepstakes under the name Applied Molecular Genetics—AMGen, as it was first known—certainly thought he was the one.

But I'm getting ahead of myself. Let's go back to the conception of Amgen. In 1978 William K. Bowes Jr., a fifty-one-year-old former investment banker, stepped down from the board of Cetus Corporation, the world's first biotechnology company. Bowes had grown increasingly frustrated with the seven-year-old firm, feeling that it had drifted off course. Over the next year or so, he began to consider what he calls a "half-baked idea" to launch a similar enterprise. Some half-baked idea.

The Bay Area native canvassed local universities for a scientist who would be interested in collaborating with him. His search took him to his alma mater, Stanford University, where a friend referred him to Winston A. Salser, a molecular biologist and physicist at the University of California at Los Angeles (UCLA) with a pedigree in genetic engineering. Over drinks, the two discussed the climate in the biotech industry and whether or not they should go forward. Perhaps the young field was already too crowded. By the end of the evening, though, they'd concluded that at least a few opportunities remained and shook hands on their new venture.

Salser's first task was to assemble a formidable scientific advisory board composed of biologists from leading California universities, while Bill reeled in investors. First to come on board were silver-haired Franklin P. "Pitch" Johnson Jr. and Raymond Baddour. Johnson, a former classmate of Bowes's at both Stanford and Harvard Business School, had founded a California investment firm called Asset Management in 1965 and had been instrumental in assisting a number of fledgling companies. Baddour, a professor of chemical engineering at the Massachusetts Institute of Technology, lent the new venture the invaluable asset of academic credibility. He would sit on Amgen's board of directors for sixteen years; Pitch Johnson, for twenty-seven. Both men imparted much valuable advice during my time as Amgen's CEO.

All told, Bowes coaxed six venture capitalists into putting up roughly $81,000 apiece in seed money. For one of them, Moshe Alafi, Amgen marked his third biotech undertaking. The prolific

Alafi had been an early chairman of Cetus. Like Bill, he'd lost confidence in the company's direction and left the board. In 1978 Alafi had cofounded Biogen—only the third biotechnology firm in the world and the first on the East Coast.

Applied Molecular Genetics was incorporated on April 8, 1980. The next step: hire a chief executive. Winston Salser suggested Rathmann, then the head of Abbott Laboratories' diagnostics division. George, with a PhD in physical chemistry, had come to the pharmaceutical giant from Litton Industries in 1975 and was instrumental in transforming what had been a lackluster division into the industry leader.

Ordinarily, Rathmann might not have been Salser's first choice, given that Abbott had no genetic-engineering program. But an Abbott colleague had piqued George's interest in biotechnology, telling him about the exciting advances being pioneered by a professor at UCLA's Molecular Biology Institute. The prof's name? Winston Salser. In a fortuitous coincidence, Rathmann wangled a six-month sabbatical in Salser's lab so that he could immerse himself in this new science. How he got Abbott to agree to the leave of absence, I'll never know. Universities may do that for faculty, but companies? Rarely.

George returned to Chicago awed by biotechnology's potential. "I could see that it was going to move ahead very rapidly," he recalls. At about the same time, Salser was telling his Amgen colleagues about the dynamic Abbott executive his laboratory had recently hosted.

Bill Bowes placed the first of many calls offering Rathmann the chief executive position. Amgen courted him throughout the spring and summer. He was suitably impressed by the company's powerhouse scientific advisory board and, most of all, by its commitment to solid science. "I remember Bill emphasizing to me, 'We're out to build a great company, not just a great stock,'" says George. "Those were convincing words." Sincere, too. Bowes's mother had been a doctor. To him, biotechnology wasn't merely another investment opportunity; he was excited by the prospect of making a lasting contribution to medicine.

The main reason it took six months to pry Rathmann away from Abbott was that he and his wife, Joy, felt the same way about the prospect of moving to California that Adele and I felt about Michigan. They hated it. Except for George's four years at New Jersey's Princeton University (where it wasn't unusual to spot Albert Einstein or J. Robert Oppenheimer strolling across campus), he was a born-and-bred Midwesterner: raised in Wisconsin, attended Northwestern University in Illinois, and logged twenty-one years at Minnesota's 3M, originally as a plastics researcher. The Rathmanns lived with their five children in a magnificent lakeside home in a Chicago suburb and were understandably reluctant to move halfway across the country. Not to mention the fact that George was perfectly happy at Abbott Labs.

Had he ultimately decided to stay there, he still would have influenced the course of biotechnology, but in a different way. To this day, not one pharmaceutical company has created a biotech division, for reasons I examine later. When George told Abbott's CEO and president about Amgen's proposal, they countered by offering him his own biotech subsidiary.

Naturally, George was flattered. There was only one hitch: "They wanted to retain 52 percent of the stock," he explains. "In the end, I didn't think it would be as much fun as Amgen, because Mother Abbott would always be in control. I really wanted to be part of a truly independent effort." In October 1980 Rathmann relocated to Ventura, California, to become Amgen's chief executive officer and sole employee. Abbott Laboratories never did pursue genetically engineered therapeutics in any meaningful way.

Although George had successfully run a division, he'd never been in charge of an entire company. In fact, several Amgen board members initially voiced reservations about hiring him for that reason. "They'd also pointed out to me—quite clearly, too!—that someone who'd worked at two huge companies might not be effective in a small company," he recalls, laughing.

What the venture capitalists didn't fully appreciate was that Abbott and 3M, both founded at the beginning of the twentieth century, operated somewhat unconventionally for such large corporations. In the mid-1970s Abbott had decentralized its bureaucratic management structure, granting some division heads far-reaching authority.

3M, best known at the time for its many tape goods and a fast-growing business manufacturing health-care products, fostered a progressive multidisciplinary approach to management. "When you got into a division at 3M," George explains, "there were four key people: the president, the vice president of research, the head of marketing, and the finance guy. As a member of the management team, you were always discussing each of those aspects, which gave you an opportunity to think like a general manager."

At Amgen, Rathmann swiftly put to rest any lingering concerns about his never having directed a company. Though first and foremost a scientist, he displayed keen business instincts; and if he didn't know something, he learned it fast.

To me his greatest strengths were an infectious enthusiasm and a prodigious power of persuasion. In the biotech world, George is known as "Golden Throat." The nickname, though well deserved, doesn't do him justice, invoking the slick patter of a traveling medicine show huckster or the Gatling gun delivery of a used-car dealer straight out of central casting. That wasn't George's style at all.

To begin with, at six-feet-four and 250 well-muscled pounds, the burly, bearded Rathmann was an imposing presence. And although he is highly cerebral, he can tailor his explanations of genetic engineering to his audience, whether a conference room of molecular biologists or a prospective investor with no scientific background.

AMGEN'S ADVENTURES IN VENTURE
CAPITAL FUNDING

It's no coincidence that U.S. manufacturers produced all of the world's first twenty biotech drugs and continue to dominate the market, as they do in personal computers and software, semiconductors, and many other fields. In the late 1970s and early 1980s, the United States boasted the technology as well as a university system for conducting research—with the help of government grants—and for turning out future scientists. Most important, it possessed the enterprising spirit that to the rest of the world defines U.S. business, if not the United States itself. Neither the National Institutes of Health nor the major pharmaceutical manufacturers gave birth to biotechnology; it was comparatively tiny start-ups like Amgen, Genentech, and Biogen. That's unheard of in most other countries.

But then, our economic system was designed to encourage the financial risk taking that fuels innovation. U.S. entrepreneurs held a tremendous advantage over their foreign counterparts in that even an untested company might one day have the opportunity to earn millions of dollars by selling publicly traded stock. That possibility is largely what entices venture capitalists to lay the foundations for new businesses, when the risk of failure is greatest. In contrast, technologically advanced countries like Japan and Germany typically did not allow businesses to pursue this route until they had demonstrated profitability and stability.

When George Rathmann began searching for funding in the fall of 1980, the U.S. venture-capital market was emerging from years in the doldrums. The more favorable climate was stimulated, in part, by two recent legislative and regulatory reforms. First, Congress hacked the capital-gains tax rate from 50 percent to 28 percent, and then the U.S. Department of Labor removed the Employee Retirement Income Security Act as a barrier to venture investing. VC financing would soon soar, from less than $600 million in 1980 to $4.6 billion in 1986.

The average first-round investment in biotechnology firms was $1.1 million, the same as the average for all industries. Yet George set his sights on $15 million. Although he'd never approached venture capitalists before, he'd once served as a scientific consultant to a small start-up launched by friends in Minneapolis. The experience, though brief, left quite an impression. "I watched how venture capitalists operated," he explains. "They always seemed to argue that you didn't need as much money as you thought you needed, and they'd hint that there would be more money down the road. Except that when you came back to them for a second or third round, they'd make it very difficult. It creates this vicious cycle where the board members hold complete control of your company. And the weaker you are, the happier they are, because they're going to get bargain-bin prices."

Such circumstances force companies to perpetually chase the carrot on a stick. A progressively smaller carrot, too, because of a stage of VC financing called *down rounds*. Here, investors' shares of equity, or ownership interest in the corporation, come at a reduced price compared with previous rounds. During flush times, a down round is a scarlet letter that shouts failure and shoddy management. Though more acceptable in a sluggish economy, it's still considered a measure of last resort. For many of those early-stage investors whose equity has just been watered down like a cocktail at a cheap tavern, down rounds are abominations.

Rathmann Makes the A Round

George Rathmann rejected the conventional wisdom that a new business shouldn't procure too much venture capital, lest its founders' stakes become diluted to the point of irrelevance. "When Amgen started, there were plenty of silver-tongued people saying to me, 'Fifteen million dollars? You don't need fifteen million dollars! You should take four or five million. Then you can get the rest of it at a premium someday, because you'll have made some real progress.'"

George's skepticism about whether *someday* would ever materialize proved to be well founded.

Because investor interest was light at first, Amgen wisely decided to pursue institutional investors as well as corporations. The first person approached, oddly enough, was Kirk Raab, corporate group vice president at Abbott Laboratories, the company Rathmann had left for Amgen. Raab, soon to be named Abbott's president and chief financial officer, was a hard-charging, cigar-chewing salesman, not a scientist. Yet he was intrigued by genetic engineering, whereas most of his researchers harbored serious doubts about its value and safety.

By sheer dint of personality, Raab convinced a reluctant Abbott board of directors to sink $5 million into the new endeavor. Good thing they did, as much for their company's sake as for Amgen's: in 1990 Abbott sold its stock for $700 million, or 140 times its original investment. By then Raab was happily indulging his fascination with biotech as the CEO of Genentech, Amgen's prime competitor.

We always suspected that a second factor motivated Abbott's decision: the Illinois drugmaker secretly worried that this California upstart might encroach on its lucrative diagnostic division. By becoming Amgen's major shareholder and acquiring a seat on our board, the company could keep a hand in—and an eye on—things. Abbott attorney Robert Weist hopped on a plane to hand-deliver the $5 million check to his once and future colleague. (First, though, he made a photocopy of it for his children to play with.) Within the year, Weist joined Amgen as general counsel.

Next, Rathmann kindled interest from Tosco Corporation of Concord, California. The independent oil and energy company had determined that the future of the oil industry lay in hard, dark sedimentary rocks called shale. An organic substance in the rocks can be converted into medium-grade oil or gas. About three-fifths of the world's oil-shale resources happen to be found in the western United States. Unfortunately, the process to extract and refine this abundant fuel source is complicated and prohibitively expensive, as several major oil companies discovered in the wake of the oil crises of the 1970s.

Tosco put up $3.5 million, crossing its fingers that perhaps biotechnology could create bacteria capable of drawing out the necessary oil-making materials. The overly simplified explanation of this theory is that genetically engineered cells would ingest—but not digest—the shale's oil-making components, which could then be retrieved in the laboratory. Tosco did not require Amgen to be involved in researching and developing oil shale, and it didn't. To date, bioengineering has yet to yield any significant breakthroughs in oil shale. Nevertheless, the company made a tidy profit on its investment.

Amgen probably benefited from the fact that its first round coincided with a milestone in the history of genetic engineering. On October 14, 1980, Genentech became the first biotech company to enter the stock market. Its initial public offering stunned Wall Street—stunned everyone—by generating $35 million and tripling its stock price on the first day of trading. The four-year-old firm's successful IPO demonstrated to venture capitalists that an investment in biotech could achieve liquidity within the preferred timetable of four to six years even if the company hadn't made a product.

George, now with $8.5 million in hand, finally went after the venture capitalists who'd been straddling the fence. Having Abbott Laboratories in his corner proved to be a coup, because it validated Amgen's scientific goals and helped convince fence-sitters to declare themselves. Pitch Johnson and Bill Bowes, two of the original investors, contributed to the first round. Then the three of them went before New Court Partners and dazzled it into investing $3 million. New Court was something of an oddity: a cross between an old-fashioned family-run partnership and a modern investment firm. The $40 million fund was managed by the wealthy Rothschild clan and underwritten by institutional investors.

On January 23, 1981, Rathmann closed the A round with a record $19.4 million in financing. A quarter century later, that is still an astronomical sum, nearly four times the average investment of $5.3 million. Making the feat more remarkable still, Amgen consisted of only three people, including the CEO. Ordinarily, by the time of a first round, a new company has already tried out a prototype of its product in the lab. George, however, couldn't point to any products or patents, only a plan. No doubt the financiers who backed Amgen were swayed as much by his personal magnetism and professional stature as they were by the company's business prospects.

Believe me, that Golden Throat nickname wasn't hyperbolic in the least. Not that his presentation to prospective investors didn't require some fine-tuning. At the very first session, someone piped up, "What are sales going to be in five years?"

"*Zip!*" he replied matter-of-factly. "There can't possibly be any sales in just five years." The financiers zipped up their wallets.

Afterward, a perturbed Rathmann collared board member Bill Bowes. "They decided not to invest, and they were good candidates. How do you explain that?"

Bowes, always the diplomat, thought for a moment. "You shouldn't let it bother you, George," he began. "But ... the next time someone asks you what the projected sales are going to be in five years, you might come up with a better answer than 'zip.'"

"After that advice," Rathmann recalls, laughing, "I still made it clear that Amgen would not have any products to show for its first five years. But I added that by then the company's value would be ten times what it was when we started, based on a couple of projects that we believed could be launched within five years. Incorrectly, it would turn out. We were looking more at a ten-year plan, which was why it was so difficult to promise a significant rate of return."

Building the Staff

With $19.4 million in the bank, Amgen now sought to build a research and development staff. Having as CEO an exceptional scientist who'd managed scientists at two outstanding corporations for more than twenty-five years certainly helped. Rathmann's charm and genuine passion for biotechnology enabled him to recruit outstanding young scientists who might otherwise have turned up their noses at the company's unspectacular digs in sleepy Thousand Oaks.

Kirby Alton, an early hire, remembers his first impressions upon arriving for an interview in the summer of 1981. "There really wasn't anything there except for George"—sitting at a desk in a corner of the lobbyless office—"and a picture of a one-story building," says the microbiologist from Georgia. "It was an artist's rendering of what the laboratory then under construction was going to look like. But George Rathmann was such an impressive, unbelievably charismatic man, I immediately felt that if anybody could build a biotech company, he could. When George offered me a job as a research scientist over dinner at a local Holiday Inn, I accepted before he'd even spelled out the terms." Alton would spend eighteen years at Amgen, eventually ascending to senior vice president of development.

The company's seemingly firm financial footing was also appealing. "Nineteen million dollars? We thought that was going to last forever!" he exclaims with a laugh.

LESS THAN TWO YEARS LATER . . .

Did I mention that when I joined Amgen as its first chief financial officer in October 1982, the company was running out of money?

I knew that going in. During my first meeting with George Rathmann, he had been more than candid about the firm's need to generate capital, and quickly. At the pace it was spending money, Amgen could last perhaps through the following summer before its bank balance hit zero.

In most industries, such news probably would have generated panic. But in biotechnology, where the *burn rate*—the monthly cost of doing business—is appreciably hotter than in other industries, hemorrhaging money was standard operating procedure. Probably every biotech teetered on the brink of financial disaster at one time or another, locked as they all were in a long-distance race to discover a marketable drug before their funding ran out. Even today, three in four publicly traded biotech companies operate with less than eighteen months' capital.

Before my arrival, Amgen's finance department consisted of a certified public accountant in private practice who showed up twice a week just to keep a general ledger. It's not unusual for a start-up venture to wait a year or more before hiring a CFO. For one thing, when you're a small company that's still years away from even contemplating going public, how will you attract someone who is suitably experienced and won't be out of his depth when the enterprise begins expanding?

Frequently, a fledgling corporation brings in a chief financial officer at the very stage where Amgen now found itself: anxious to replenish its coffers. When George was selling me on joining the company, he'd observed, "You know, you'd have a great advantage over our other employees. You'd be betting on yourself to raise the money we need to stay in business, whereas everybody else would be betting their futures on a complete stranger." No pressure there, right?

Projections that the funds raised would carry Amgen through 1984 underestimated by about half a biotech R&D's insatiable appetite for money. At the end of 1982, our tank was already three-quarters empty, with roughly $5 million left.

The fierce burn rate was a concern throughout the industry, and not only at Amgen (see "Tick, Tick, Tick: Burn Rate"). In the 1980s, the average cost of bringing a genetically engineered drug to market ranged from $25 million to $75 million. A decade later, developing a comparable product exceeded $100 million. By then, companies had grown. Early projects may have been the work of a single research scientist and a handful of lab assistants; now it was common for project teams to consist of fifty or more people. The expense of con-

Tick, Tick, Tick: Burn Rate

To calculate a business's burn rate, look at its most recent form 10-Q, the quarterly financial report that all public companies must file with the federal Securities and Exchange Commission (SEC) three times a year. (No 10-Q follows the end of the fourth quarter, because that is when a company submits its annual report, or 10-K.)

For an estimate of its annual net loss, you multiply the business's quarterly net loss by 4. Next, total the available cash. Then divide the latter figure by the first number to see how long the company has until its last nickel runs out. You can make a number of adjustments—such as adding back noncash charges like depreciation—but the results don't change much.

Here's a quick example, using the imaginary 10-Q of fictitious toy retailer Woe Is Us:

- $8 million (quarterly net loss) × 4 = $32 million (annual net loss)

- Cash and other assets = $40 million

- 40 ÷ 32 = 1.25 years, or 15 months, before bankruptcy looms

structing laboratory space nearly doubled, to more than $500 per square foot. And a piece of equipment that used to run, say, $25,000 often exceeded $1 million.

Those figures cited for the average cost of developing a new drug don't take into account the largest expenditure of all: the millions poured into promising agents that never pan out. According to the Pharmaceutical Research and Manufacturers of America (PhRMA), the trade association for the country's leading pharmaceutical research and biotechnology companies, for every five thousand compounds that show promise in the laboratory and in animals, only five will advance to testing in human beings. Of those five hopefuls, only one will go on to win the blessing of the U.S. Food and Drug Administration and land on your pharmacy shelf.

When you factor in the cost of failures, as researchers at Tufts University did in a 2003 study of drug development costs, the total expenditures of each federally sanctioned medication—prior to approval—averaged $138 million in 1979, $318 million in 1991, and $802 million in 2003. Those numbers are somewhat inflated, because the researchers added interest for each year of research and development. A more appropriate figure would be in the vicinity of $500 million (without interest) per new medication—still an enormous outlay.

Drug Development Phases

In many businesses, the solution to the problem of high overhead is simple: cut overhead. Speed up production. But drug manufacturers don't set their own standards; the government does. Drugmakers are bound by the FDA drug-approval process, which requires extensive *preclinical* testing in the laboratory and in animals, followed by three phases of evaluations in patient volunteers. (In medicine, the word *clinical* denotes human involvement, whether it refers to investigational studies, diagnostic procedures, or treatments.) Later in this book I'll walk you through each stage, but briefly, a *clinical trial* is designed to answer various questions concerning a compound's safety and efficacy.

Table 1-1 outlines the three phases of clinical testing. The numbers of patients and the study duration are for a highly efficient drug company testing a best-case product—one that is safe and effective, with no anticipated problems. Many investigations require even more patients and take years longer.

Before clinical trials even begin, the company has invested three to five years in research, drug design, and preclinical testing.

TABLE 1-1

The three phases of clinical trial testing

Phase of testing	Attempts to answer these questions	Number of patients	Duration of study
Phase I	• At what dose is the drug safe, without producing unwanted side effects? • How should the drug be administered (orally, by injection, and so on)?	• 20 to 200 healthy volunteers	• 6 months to 1 year
Phase II	• Does the drug show evidence of being effective? • What is the correct dosage?	• 200 to 500 healthy volunteers and patients afflicted with the disease the drug is intended to treat or prevent	• 1 to 2 years
Phase III	• Does experimental data support substantial efficacy with high statistical significance? • Does long-term usage lead to any side effects?	• 300 to 5,000 or more patients with the same medical condition	• 2 to 3 years

Then tack on roughly one and a half years at the end of phase III to prepare the *new drug application* (NDA)—which can be as long as 500,000 pages—and then wait a year while the agency reviews it. All told, the path to commercial licensing takes eight to fourteen years. In the interest of public safety, there's no cutting corners, nor should there be.

Now here's the part about biotechnology—and drug development in general—that someone who thrives on predictability would probably find difficult to accept: when trying to create life-changing medications, especially for applications that haven't been tackled before, you can do everything "right"—couple the best science with hard work and impeccable execution—and yet the project may implode at any point, without warning, leaving you with nothing.

Pharmaceutical research and development presents the reverse challenge of R&D at, say, an engineering-based company. It's a more difficult challenge, too. In engineering, little doubt exists that a desired product can be created; the uncertainty lies in what it will cost and how many customers will buy it and at what price. In drug R&D, you know in advance that there's a need for the product and that the health-care system will pay for it at a reasonable price. The big question is, Can you do it? I believe that Amgen was much better than its competitors at R&D decision making, where there's a wide gap between capable management and poor management. You'll learn more about R&D management in chapter 3.

I liken the process to a marathon. Failure can come immediately out of the gate, during preclinical studies, or in a phase III clinical trial, with the finish line almost in sight. Early failures are relatively inexpensive, but late failures can be extraordinarily costly. Even after FDA approval is granted, a drug may have to be withdrawn from the market because of unanticipated side effects, and subsequent lawsuits can tally in the billions of dollars.

TIME FOR A SECOND ROUND—RIGHT?

There was a good reason Amgen was consuming capital at an alarming rate. As Bob Weist, our general counsel, points out, "We were making progress faster than was originally anticipated, which meant that we had to hire more employees sooner."

George Rathmann—keenly aware that companies like Genentech had a five-year head start (not to mention millions of dollars from its initial public offering)—wasted no time in trying to compete. "We had a lot of incentive to move rapidly," he reflects. "Genentech was gigantic compared to us. In fact, some people used to refer to the biotech industry in general as Snow White and the Seven Dwarfs—Snow White, of course, being Genentech. The pervasive feeling was that the rest of us were going to stay dwarfs forever unless we worked very hard, followed a sound strategy, and were blessed with some good luck."

When the need to raise additional money became painfully apparent, in the fall of 1982, George naturally assumed that it was time for a second round of venture capital. Biotech companies routinely returned to the same well for financial sustenance twice, three times, sometimes even a fourth time. A second round was typically expected to bring in $5 million to $14 million.

Rathmann turned to Frederick Frank of Lehman Brothers. Frank, a legendary name in the venture-capital and biotech worlds, has been an investment banker since 1958. After eleven years at Smith Barney (now Salomon Smith Barney), he moved to Lehman Brothers and has been there ever since.

George wanted to know how to initiate a successful second round.

"Oh, it's not hard," Fred said confidently. "You've got a great thing going here, George. Just ask your investors to offer one dollar for every four dollars they put up last time. Do that, and you'll have raised around five million, which should give the company breathing room for another couple of years."

Collaring the original financiers couldn't have been simpler, because four out of the five major VCs sat on our board: Pitch Johnson's Asset Management; Bill Bowes's company, U.S. Ventures; Kirk Raab of Abbott Laboratories; and New Court Partners' representative, Jim Blair. Tosco Corporation, not wanting to incur the liabilities that come with being a board member, had declined a seat. Of the four, Blair was the most vocal in expressing his concern about Amgen's burn rate.

Although Rathmann hadn't yet officially been declared chairman, he essentially functioned as one and therefore conducted board meetings. "We're going to run out of money in about eleven months," he announced at the November meeting. He then recounted Frank's one-dollar-for-every-four-dollars strategy.

According to George, "The room went *dead* quiet. Not a single venture capitalist had any appetite for putting more money into the company. I thought, 'Holy smoke!' It was extremely scary."

Now what? Try elsewhere? Not likely. If no first-round investors saw fit to reinvest, why would a newcomer? That was a tough sell then and a tough sell today. Scarier still was the board's ominous directive that it wanted to see a contingency plan at the first meeting of 1983. To us, *contingency plan* could mean only one thing: laying off scientists. There was virtually no one else to let go. Except for a couple of secretaries (George's doubled as head of human resources), the staff of fifty belonged almost entirely to research and development.

Rathmann summoned the four senior officers to his office: along with me, he called in Bob Weist, research director Dan Vapnek, and Noel Stebbing, an Englishman who'd defected from Genentech to become our vice president of scientific affairs.

"I will not accept any layoffs," George said firmly. "Not one. It would be the kiss of death." He explained that at one time, while he was at Abbott, budget cuts forced all divisions, including his, to dismiss employees. Rathmann reluctantly had to let some scientists go. The blow to morale was devastating. "Factory workers get laid off, not *scientists!*" Top researchers shunned the drugmaker's job offers for years afterward, and Rathmann vowed then that he would never again pink-slip R&D personnel.

He proposed that if the board insisted on staff cuts, all five of us would resign immediately. Now, this was hardly a room full of youthful radicals. But being part of a company that develops medications for enhancing or prolonging human life tends to revive one's idealism. We all nodded in agreement.

However, there was still the matter of presenting a contingency plan to the directors. "What if we take the company public?" I said. I'd been privately discussing the prospect with every senior investment banker I knew—all two of them: Lehman's Fred Frank and Bob Hotz of Smith Barney. Frank had pulled the strings for the second IPO by a biotechnology company, in March 1981, when the Bay Area firm Cetus Corporation raked in an unbelievable $107 million—still an all-time industry record. Both men said essentially the same thing: an IPO was possible, but only if the climate for IPOs improved.

How an IPO Works

The process of a company's going public makes for a fascinating study in human psychology. It's remarkable how investors, normally an analytical lot, can get swept up in often groundless euphoria over a business or field and lose all sense of reason.

Under the Securities Act of 1933, every company conducting a public offering is required to file a registration statement that discloses all pertinent information about its business, finances, and so on. Beyond that, it is strictly a case of buyer beware, as was demonstrated in gruesome fashion by the e-commerce feeding frenzy of the late 1990s and the subsequent indigestion brought on by the swift collapse of many dot-coms. Regardless of the industry involved, the story line usually plays out pretty much the same.

The cycle gets rolling when one strong company dares to test the waters. It boasts genuine prospects, solid management, and powerful investment bankers, and its public offering is reasonably successful. Next, another upper-tier business follows suit and then maybe another, forcing the IPO window of opportunity wide open. Eventually, all the big fish in what is a rather small pond get snapped up, and subsequent public offerings feature progressively weaker companies. Investors, intoxicated by the rapidly rising prices of the recent past, don't catch on until they hook some scrawny minnows represented by third-tier investment banks. When enough casualties have piled up, the cycle groans to a halt.

Here's an example: after Cetus Corporation's spectacularly successful IPO in March 1981, speculation ran wild about how many millions a Washington biotech firm called Genetic Systems Corporation would fetch in its offering, scheduled for April. One hundred ten million? One hundred fifty? More?

It wasn't even close. Genetic Systems hobbled away with $6 million, and a May public offering by Ribi Immunochem of Montana grossed a microscopic $1.8 million. The proceeds probably didn't last the summer. And with that—*thunk!*—the window slammed shut. Its reverberations lasted a year, which passed without any activity.

An IPO for Amgen?

Greed springs eternal, however, amnesia sets in, and before long the sequence revs up all over again. That's where we stood at the beginning of 1983: three respectable biotech public offerings in a row over the previous six months, a favorable sign. Biogen was due to step up to the plate next, in March.

Two other recent events boded well for the biotechnology industry in general: at the end of October, Genentech received FDA approval to market the world's first genetically engineered drug, Humulin, a synthetic form of the human hormone insulin. Men and women with type 1 diabetes inject themselves with Humulin to help prevent dangerously high levels of glucose, the body's principal fuel source, from building up in the bloodstream.

Then, four days into the new year, Congress passed the Orphan Drug Act of 1983, a law granting financial incentives to drug manufacturers to develop medications for treating less-common health problems. Given the enormous cost, drugmakers could expect to lose money on products aimed at these disorders, which the bill defined as any condition affecting fewer than two hundred thousand Americans. Consequently, whole groups of patients were being neglected, including those with such familiar disorders as muscular dystrophy, cystic fibrosis, Tourette's syndrome, and hemophilia. In all, six thousand ailments met the criteria for rare-disease status.

Makers of conventional drugs probably let out a mild hooray, but for the biotechnology field the new legislation was a godsend, because most of its early candidates were intended to take on orphan diseases.

With some trepidation, George Rathmann convened the Amgen board for the January meeting. The directors were eager to see the contingency plan they'd requested. They expected to hear about massive layoffs and other cost-cutting measures. Instead, I calmly informed them that our contingency plan was to enter the IPO on-deck circle and take Amgen public.

Had we been in a Warner Bros. cartoon, you would have heard crickets chirping. The board members looked at one another, perplexed. One of them finally broke the silence: "How can you possibly think of having a public offering?!" he spluttered. "You have nothing to brag about, no products even remotely approaching the marketplace!"

When I explained that the esteemed Fred Frank of Lehman Brothers felt that it was possible, the board members softened a bit. To their credit, they agreed to discuss the proposal again at the March meeting, with three provisos: that an investment banker had been lined up, that they were supplied with a specific plan and time line, and that the dreary economic climate had improved.

Luckily for us, the IPO market continued to recover, with Biogen commanding an exceptional $57.5 million the day it debuted on the NASDAQ exchange. The directors gave us the go-ahead we were looking for. They never did force us to implement those staff cuts; nor did they ever find out that Amgen's five senior managers had been fully prepared to walk if they had.

2

Amgen Goes Public

IT IS NO EXAGGERATION to say that Amgen's entire future hinged on a successful initial public offering. Fred Frank wanted to know how much capital we hoped to raise. "As much as possible!" I told him, recalling a nugget of wisdom dispensed by Bill Bowes. "I've heard of lots of companies that ran out of money," he once said, "but I've never heard of a company that ran out of stock certificates." Anything less than, say, $25 million would be too little to sustain us for a significant time or to impress Wall Street.

I'm going to walk you through Amgen's IPO. Maybe this isn't relevant to your career at the moment. But at some point, you might be a senior manager at a company about to embark on this route, and you'll be expected to pitch in. Even if you're not directly involved in the process, you certainly want to have a basic understanding of what's going on. After all, the outcome of a company's public offering affects every person who works there.

The freewheeling late 1990s painted a surrealistic picture of the IPO. Today's business-school graduates, lacking the historical perspective that comes with age, may not fully appreciate what an aberration those years were. No doubt many of them have read the seductive stories about self-promoting entrepreneurs charming investors out of millions of dollars and are crossing their fingers that history will repeat itself.

I wouldn't count on it, certainly not soon. In 1999, at the height of Wall Street's giddy infatuation with e-commerce and, to a lesser extent, the technology sector, 457 IPOs raised $69.2 billion in financing. During less hallucinatory times, a business usually was six or seven years old before it took the giant step of selling shares on a recognized stock exchange. You can subtract a few years if the firm is part of an emerging industry, as Amgen was. But in the mass delirium of the high-tech bubble, online media company theglobe.com commanded $27.9 million after four profitless years, and online pet-supplies store pets.com was still in the terrible twos when it raked in $82.5 million. Who could blame young people for starting to believe that an IPO bonanza was virtually one's birthright just for showing up at work?

On Friday, April 14, 2000, a 600-point free fall in the Dow Jones average abruptly ended the longest peacetime bull market in U.S. history. The NASDAQ composite index, which had been slipping since March, shed 355.61 points, its largest single-day descent on record. It was as though investors had sobered up after a long bender and took a close look at some of the companies they'd bedded during the past few years. When IPO activity is unusually high, as it was then, neither investors nor the investment banks overseeing the process (the underwriters) have adequate time to fully research the organizations and their management teams. Flaws, some of them significant, get overlooked: too much flab, too little going on upstairs, and so on.

In the less-forgiving light of Wall Street's new dawn—and minus the heat of the moment—hot prospects can turn out to perform dismally in the boardroom. More than five hundred e-commerce retailers were tossed on the corporate bone pile in 2000 and 2001. There was plenty of blame to go around for the dot-com debacle, starting with inexperienced executives who couldn't master even the rudiments of running a business—or were openly contemptuous of them. Fingers also must be pointed at the underwriting syndicates for championing these subpar companies, and at besotted investors for throwing money at them. Presumably everyone learned a lesson, because the next three years produced only 266 initial public offerings, about half the total in 1999 alone.

NO TIME TO LOSE

A successful initial public offering typically takes at least six months, and that's assuming the stars are all in alignment: a strong stock market and an organization with its house in order. Yet Amgen pushed its IPO through in half that time.

Why the rush? Simple: since Wall Street is subject to outside forces, you have no way of forecasting whether today's sunny conditions won't darken a month from now, closing the IPO window. Believe me, I know. In 1972, my second year as chief financial officer at System Development Corporation (SDC), the board of directors concluded that the time was right to take the company public. The gradual withdrawal of U.S. troops from Vietnam was nearing completion, and that was expected to jump-start the economy. An investment banking syndicate was promptly pulled together, the appropriate documents were filed with the Securities and Exchange Commission, and so on, until we were only two days away from the *effective date:* the day of an initial public offering.

Then, just before Christmas, President Richard Nixon ordered U.S. B-52s to resume bombing the North Vietnamese capital of Hanoi, ending a four-year lull. The turnaround in U.S. military policy sent Wall Street into a spin. Smith Barney, SDC's lead underwriter, was willing to go ahead with the offering; however, it cautioned that any undertaken at that time probably wouldn't be very successful. The board wisely decided to wait. And wait.

Although the resumption of bombing helped hasten the war's end in a matter of weeks, the United States entered its worst stock-market decline in more than thirty-five years. When six months passed with no revival in sight (it would take nearly two years just for the market to bottom out), SDC reassessed its strategy and elected to sell the company outright.

Mindful of how a military action halfway across the globe had torpedoed SDC's IPO forty-eight hours before showtime, I informed Amgen's lead investment bank, Smith Barney, that we intended to condense six months of preparation into three. When one of the outside attorneys handling the public offering read the schedule we drew up, he rumbled, "This is impossible!" His law firm was already shepherding five other IPOs the day it began working on ours.

"Sorry," I told him. "We're going to meet these dates, so you're going to have to meet them too. In fact, we're going to set a Guinness world record for the fastest initial public offering ever." As often happens when a challenge is dismissed as impossible, all deadlines were met, on both ends.

You don't want to sacrifice performance for speed, though, because filing inaccurate or incomplete documentation with the SEC constitutes a serious offense. Also, an unrealistically narrow timetable could lead to missed deadlines, forcing the IPO to be postponed. Will the window still be open by the time you get back on the calendar? Maybe, maybe not. Companies don't always appreciate the importance of timing when pursuing a public offering and go about their business as if they have all the time in the world. Even some veteran underwriters proceed at a leisurely pace unless management cracks the whip.

If your organization has been behaving like a public entity long before it registers with the SEC, you stand a good chance of sailing through the process with a minimum of ulcer-inducing moments. For instance, as soon as a company resolves to cross over from private to public, it should get right to work on the following, if it hasn't already:

- *Hire a chief financial officer.* Preferably, your CFO should be experienced in IPOs.

- *Develop relationships with seasoned underwriters, attorneys, and accountants.* Lehman Brothers' Fred Frank generously dispensed sage advice even though we threw in our lot with Smith Barney. The interest from the latter came about, in part, because I'd known its head of corporate financing, Bob Hotz, for years. Coincidentally, Hotz had been the underwriter for the ill-fated System Development Corporation public offering; the two of us had worked together closely and developed a lasting mutual trust and admiration. Otherwise, there's no telling whether Bob could have persuaded his colleagues to take on an unproved company like Amgen in such an uncertain IPO market.

- *Employ an outside accounting firm to audit the company for at least the past three years.* A business that neglects to get an independent audit rolling well in advance of filing with the SEC will not only incur needless expenses but also may be shocked to discover that company performance has been falling short of expectations. If the clock is ticking down, though, there's no time for improving matters.

- *If necessary, give your board of directors a makeover.* Under the Sarbanes-Oxley Act of 2002, an organization's board must be genuinely independent. Members may not accept any fees from the company or one of its subsidiaries for, say, consulting. Amgen, from its inception, always practiced exceptional corporate governance. For example, we wouldn't admit to the board anyone from a company that did business with Amgen, whether a bank, a law firm, or an advertising agency.

Realistically, are people who profit from an association with a company truly going to speak their minds or perhaps take issue with a position held by the CEO?

If the chief executive is secure enough to welcome opposing viewpoints—a trait of great leaders and consequently of great companies—it shouldn't be a concern. But the mere appearance of a possible conflict of interest is enough to undermine your business, and not only with federal regulators. Put yourself in an investor's shoes: would you feel confident purchasing stock in an organization whose board was stacked with the founder's relatives and old college roommates? I wouldn't.

A distinguished, autonomous board lends a company prestige. I can tell you that Amgen's initial public offering unquestionably benefited from the presence of well-respected academics and businessmen like Raymond Baddour and New Court Partners' Jim Blair. These men were offered more seats than an expectant mother on a crowded bus. Investors could therefore infer that Amgen must have something going for it; why else would folks of this caliber sit on its board?

- *Make sure that company policies concerning executive loans and stock-option plans conform to SEC regulations.* Sarbanes-Oxley prohibits publicly traded businesses from making certain personal loans to directors and executive officers. Before the offering, management should consult its legal department to learn which loan arrangements will be off-limits after the company arrives on Wall Street, and bring its practices into line.

Conducting business like a public company long before you become one instills invaluable discipline in managing earnings. It also affords you some breathing room should a problem crop up—which, in accordance with Murphy's Law, you can pretty much bank on.

Amgen's IPO pursuit was nearly derailed before we'd even left the station, and believe it or not, the hand throwing the switch belonged to one of our own directors.

Abbott Laboratories, you'll recall, bankrolled roughly one-quarter of our first venture-capital round in 1980, more than any other shareholder. At the time, the two companies signed a letter of agreement granting Abbott the right of first refusal on some Amgen products. The letter also stipulated that a definitive legal document spelling out the details would be drawn up at a later date. Well, it never was.

Now, two years later, we were on the eve of filing with the SEC, and Abbott's president, Kirk Raab—an Amgen board member!—said that he would sue if we didn't honor the letter. As per Abbott's interpretation, this entitled it to license any Amgen product merely by matching whatever terms we'd negotiated with another company.

Our position was simple: no! Amgen had been spending its own money on R&D and would continue to year after year. It was never the intent of the original agreement that Abbott could cherry-pick whichever products it fancied, including those not even conceived at the time of the signing. This is what we proposed: "If you want to exercise your right of first refusal, we'll give you one opportunity now. Here is a list of everything our scientists are working on. License what you want, but you have no claim to them after that, or anything else."

Abbott responded by making good on its threat and taking Amgen to court. The pharmaceutical manufacturer probably figured it had us over a barrel, assuming that we couldn't go forward with the IPO until the matter was settled. However, I convinced Smith Barney to hold the stock offering despite the dispute. Furthermore, the underwriters would attend our March 1983 board meeting and state their decision in person. I suggested to George Rathmann that we address the pending lawsuit at the end, after the discussion about whether to finalize our plans for the IPO.

To be fair, Kirk Raab had always been supportive of Amgen, and certainly he found himself in an awkward position. Glancing at the written agenda, he protested: "I think this agenda is backward. How can we discuss the public offering until we've discussed the Abbott-Amgen lawsuit? You can't conduct the IPO without a settlement."

That's when the investment bankers made their cameo appearance, effectively kicking Abbott's legs out from under it. The showdown was resolved amicably a few days later and on very favorable terms for Amgen. However, it was an eye-opening lesson that corporate partners don't always act like partners.

With that crisis behind us—and it was a true make-or-break moment in the company's history—we were free to set our sights on Wall Street.

ON WITH THE SHOW

The action really ratchets up during the final two to four weeks, when senior management barnstorms across the country, speaking to roomfuls of financial analysts, brokers, and potential institutional investors assembled by the underwriter. The series of presentations, fittingly dubbed the "road show" and sometimes the "dog and pony show," epitomizes capitalism in its rawest, purest state.

A company's representatives have approximately thirty minutes to promote interest in their stock offering—no small feat. Today most dog and pony shows incorporate PowerPoint visuals—a technological leap from the Kodak Carousel 35-millimeter slide projector that George Rathmann and I toted in 1983. Usually the CEO commands the spotlight, but we wanted to emphasize Amgen's managerial depth. When the attendees bombarded us with questions, George fielded the ones related to science (for more, see "A Brief Biology Lesson: Recombinant DNA") and I handled the queries about our finances.

A Brief Biology Lesson: Recombinant DNA

The chemical *deoxyribonucleic acid (DNA)*, which makes up the more than thirty thousand different *genes* in the human body, is analogous to a software program designed to create and sustain human life. Everything about us, from eye color to perhaps a preordained susceptibility to a health problem, is encoded at conception by the DNA in our cells.

Recombinant, essentially a synonym for "genetically engineered," refers to the scientific method of transferring DNA from one type of organism into another and then growing these synthesized cells in large numbers.

"How long is it going to take to get your first product on the market?"

"It's hard to say. Probably at least five years from now."

"But you'll run out of money before then. What will you do in that case?"

"We'll either strike up a licensing deal with a pharmaceutical company or have another public offering—whatever the circumstances dictate."

Because Wall Street knew next to nothing about genetic engineering, the questions about Amgen's product development were unsophisticated by today's standards. (Not long after, investment firms began hiring PhDs and MDs as securities analysts and handing them the biotech beat.) So someone might pipe up, "If your drugs can be administered by injection only, aren't you worried about what will happen when the Big Pharma companies come out with pills to treat the same medical conditions?"

"No," Rathmann would reply, "because it's scientifically impossible to make a pill that does what recombinant protein drugs can do." If pressed, he'd explain that conventional oral medicines rely on small molecules, which work by blocking biological processes in the body, such as inflammation. The therapeutic proteins that defined medical biotechnology for its first twenty years are extremely large molecules. They exert the opposite effect, stimulating specific biological activities. In the introduction, I described how epoetin alfa, Amgen's genetically engineered version of the human hormone erythropoietin (also called EPO), combats anemia by stimulating production of red blood cells. It takes a large molecule to bind to the erythropoietin receptor on the surface of a cell in the bone marrow so that it can signal the cell to mature into a healthy red cell.

Unfortunately, the digestive juices in our gastrointestinal tract easily dismantle large proteins, and that is why these agents must be injected directly into the blood. Small-molecule drugs survive the tour through the GI system, but no one has ever developed an oral medication that can activate a receptor.

Did every attendee walk away truly understanding the essence of biotechnology? No. But to be honest, they were there to assess the caliber of Amgen's management team as much as (if not more than) our science or business plan. Investors have two timeworn sayings: "Bet the jockey, not the horse" and "The 'A' management team with the 'B' idea is better than the reverse."

The Benefit of Our Experience

Much of Amgen's success in raising capital can be attributed to the fact that every one of our senior managers had worked for large corporations. As a result, even when Amgen consisted of only fifty employees, we had the organizational discipline of a far bigger company, with salary grades, annual performance reviews, monthly reports, and budgets that were taken seriously. All the things that start-ups rarely do, we did; to us, it was second nature.

What also set Amgen apart from our competitors was George Rathmann's background. As Fred Frank points out, "At many biotech companies, the ideas for the science came from academic institutions, and the people who founded the company were academics, with no industry experience. George, on the other hand, had extensive industry experience from his time at 3M and Abbott Labs, and that clearly resonated with investors."

An IPO's success rides heavily on your poise and credibility while espousing your company's virtues at each stop of the road show, particularly during the question-and-answer session afterward. So it's vital that you come well prepared. Shortly before Rathmann and I flew to our first scheduled meeting, the underwriting syndicate asked whether we would give our presentation to a group of its people. Once there, we realized that the audience was window dressing; the bankers had papered the house, as they say on Broadway, just to see how well we did. Afterward they critiqued everything from our slides to certain turns of phrase. Underhanded? You bet. But I was glad they'd tricked us into an impromptu rehearsal.

Bob Hotz encouraged us to sum up Amgen's story in thirty seconds, as if we were pitching a movie idea to a Hollywood producer. We needed something short but compelling that a broker could repeat to his clients. We decided to position ourselves as a second-generation biotech company committed to improving upon nature.

Let me explain. First-generation companies like Genentech were trying to clone replicas of existing DNA molecules. One advantage Amgen had over its competition was that a member of our scientific advisory board—chemist Marvin Caruthers of the University of Colorado at Boulder—had been instrumental in devising a revolutionary technique for producing DNA molecules from scratch, so to speak. In theory, this process would allow us to go beyond nature and readily design a better molecule than evolution had created. At the time, no other biotech firm possessed this capability.

On the Road

The hit-and-run itinerary of a road show is exhausting but exhilarating. You're generally out for several days two weeks in a row and home on weekends, because nobody turns out for a presentation on a Saturday or Sunday. *Or* a Monday or Friday. That leaves Tuesday, Wednesday, and Thursday—but not later than three or four in the afternoon. As a result, you're limited to about two performances a day.

Common sense dictates that your schedule take you in the direction of the key city; for us that was New York. Presumably by that time you've sharpened your presentation and know which questions to expect. It's the same logic of having a theater company open in New Haven, Connecticut, to work out the kinks before bringing the show to the Great White Way.

One of our first stops was a luncheon in San Francisco for three hundred investors. It goes without saying that when you're trying to stir up interest in your company, it's helpful not to keep would-be buyers waiting. Around the time we should have been landing, the pilot announced that San Francisco International Airport was fogged in, forcing us into a holding pattern.

We still had plenty of time, so none of us was worried. But our composure changed in a hurry when the pilot's voice came over the intercom again to inform us that the plane was running low on fuel and would have to make an unscheduled pit stop in San Jose, fifty miles south. "Once we're back in the air, we'll still probably have to keep circling for at least another hour," he added. "Maybe more."

It was quickly decided that our group would squeeze into a taxi to complete the rest of the trip. When we touched down in San Jose, however, the plane sat on the tarmac, waiting to be refueled. Now George Rathmann and I began looking at our watches obsessively.

I approached a flight attendant. "We really need to get off this plane. Otherwise we're going to be late for a very important meeting."

"You *can't* get off," she huffed. "There aren't any stairs."

Just then the handle of the cabin door began to turn, seemingly by itself. The door slowly creaked open to reveal an airline mechanic standing atop a portable stair ramp. He looked as surprised to see us congregated by the door as we were to see him.

In a scene right out of an old Keystone Kops movie, the four of us eyed one another and then looked back at the flight attendant. "Thank you very much!" we chorused. With that, we nudged aside the puzzled mechanic and sped down the stairs and into the passenger terminal. An hour and a half later a Yellow cab deposited us at the door of the hotel with minutes to spare. I don't remember how much the taxi fare came to, but whatever it was, it was a bargain. Thank goodness we'd listened to our underwriter's strict orders to pack lightly and bring only carry-on luggage. Never check your bag; the schedules are too tight to have to deal with a lost suitcase.

In all, we visited six cities. While you're center stage, the investment bank's sales force buzzes about the room gauging the level of interest in the offering. No hard sell is allowed: securities law prohibits stockbrokers from accepting orders, and investors' verbal indications of interest are nonbinding. By the end of the tour, though, the underwriters should have a pretty accurate reading of the number of shares they can expect to sell and at what price.

HOW MANY SHARES AND FOR HOW MUCH?

According to Bob Hotz, the demand for Amgen's forthcoming IPO appeared extremely strong. "We're oversubscribed. We could either sell more shares or sell the same number of shares at a higher price. Which option do you want us to do?"

"Whichever will get us the most money," I said.

"Then sell more shares."

End of discussion. Most companies would have preferred the other, less diluting route, but we didn't know when the next opportunity to raise funds would come along.

Even with the public offering days away, you still don't know the exact selling price per share. On the registration statement to the SEC, your underwriter provides a ballpark figure—say, $14 to $16—based primarily on the company's value. However, because biotech firms were expected to dwell in the red for years, traditional formulas for estimating worth, such as book value, were obsolete. At the time of Amgen's IPO, says Fred Frank, "there were very few analysts and no precise, well-accepted models of valuation. In fact, they could be rather idiotic. Some early analysts valued companies at $1 million per PhD; others based their valuations on $1 million per employee. It took a while before they got down to discounted cash-flow models," a perennial Wall Street favorite.

For a major investment firm, the ideal starting point falls between $10 and $25 per share, with a stock split—or, more commonly, a reverse stock split (explained in a moment)—undertaken shortly before the offering. In the end, however, a security is worth only what people will pay for it. Therefore, investor feedback figures prominently in determining the final price, which is fine-tuned based on prevailing market conditions as well as the sometimes irrational buying practices peculiar to Wall Street.

For example, there's an unspoken maxim that many investors won't buy fewer than one hundred shares of a stock. If you set the share price too high, they may consider the stock overpriced and bypass your offering. But if you set it too low—$10 being the Mason-Dixon line of respectability—your offering risks being perceived as a second-rate investment. You know how sometimes you'll be shopping, and you find the item you've been looking for at a dirt-cheap price? At first you're delighted: what a bargain! Then a voice of doubt starts whispering, *If it's so inexpensive, the quality must not be very good.* The same outlook may dissuade investors from purchasing a stock.

Therefore, a company seeking to reap $25 million from its IPO would be better off selling 1.67 million shares at $15 each than 2.5 million shares at $10. With a $10 IPO, if the stock price drops even slightly, it's now in single digits and treading perilously close to the $5 minimum for maintaining respectability.

According to Fred Frank, the Sigmund Freud of investor psychology, a successful public offering is usually oversubscribed by a ratio of about 3 to 1. He explains: "The way it works is that if an institutional investor calls me up and says he is interested in one hundred thousand shares, and I agree to sell him that amount, his reaction is likely to be, 'You must not have much demand if you're going to give me everything that I want!' As the underwriter, I want to allocate to all interested parties a modest proportion of what they've asked for." The hope is that they'll satisfy their hunger by filling up on additional shares after the IPO, and at a richer price.

BACK AT THE RANCH

An investment firm typically trims 10 percent to 20 percent off the stock's estimated value to provide an incentive for institutional buyers and to reward investors with a quick if modest appreciation. In addition, underpricing, or "leaving something on the table," serves as a buffer against a weak post-IPO market and helps protect the underwriter in case a dissatisfied investor complains that the issue was overpriced.

Amgen's securities would have sold at $9 per share, which was lower than we'd wanted. To double the price, we executed a *reverse stock split:* an employee with options for one thousand shares would now be entitled to five hundred shares. Some of our scientists grumbled that they must have been cheated somehow; they didn't like the idea that their number of shares had been reduced, even though the monetary value remained exactly the same. But overall, the atmosphere in Thousand Oaks was surprisingly calm during the weeks leading up to Friday, June 17, 1983.

Throughout the winter and spring, we'd regularly kept Amgen's people—now numbering one hundred or so—apprised of where the company stood financially and the status of the IPO. Researcher Kirby Alton recalls, "Everyone knew that Amgen was running out of money, but I guess we were all young and naive enough to assume that it would all work out. So we just kept pressing on, which, when you think about it, was an amazing thing. It's really a credit to senior management that they were able to keep everyone focused on the work while all of this behind-the-scenes activity was going on."

THE BIG DAY

In a *firm-commitment* agreement, whereby the underwriting syndicate buys all available shares regardless of its ability to sell them to investors, the effective date of the public offering is more or less anticlimactic. We knew going in that Amgen would be issuing 2.35 million shares at $18, for a total of $42.3 million in proceeds. Nevertheless, that Friday contained more drama than an episode of TV's *Dallas*.

I'd asked Smith Barney whether I could be present on the trading floor of its New York headquarters throughout the offering. I had no ulterior motive; I just thought it would be an interesting experience. Was it ever.

At eight in the morning, an hour before NASDAQ's opening bell sounded, sell orders started trickling in from some major institutional investors. Possibly they'd felt that the stock wasn't going to go up on its first day. To protect themselves against a short-term loss—it couldn't get any shorter—they could unload it to the syndicate, which was obligated to buy back the shares.

On Wall Street, word spreads faster than a White House leak. After a few more calls like that, tempers started flaring, because the traders could see that we were off to a rocky start. "Who's the son-of-a-bitch salesman that sold these shares to this guy?" one trader railed. "Make sure he doesn't get a commission on 'em!" By the time the market opened, sell orders were pouring in. Meanwhile, I was sitting there, watching the commotion around me and thinking, "What the hell happened? This whole thing is a disaster!"

Far from it, actually. On the negative side, the price per share dipped to $16.75 by the end of the day. Our syndicate struggled to maintain the offering price, but it proved to be impossible. At one point, though, the price had plummeted to less than $10, so we had to be thankful that it recovered in the afternoon. Normally, investors hope to see a gain of approximately 15 percent on the first day of trading; needless to say, we disappointed them.

Still, we achieved what we'd set out to do: put Amgen back on solid ground financially for some time to come. Our $42.3 million in proceeds might seem like small potatoes compared with the sums raised in the heady 1990s, when the *average* IPO fetched $67 million and made instant millionaires out of mailroom clerks (or so the breathless media coverage had us believe). At the time, however, it ranked as the industry's third-highest public offering.

I flew home to California satisfied with how everything had turned out. The accomplishment would shine brighter still in a year or so, when it became clear that we'd slipped under a closing IPO window by a whisker. That summer, public offerings by Immunex (a biotech firm that Amgen acquired many years later) and Chiron de- livered only $16.5 million and $17 million, respectively, while in November the Immunomedics company's paltry $2.5 million IPO signaled the end. The window would not budge open again for two and a half years.

Oh yes: Remember those five companies whose public offerings were already in progress when we were just getting started on ours? Amgen beat them all. In fact, a couple of the procrastinators didn't make it to Wall Street at all before the window came down like a guillotine, cutting them off from millions of dollars in financing.

CHAPTER **3**

The Business of Science Meets the Science of Business

WITH AMGEN'S FINANCES stabilized for the foreseeable future, we returned our attention to the business of science, minus the distractions of the past several months.

When you have an organization staffed almost exclusively by scientists, as Amgen was for its first seven years, perhaps it's only natural that its business approach would be unorthodox. It's fair to say that at many companies, if not most, sales and marketing dominate corporate strategizing; the scientific or creative end may be behind the wheel, but ultimately the sales-and-marketing people commandeer the road map, barking out directions from the passenger seat.

Not so in the field of biotechnology—and certainly not at Amgen, where even the company's location was chosen in part to attract first-rate scientists. Our Thousand Oaks headquarters sat more or less equidistant from the three principal research centers in Southern

California: the University of California at Los Angeles (UCLA), the University of California at Santa Barbara (UCSB), and the California Institute of Technology (Cal Tech), in Pasadena.

The scientific mind-set permeated Amgen's operations to create a highly efficient science-based business model. Many companies now incorporate elements of science in the workplace, although they may not be conscious of it. What is test marketing if not an experiment conducted to gauge, say, consumers' response to a planned product? Rarely, though, do businesses rely on science to help shape decision-making procedures and internal policies. We did. I'll give you an example of what I mean.

This is jumping ahead a bit, but in 1992, my fourth year as CEO, Amgen was struck by twin tragedies. First, our manager of sales and marketing, Paul Dawson, died of a heart attack. Immensely talented and popular throughout the company, Paul had been hired as our first vice president of sales and marketing in 1987, when Epogen looked to be a year away from winning FDA approval. He built Amgen's sales and marketing from the foundation up. Even more impressive: You know how some managers shine during a business's upward climb but seem to lose their footing once large-scale success arrives, bringing with it exponential growth and change? Paul kept pace the whole time, and we had expected him to lead Amgen sales and marketing for years to come.

We were all still reeling from the shocking news when Thomas Beard, vice president of sales, also suffered a heart attack. He survived, thankfully, but his health was impaired to the degree that he could not continue in such a demanding position.

We could have tapped an outsider to succeed Paul Dawson, but that would have required months of searching. What's more, Amgen was in a crucial period, having only recently launched its second product, filgrastim (Neupogen); we couldn't chance hiring an unknown and then discover that the person wasn't going to work out.

Fortunately, one of the best pure managers I'd ever known had been with the company since 1981. He was a scientist, though, and hadn't shown any interest in business, much less sales and marketing. Dennis Fenton had come to Amgen as a thirty-year-old bench researcher. A refugee from conventional pharma, he'd spent four frustrating years at Pfizer, in sleepy Groton, Connecticut ("Rotten Groton," he jokingly called it)—not the most exciting environment for an avid surfer with a budding interest in genetic engineering.

"Pfizer was going in that direction at a glacial pace," Fenton recalls. "One day I saw a tiny ad in the *Simi Valley News*: 'Applied Molecular Genetics Seeks Scientists.' Pretty general. I thought, 'Hmmm, I might fall into that category.' The address was in Newbury Park, California; I'd once eaten at a famous hamburger joint there called Du-Par's while on vacation. That was enough to encourage me to send in my résumé. And lo and behold, George Rathmann invited me out for an interview and hired me."

At the time of Paul Dawson's death, Dennis was serving as vice president of operations in charge of process development, as well as building and overseeing our manufacturing facilities. The thought of entering sales and marketing had never grazed his mind. That would explain his dumbfounded expression the day I called him into my office and asked, "Dennis, have you ever considered the possibility of running sales and marketing?"

"Gordon?" he said, waving at me as if to jolt me back to reality. "It's *me*—Dennis. You're talking to *me* about sales and marketing."

"I know."

He might not have envisioned himself in that capacity, but I believed he was exactly what Amgen needed, for a couple of reasons. First, although the sales and marketing department was in good shape in many ways, it was not well organized. I knew that Dennis would quickly tighten things up and get everyone singing from the same page. He would promote the right people and transfer others, establish more internal structure, devise plans and teach people to follow them—in short, create a smooth-running organization. Then, after a couple of years, he could return to operations and leave a well-disciplined sales and marketing department as his legacy.

Thinking back to that afternoon in my office, Dennis says, "Gordon proceeded to sell me on the idea. He spoke enthusiastically about how much I could learn, and how it would be fun, exciting, different. I didn't have any doubts about that. My big fear was that I would fail and wind up having to leave this company that I loved."

I sensed his misgivings. "You're *not* going to fail," I told him. "I wouldn't offer you the job if you weren't able to do it. Trust me; just try it. If it turns out to be a mistake, it's *my* decision, *my* fault, not yours. You'll go back to your old job or another one within the company." Regarding his other major concern about switching to sales— "But Gordon, I don't even own a suit!"—that could be rectified easily enough.

Dennis needed reassurance that he would succeed. Who doesn't from time to time? Although assuming the reins of sales and marketing was "the single hardest thing I ever did in my life," Dennis says, he shepherded Amgen through the crisis brilliantly. Being a PhD in microbiology, he also implemented the scientific approach to problem solving, as might be expected.

He started by speaking at length with the staff—listening more than talking, as a good manager should—soliciting their opinions about how the existing systems might be improved.

I should explain here that pharmaceutical sales isn't like hawking vacuum cleaners door to door. Our clients are physicians, and a fast-talking salesperson with a slick sales pitch would do more harm than good. What doctors respond to is accurate information anchored in science, and hold the hype. Because they're busy, they seldom have time to read the latest studies in medical journals. Amgen's sales and marketing people may not be MDs or PhDs, but they know their product inside and out; more like educators than salespeople, their primary function is to teach health-care professionals how to use the company's medications most effectively.

As reps of a two-product company, our salespeople split their time between visiting dialysis facilities to talk to nephrologists (doctors who specialize in diagnosing and treating kidney disorders) about Epogen and then dropping in at oncologists' offices to discuss new developments regarding Neupogen in cancer treatment. That's a tremendous amount of highly technical information to absorb. One of the biggest challenges, according to the staff, was determining how much time to devote to each product.

One day at a sales and marketing meeting, Dennis posed this question: "Have you ever considered dividing the sales force so that each of you can focus on one product?"

From the incredulous response, you would have thought he'd proposed that from now on all Amgen reps rollerblade to their appointed rounds.

"No, never!"

"It's a bad idea."

"The salesmen wouldn't go for it."

"Other companies don't do that."

"This way is more fun."

"That might be true," Dennis replied evenly. "But we're a science-based company. Why not run an experiment? Let's take two districts at random and have each of their people sell only one product for a while—say, six months. Then we'll see which way works best. If it doesn't pan out, we'll go back to the way things were. But at least we'll know the true answer instead of speculating."

Everyone agreed, even though the one-product-per-salesperson approach flew in the face of conventional wisdom. (The industry standard was three to four products per rep.) The results of Fenton's experiment surprised everyone. Our salespeople discovered that they preferred representing a single drug after all. Not only that, but they were more effective, and that led us to reconfigure the entire national sales force.

THE SCIENTIFIC METHOD

Designing an experiment to help resolve a business problem is simple, at least compared with structuring a clinical trial for testing a new drug's safety and effectiveness. But how frequently do companies do it? Not very often. They may try out new ideas, but few actually conduct formal experiments in the way that scientists would:

Step 1: define the question you hope to answer. As Dan Vapnek, Amgen's longtime head of research, used to say, "If we knew the results we would get from an experiment, we wouldn't *run* the experiment." That's what an experiment is: the creation of a controlled environment in which to evaluate a hypothesis. Our question was straightforward: will the sales force feel more comfortable and be more productive representing one product rather than two?

Step 2: determine the particulars of conducting the experiment. As a general guideline, the larger the sample size (the number of participants), the greater the accuracy, but the smaller the sample size, the lower the cost. In testing new medications, for example, studies of fewer than twenty patients are considered preliminary or suggestive at best.

Our informal sales study was analogous to an investigational drug trial in that it compared the current standard (having all salespeople promote both Epogen and Neupogen) with the untested method (having them promote one drug). The first group is referred to as the *control group,* while the volunteers assigned to the experimental arm belong to the *study group.*

The trickiest part of designing any study is to minimize factors that could cloud the issue. Although you can never entirely eliminate bias, assigning participants to either the study group or the control group through a random process—such as a lottery system or picking names out of a hat—reduces the chance that the study's coordinators might subconsciously create groups that are not evenly matched.

In addition to randomizing subjects, the other major consideration for ensuring an objective measurement is to even the playing field as much as possible. If, let's say, a clinical trial pits a new chemotherapy drug for early-stage colorectal cancer against the established intervention, both groups should have equal numbers of patients with similar characteristics. The researchers would want to enroll men and women with the same severity, or stage, of disease; the same treatment history (surgery to remove the tumor and no previous history of chemotherapy); and the same current protocol (postsurgical administration of the experimental or standard drug regimen; no radiation therapy). In this way, if a significant benefit emerges, you can be reasonably confident that it is not a mirage but is attributable to the investigational agent—the only major difference between the two groups. For our experiment, it was essential that the drug reps in each group had similar numbers of clients and similarly sized territories.

Step 3: Determine how you will measure the results. For an informal study such as this one, you might use the following tools:

- A simple survey rating the sales staff's satisfaction on a scale of 1 to 5

- A comparison of actual sales versus sales from the prior period

- A comparison of actual sales with the sales quotas

LISTEN TO YOUR DATA

After you've compiled and analyzed the evidence, heed what it tells you. That might be difficult if you consider yourself an intuitive business executive and prefer to go with your gut. Maybe all this reliance on data for making decisions sounds duller than sitting next to the boss at the annual managers' weekend retreat. Maybe you think it would stunt creativity and the open exchange of ideas.

To the contrary: the scientific approach fosters free thinking. When you allow the results of a quality study to guide decision making, it depersonalizes the issue, taking it out of the realm of "good idea," "bad idea," and, most poisonously, "his idea" or "her idea." Look at it this way: the idea won enough support to warrant being put to the test. It may still be valid—or not. The important thing is that you're evaluating the idea and not the person who proposed it. You tried the experiment, and it didn't work; now discuss what the results can teach you and move forward.

As Dennis Fenton points out, "Most companies run away from failed ideas, as though they exude a stench. If you're science based, analyze what went wrong. Was the design of the experiment flawed? Did the experiment prove that the hypothesis was correct, or incorrect, or did it leave us without an answer? Another question to ask is, Was the experiment conducted properly? Regardless of the results, your company will get progressively smarter if it uses the scientific method."

When ideas become too closely associated with individuals, people start digging in their heels. In reality, they're no longer defending their idea; they're defending themselves and perhaps defending or attacking others. Using the scientific method makes it easier to decouple what's best for the organization from what's best for the individual. Another benefit: experimentation allows you to arrive at decisions based on a sample. To test Dennis's hypothesis, Amgen didn't have to overhaul its entire sales force—only two districts.

If you act on the results of your experiment, you'll make the right decision far more often than not. Doesn't every company do that? No. How many times have you seen someone embrace data that supports a preconceived conclusion while ignoring data that contradicts it? If too many people in an organization become overly invested in their own ideas, the company will have fewer ideas to consider, and it will take forever to evaluate the ones that are put on the table.

SCIENCE DRIVES PRODUCTION

That Amgen's culture was science driven from the top down was most apparent in the resolve to let research and development dictate our product line. This runs counter to the way things are done at conventional pharmaceutical companies. Typically, a desirable patient population is identified. Then the firm's scientists are set out like dogs on a scent to see whether they can dig up a new way to treat the condition. It doesn't have to be groundbreaking, only enough of an advancement to muscle its way into, say, the $1 billion migraine drug market or the $3.5 billion osteoarthritis drug market. Two notable exceptions are 3M and Abbott Laboratories, where, not coincidentally, George Rathmann had spent his career before coming to Amgen.

Biotechnology firms were trying to develop landmark drugs that either were the first of their kind, like Epogen and Neupogen, or that marked a significant advance over what was available. Coming up with a slightly better product and trying to win the competitive battle through superior sales and marketing might have been acceptable for big pharmaceutical companies, with their large and highly effective sales forces, but any biotech firm following that strategy was certain to fail.

To develop revolutionary drugs, we had to go wherever the best science led us, whether the destination happened to be a huge market or one of more modest size. The entire biotech industry operated on a measure of faith that recombinant drugs would mark an unparalleled advance in medicine and would benefit from strong patent protections, so that even if the numbers were small there would be scant competition. We could become the large (genetically engineered) fish in the small pond and, with some luck, perhaps the largest fish in the ocean.

For example, Epogen's original consumer base was composed of men and women forced onto kidney dialysis by end-stage renal disease (ESRD), a patient population that barely exceeded one hundred thousand the year the drug entered the market. At the time, nephrologists had nothing to offer the nine in ten dialysis patients who suffered from chronic anemia so severe that many of them didn't have the energy to get out of bed. Therefore, you can imagine the demand for a drug that restored their red-blood-cell counts to near normal. Since that time, the number of people on hemodialysis has more than quadrupled; in addition, Epogen has acquired FDA approval for other uses, including chronic anemia brought on by AIDS, cancer, and cancer treatment.

If not for the passage of the Orphan Drug Act of 1983, it's questionable whether the pharmaceutical industry could afford to serve small patient populations such as the ESRD community. The cost of developing a new drug is the same whether the number of potential users totals in the millions or only a few thousand. Coming up with treatments for rare disorders is almost always a money-losing proposition.

In the United States, the drug manufacturers themselves foot most of the bill for medical research. Public law 97-414, spearheaded by Rep. Henry Waxman (D-CA), offered seven years' patent exclusivity to drugmakers that were willing to invest in discovering new treatments for any of the six thousand or so orphan diseases: those that affect fewer than two hundred thousand people.

This seven-year exclusivity took effect the day the drug was licensed for commercial use. Non-orphan medications are limited to twenty years of patent protection from the day the patent application is *filed*. (Until 1995, the term of a patent was seventeen years from the date it was issued.) But it can easily take ten years or more for a product to surmount all the hurdles on the road to FDA approval, so in reality the standard patent protection often turned out to be about the same as the seven years provided by the Orphan Drug Act.

The bill quickly achieved its intended effect: from 1983 to 2007 more than 280 conventional drugs and biologics for orphan diseases have been introduced as opposed to only 10 in the previous decade. Japan admired the legislation so much that it adopted its own, but for 10 years.

AMGEN'S FOUR-PRONG STRATEGY FOR MANAGING RISK

Epogen was one of several products on the drawing board at the time of Amgen's IPO. From the start, George Rathmann had wisely sent his researchers scouting in four directions: human health care, human diagnostic testing, animal health care, and specialty chemicals. Initially the four-prong strategy didn't sit well with some board members, in particular Jim Blair, who wanted the company to be more market driven and to concentrate on a single product or a few products at most. Blair's objection to building a multifaceted product portfolio was difficult to understand, because Genentech, Biogen, and most of our other chief competitors had adopted that strategy. Tensions sometimes flared at board meetings, where for three years George was barred from stating his opinion that Amgen should aspire to be more like a pharmaceutical company than an R&D boutique.

Not many people understood what we and the other biotech firms were doing. With no existing data to dictate which areas we should pursue, it made sense to dabble in each and decide which ones looked the most promising after some facts were known. We understood from the outset that we couldn't afford to spend too much time and money on multiple areas; those that didn't pan out would be dropped early. Our R&D decisions would be based on our own scientific evidence.

Ultimately the tug-of-war went Rathmann's way, as it should have all along. There was never any disagreement that our long-term success hinged on developing drugs designed to treat people. But because income from this area was a good decade away, clearly we needed to pursue other avenues of revenue.

Most of them, such as animal therapeutics, turned out to be dead ends. That one surprised many of us. The entire biotech industry had been banking on genetically engineered animal medications as quick moneymakers, on the assumption that the government approval process would be far shorter than it was for human drugs. What no one took into consideration was the endless red tape involved in having to obtain a license not only from the FDA but also from the U.S. Department of Agriculture (USDA). More than a dozen human products reached the marketplace before the first biotech animal drug was approved.

Amgen's forays into this field yielded little except three great yarns.

Arbor Acres, a poultry breeder, invested in our chicken growth hormone project. The study had been farmed out, so to speak, to local chicken growers. Although virtually everyone believed that the substance would make the birds grow faster, it didn't. Our disappointment was compounded by the fact that one of the farmers died of a heart attack while feeding the fowl right there in the farmyard, and apparently his body went undiscovered for two days. Naturally the *National Enquirer* couldn't pass up the story: "Giant Genetically Engineered Chickens Peck Farmer to Death!" trumpeted its headline. Not exactly the kind of publicity that a company goes chasing after.

A few years later, the SmithKline pharmaceutical company funded work on a porcine growth hormone that it hoped would produce leaner pigs. It did. Scientist Burt Ensley, another of Amgen's earliest hires, recalls, "The animals had almost no fat on them. But because of that, the concern was that they probably wouldn't taste as good. So, to find out, we ate the experiment."

Befitting a company of scientists, we turned one of our Friday barbecues into a randomized single-blinded study, better known as a taste test. People's plates were piled high with either porcine somatropin (PST) center-cut pork chops or "control" pork chops, although no one knew which was which. This being a tightly controlled trial, each piece was cooked to the same internal temperature and cut into similarly sized pieces.

After dinner, everyone filled out a detailed survey pertaining to taste, juiciness, texture, and so on. The ultralean meat compared favorably with the ordinary fatty pork in every category. Unfortunately, the growth hormone turned out to be a pig in a poke, because 2 percent of the animals developed peptic ulcers. That mortality rate was considered too high.

In addition, we were unable to develop a long-term sustained-release version of the hormone, which would have required only a single treatment every thirty days. Farmers weren't interested in a product that had to be administered more frequently than that. And so the project had to be scuttled. (Strangely enough, the porcine growth hormone did make salmon grow faster.)

Not long afterward, Amgen decided to close the barnyard door on animal therapeutics. The only salable product to emerge from the program was a bovine growth hormone, licensed to the Upjohn Company, that made cows produce more milk. We decided to showcase the success in our annual report and put a photograph of a beautiful dairy cow on the cover.

There weren't any cows to be found within a country mile of Thousand Oaks, so we arranged to fly to Kalamazoo, Michigan, and take a picture of one of Upjohn's animals. In preparation for the shoot, the Upjohn people cleaned their dairy facility until it was as spotless as an operating room. This was going to be a great photograph.

When it was time to bring out the star, however, the poor animal slipped on the wet floor, landing spread-eagled. She lay there for thirty minutes while Upjohn employees pushed and tugged. They were visibly embarrassed; we bit our cheeks not to laugh out loud. The annual report cover was not graced by a dairy cow after all. Nor did our partnership with Upjohn ever get on its feet. For some reason, the pharmaceutical giant decided against selling the bovine growth hormone. The product is on the market but is sold by another company.

OUR FORAY INTO SPECIALTY CHEMICALS

In the specialty-chemicals field, Burt Ensley could claim responsibility for one of our early successes. As sometimes happens in science, it was the result of a happy accident. "You can use bacteria to make a number of products in the laboratory," he explains. "For instance, benzene is a fairly nasty chemical." Carcinogenic, too. "But exposing it to bacteria can turn it into lots of interesting things, like catechol, a substance used in photo developer, dyes, pigments, and tanning agents."

Ensley notes that one product his group was working on was naphthalene. "There's a bacterium, *Pseudomonas,* that grows on naphthalene and causes it to decompose into something useful called alpha-naphthol. But the bacterium wouldn't quit there; it would proceed to eat the alpha-naphthol. We wanted to try stopping it. How to do that was not well known back then. We extracted the genes from this bacteria and cloned them in a sample of E. coli bacteria. When we did that, the bacteria started turning bright blue. Now, we had absolutely no idea *why* this should have happened."

Eventually another scientist guessed that perhaps we were inadvertently making indigo, a plant-derived dye that is used to color blue jeans. That turned out to be right. When we compared the product to a small amount of indigo, we discovered that the two materials were identical. Apparently the bacteria were converting something in the E. coli into indigo.

"So, *voila!*" says Ensley. "Just like that, we were out of the naphthol business and into the indigo business." His team's unexpected discovery landed on the front page of the prestigious international journal *Science*.

What made for intriguing science did not translate into a profit, however, but not because there wasn't interest in a substitute for the dye. Ultimately, we learned that there were only three major manufacturers of indigo in the world: one in the United States, one in Europe, and one in Japan. They didn't seem to compete much in one another's home market, and although the selling price was $12 per pound, our analysis showed that each of the three might have manufacturing costs as little as $4 per pound. Given our process, we couldn't hope to go that low. We suspected that if we ever became a serious competitor, the $12 price would drop very far, very fast.

The lone financial success from specialty chemicals came in laundry detergents, of all things. Procter & Gamble, Lever Brothers, and their competitors were concerned that the stain-removing enzymes they advertised prominently tended to degrade in less than a month. Amgen scientists fashioned a biotech-based enzyme that was hardy enough to stand up to the harsh environment of a liquid detergent. Genentech also came up with a suitable enzyme.

Detergent enzymes couldn't create huge opportunities for biotech companies, however, and we didn't have any other product candidates. Genentech off-loaded its enzyme to Corning, while we licensed ours to Kodak, which had been bankrolling the specialty-chemicals program. And with that, the biotech industry acknowledged another blind alley. At least the diagnostics program, funded by Abbott, was chugging along quietly on the strength of a few laboratory test kits.

AN EXCEPTION TO THE RULE

The only program in which Amgen put a substantial amount of its own money was the big one—human therapeutics—where we had five contenders: recombinant alpha-interferon and gamma-interferon, a hepatitis C vaccine, a skin-growth factor (epidermal growth factor, or EGF), and erythropoietin. None of the five was a sure thing, but you'd have to name erythropoietin the runt of the litter. In the summer of 1983, nearly two years after scientist Fu-Kuen Lin and his small team began working on the project, they still had not been able to identify the gene responsible for the hormone that stimulated red-blood-cell production. Like every other biotech enterprise, we were desperate for one product to shine so brightly in the laboratory that it would support the entire company. Adding to the pressure in the case of erythropoietin, other firms were hot on our heels. In a race like this, where finishing first brings exclusive patent protection, there is no such thing as second place. It's all or nothing.

By now, you probably have a good sense of how devoted George Rathmann was to his scientists. But he also knew that scientists, with their innate enthusiasm and their sometimes obsessive nature, would go on trying to develop a product for eternity unless a time limit was imposed. What made Amgen unique among biotech companies was that projects were expected to show some progress within a pre-scribed time, or else they had to be reevaluated. In the aftermath of our successful IPO, it looked as if erythropoietin might have reached the end of the line.

Based on the evidence, terminating the project increasingly appeared to be the logical decision. For all the efforts to prevent information leaks, word had spread throughout the industry that no company was close to pinpointing the gene. Perhaps it couldn't be done; after all, scientists had been searching in vain for EPO since the 1930s. When one of our competitors bailed out to preserve its limited resources, Dan Vapnek and Noel Stebbing strongly recommended that we do the same.

George wouldn't hear of it. "We can't quit," he said adamantly. "These scientists have been working on this project day and night, seven days a week for more than two years! They still believe they can do it. We can't just pull the rug out from under a team of people who are that positive and who are working that hard. We have to assume that they know what they're doing and let 'em keep going."

From a scientific standpoint, Vapnek and Stebbing were absolutely correct. However, George astutely judged that despite Amgen's dedication to data-driven decision making, this was one instance when the people factor took precedence. It also illustrated an important Amgen principle: "Every rule, policy, and procedure has exceptions."

4

From IPO to EPO
in Four Months

FU-KUEN LIN, THE son of an herbal-medicine doctor, emigrated from his native Taiwan to the United States in 1967 at the age of twenty-six to study plant pathology. After he graduated from the University of Illinois in 1971, his postdoctoral work took him on a winding course through the Midwest, back to Taiwan for a couple of years, and then through the southern United States. While at the Medical University of South Carolina, he began conducting experiments in genetic engineering.

In 1981 Lin answered the same help-wanted ad as Dennis Fenton—this one appearing in the pages of *Science* magazine—and became Amgen's seventh scientist. He was offered a choice of assignments. It is a testament to his adventurous nature that the soft-spoken biologist asked to work on cloning the elusive erythropoietin gene. Of our five human-therapeutic projects then under way, EPO was the only one for which the difficult step of identifying the gene had yet to be accomplished.

At least six other companies, including Biogen and Genetics Institute (GI), were in pursuit of the erythropoietin gene, one of the Holy Grails of the nascent biotechnology industry. Amgen held a slight edge in that sixty-year-old Eugene Goldwasser had agreed to serve as a consultant.

Goldwasser, a biologist at the University of Chicago, discovered the hormone's existence in 1977 after more than twenty often frustrating years of research. As far back as 1906, scientists had suspected that a substance in the blood instructed the bone marrow to churn out replacements for expired red blood cells at two million to three million per second. But with more than two hundred proteins in the circulation, no one could find the biochemical messenger named after *erythropoiesis,* the Latin word for red-cell production.

In the late 1950s, Goldwasser and his team of researchers determined that the kidneys were the body's source of EPO. They figured this out through process of elimination, surgically removing different organs from laboratory rats and waiting to see whether their red-cell counts dropped precipitously. As suspected, the animals whose kidneys were removed developed severe anemia.

The Brooklyn-born Goldwasser speculated correctly that if you induced anemia in an animal by injecting it with an agent that destroyed red blood cells, the kidneys would attempt to correct the imbalance by secreting additional EPO into the circulation. Where he erred was in assuming that a large surplus of erythropoietin would turn up in the blood, which hopefully could then be isolated and injected into anemic rats as a cure. The "enriched" blood samples he withdrew contained only trace amounts of the hormone, too little to be isolated using the available technologies and equipment.

Goldwasser might have remained stranded had not a Japanese researcher read a paper Goldwasser had published. By this time, 1973, the growing suspicion was that excess EPO showed up more in urine than in blood. Certainly urine contained smaller amounts of other proteins, and that would make separating EPO easier. The researcher, Dr. Takaji Miyake, offered to collect urine samples from patients who suffered from a rare blood disorder called aplastic anemia. The idea was that their defective marrow produced insufficient numbers of red cells; consequently, their kidneys produced additional EPO, thereby increasing the level in their urine.

Eighteen months later, Miyake arrived in Chicago bearing a shoebox-sized package of dried urine. Goldwasser was able to cull from it a small amount of purified erythropoietin. When the specimen was injected into the anemic lab rats, it stimulated their bone marrow to produce red cells, just as Goldwasser had theorized twenty years before.

A little EPO goes a long way in a mouse; human kidneys produce the hormone in minuscule amounts. It took 675 gallons of urine, courtesy of Miyake, to yield a mere 8 milligrams of pure erythropoietin. Clearly, not enough EPO could be extracted from urine samples. Goldwasser briefly considered cultivating kidney cells and trying to manipulate them in the laboratory to generate the hormone, but despite some initial promise, nothing came of this process.

He knew he didn't have the resources to pursue the next major step on his own and started looking for a pharmaceutical company to partner with. In retrospect, it's hard to believe that Goldwasser was unable to interest Parke-Davis in his research; and Abbott Laboratories, where George Rathmann worked (but in diagnostics, not therapeutics), rejected the biologist's solicitations more than once. When Goldwasser told his employer, the University of Chicago, about his patentable discovery, the administrators there didn't bother to return his phone call—shades of the Mayo Clinic's failure to patent cortisone in the 1940s and subsequently losing millions in income.

Biogen approached Goldwasser before Amgen did. He turned down Biogen, unimpressed with the caliber of the company and its scientific advisory board. You have to wonder why, because most observers at the time would have rated Biogen one of the industry's top firms. In any event, Amgen and its star-studded scientific advisory board convinced him to cast his lot with us. That was an early example of how recruiting the best people brings rewards in addition to its obvious advantages. It can help do the following:

- Draw to the organization other talented professionals who want to play on a winning team
- Attract desirable licensing opportunities
- Interest the most successful companies in forming business relationships

Certainly Amgen's people were one of the keys to its sustained success over the years.

A NEW OPTION: GENETIC ENGINEERING

By the dawn of the 1980s, a new possibility had opened up for making EPO a practical treatment for anemic patients. That the science was so advanced is astounding when you consider that only twenty-five years had passed since James Watson and Francis Crick, a pair of researchers at England's Cambridge University, had determined the structure of DNA, the biochemical that encodes the genetic information of all living organisms.

To appreciate this remarkable manmade process for unlocking the body's natural secrets, it helps to first aquaint yourself with some basic cell biology. High school biology students have been learning it for years. I promise to keep this short and simple, but you may pick up enough to help your children with their homework.

Your body is made up of roughly 100 trillion cells. All of them, with the exception of red blood cells, contain the complete genetic blueprint for creating and sustaining human life, referred to as the human *genome*. Imagine that you're looking at a single cell magnified 100,000 times through a powerful microscope. Within its membranous wall lies the command center known as the *nucleus,* home to twenty-three matched pairs of threadlike *chromosomes;* you inherit half of each pair from your mother, and half from your father.

A chromosome holds about 1,000 genes, on average, although the number varies—from chromosome 1, the largest (with an estimated 2,100 to 2,800 genes) to chromosome 21, the smallest (with 200 to 300 genes). A *gene* is simply a short, tightly coiled segment of DNA. Every cell is packed with about six feet of DNA, which measures only about one-millionth of an inch wide.

The DNA molecule (as first described in 1953 by Watson, an American biologist, and the British physicist Crick), resembles a ladder that has been twisted into a corkscrew shape—the famed double helix (see figure 4-1). Its long rails consist of sugar and phosphate,

FIGURE 4-1

The ladder of life

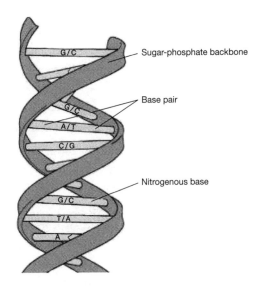

Source: Illustration courtesy of the National Institutes of Health.

and each rung is constructed from a pair of similar chemical *bases*—either *adenine* and *thymine,* or *guanine* and *cytosine* —bonded together by hydrogen (see figure 4-2). Typically, a gene is made up of several thousand bases along the length of a DNA strand.

The DNA in each cell functions as a set of instructions, and it programs its cell to produce *proteins.* These complex molecules, composed of a chain of smaller building blocks called *amino acids,* participate in the structure, function, and regulation of your body's cells, tissues, and organs.

You can think of DNA as a language having only four letters—*A, T, G,* and *C*—each corresponding to one of the chemical bases:

A = adenine

T = thymine

G = guanine

C = cytosine

All proteins are built from a combination of twenty amino acids. The order of As, Ts, Gs, and Cs spells out which acids will be assembled in which sequence to form a given protein. DNA also governs how much of the protein will be manufactured by your cells, as well as when, why, and where in your body.

A four-letter alphabet might seem limited. But don't forget that computers can perform highly complex tasks by using a language consisting of only two characters—the numbers 0 and 1—sometimes called binary code. Our biological language is further simplified by the requirement that each "word" contain exactly three letters. For example, the three-letter word, or *codon,* UGG translates into an order for the amino acid tryptophan; two three-letter words—UUU and UUC—are both codons for the amino acid phenylalanine. Other amino acids are associated with as many as three, four, or even six different codons.

FIGURE 4-2

The structure of DNA

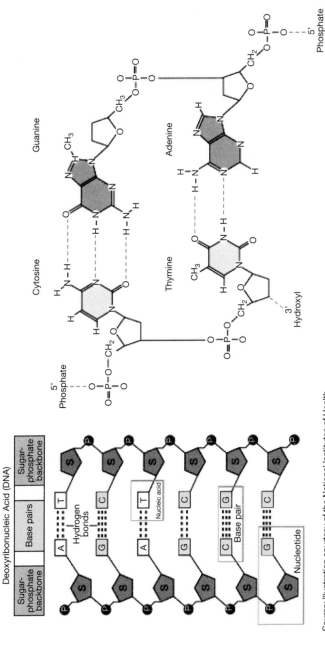

Source: Illustration courtesy of the National Institutes of Health.

Why does nature contain this redundancy? Is it only a meaning-less artifact of evolution? The answer is that different organisms pre-fer different codons. Here's why this is important for manufacturing biological products: if, say, yeast is used as the production system for a human protein, the production yields of that protein are greater if you construct a gene using only the codons preferred by yeast rather than the codons in the human gene. Many people believe that differ-ent organisms use different codons for the same amino acids to en-hance the ability of the body's immune system to distinguish friends from foes.

A gene, then, can be thought of as a sentence made up exclusively of these three-letter words. Mathematically, with four letters and with three-letter words, there are sixty-four possible combinations of codons, in addition to three *stop codons* for denoting the end of a gene, much like a period at the end of a sentence.

RECOMBINANT DNA TECHNOLOGY: CUT AND PASTE

The basic process of using recombinant technology to manufacture a therapeutic protein is as follows: you locate the gene (genetic in-structions) for producing the desired protein; you cut out this gene or manufacture it in the laboratory; then you insert the gene into a cell that will mass-produce the protein coded by the gene. In essence, you turn the cell into a tiny protein factory.

In April 2003, fifty years after Watson and Crick's landmark discov-ery, an international consortium of scientists finished sequencing the approximately three billion base pairs that make up the approximately thirty thousand genes in the human genome. This blueprint for hu-manity is more than 99 percent the same in every person on earth.

As of the mid-1970s, however, only a few hundred genes had been mapped to their exact locations on particular chromosomes. The sequence of base chemicals on one side of the DNA ladder *complements* the other: adenine complements thymine, and guanine complements cytosine. For example, if one strand reads AGCGT, we know that the other reads TCGCA, and vice versa. Therefore, it's not necessary to identify the counterpart of any one sequence. Nevertheless, pinpointing the code for a specific gene was a time-consuming, painstaking process.

In 1978 molecular biologist Dr. Herbert Boyer, cofounder of Genentech, created the first recombinant gene: a genetically engineered version of the DNA that produces the human hormone insulin, located on chromosome 11. Insulin—like erythropoietin, an essential hormone—enables our cells to absorb the simple sugar glucose, the body's principal source of energy. Following a meal, glucose builds up rapidly in the blood. The pancreas, detecting this, floods the circulation with insulin. People with diabetes make too little of the hormone or none at all, causing excess glucose to accumulate in the blood—a state known as *hyperglycemia*. Most of the 14.6 million diagnosed diabetics in the United States manage to keep their blood-sugar levels within a safe range through dietary restrictions alone or through diet plus insulin injections or other medications. Repeated episodes of dangerously elevated blood glucose can eventually damage multiple body systems, leading to severe complications such as cardiovascular disease, blindness, and nerve disorders.

The method for isolating a targeted gene is difficult, laborious, and complicated. Here it is in executive summary form: Boyer examined human pancreatic cells to determine the genetic code for insulin, 110 amino acids long. The next step—combining the insulin DNA and that of another organism—had been pioneered five years earlier by Boyer and scientist Stanley Cohen. First, a delivery vehicle is fashioned from a small ring of bacterial DNA called a *plasmid*. Plasmids can be moved from one cell to another even when the recipient cell belongs to a different species. This makes them ideal for smuggling DNA, like a microscopic Trojan horse, into a target cell.

A portion of DNA is cut out of the plasmid (imagine an *O* made into a *C*), not with a snipping tool but with *restriction enzymes.* Still other enzymes are used to splice the insulin gene into the opened ends of the plasmid. Then the plasmid-gene combination is sealed inside a single-celled organism capable of rapidly replicating itself, such as bacteria, yeast, or mammalian cells. In Boyer's time, all this was done by hand. Now automated equipment can make thousands of pieces of DNA within hours, but then, it was a major project to create only one.

Boyer chose *Escherichia coli*—yes, the same E. coli that, if you ingest its harmful strain in tainted hamburger or apple juice, can induce fatal damage to your kidneys and digestive system. But the E. coli bacterium used in recombinant engineering is extremely weak and safe. (For Boyer and Cohen's historic first effort at cloning, in 1973, they placed a plasmid containing genetic material from an African clawed toad inside the bacterium.) Each time the cell divides, its imported DNA instructions for manufacturing human insulin are passed down to the next generation. Before long, you have billions of cells harboring the insulin gene.

Animal insulin, for injection beneath the skin, had been available to diabetics since the early 1920s and was extracted in large amounts from pig pancreases when the animals were slaughtered. It was used to treat diabetes with good success, although few patients were aware that they were injecting themselves with pig insulin. The insulin hormone in pigs is so similar to human insulin that it can be used in people, but it is different enough that some patients developed reactions to it. In addition to causing painful inflammation at the injection site, this compromised the treatment's effectiveness. Humulin, the first drug produced through biotechnology, was hailed as a significant improvement; it is identical to human insulin, so the body's defense system pays no attention to it.

LIN'S PREDICAMENT

When Genentech's Humulin went on the market to great fanfare in late 1982, Fu-Kuen Lin had been struggling for more than a year to locate the EPO gene without success and with little cause for optimism. The chief problem that he and his research associate, Chi-Hwei Lin (no relation), faced was that they had little of the natural product to work with. As George Rathmann explains, "It's always easier to sequence a molecule if you have lots of it. Unfortunately, Gene Goldwasser was sending us only a half milligram of EPO at a time, which just wasn't enough."

Somehow, word of our experiments reached The Dow Chemical Company, which proposed becoming Amgen's partner. What could the giant corporation bring to the collaboration? Tens of thousands of gallons of human urine partially purified to contain high concentrations of erythropoietin. It seems that Dow had contracted with the Italian army to collect urine from some fifty thousand soldiers.

A sample was sent to us, but despite the company's claims, the EPO levels turned out to be no greater than that of normal urine. The people at Dow Chemical were so embarrassed that we never heard from them again. Transforming new technology into a successful business is never simple, quick, or without numerous failures.

In the summer of 1983, while Amgen was still riding the euphoria of its initial public offering, Dan Vapnek argued that Amgen should discontinue the EPO project and devote our limited resources to other endeavors. He wasn't the only scientist to feel this way. Based solely on science, we probably should have stopped. But there was another important aspect of this decision: the human factor. And that strongly supported continuing.

"Fu-Kuen's lab bay was right next to mine," Kirby Alton recalls with a laugh. "Sometimes I would come in at weird hours because of an experiment that I was working on, and there was never a time when either he or Chi-Hwei was not there. I'm talking about the first four years of the company! They worked very, very hard, all of the time."

George Rathmann understood firsthand the gambles inherent in any kind of research. Scientists are like anglers, casting their fishing lines for answers in a vast sea of data. Failures far outweigh successes, and it's common for years of experimentation to pass without a bite. A chief executive who wasn't accustomed to the incremental pace and unpredictability of drug development might have grown impatient and scuttled the program prematurely. Rathmann couldn't bring himself to fold the program, mostly out of respect for Lin's dedication.

He did, however, issue an ultimatum. "Nobody was questioning how good Fu-Kuen was or how hard he worked, but the program was not moving," he reflects. "I told everybody involved that if we didn't see significant progress within sixty days, we'd have to get out of the erythropoietin business—not as a threat but as a statement of fact." He continues, "Sixty days was an arbitrary number picked out of thin air. I'd encountered situations like this before at 3M and at Abbott, and setting a deadline usually had very beneficial results. I knew it would get things in gear that otherwise would have been taken for granted."

The number 1 priority was to appeal to Eugene Goldwasser for more erythropoietin. "He was very reluctant to part with it, which was understandable," says George, "because as long as he had the world's only supply of EPO, people would beat a path to his door. But our people went to see Gene and insisted that he give us more material, because what we had wasn't enough to do the job. Now, if they'd thought the project had another year, they probably wouldn't have done that as quickly as they did. It turned out that he had much more than we thought."

The extra supply provided Fu-Kuen Lin with additional information regarding a portion of EPO's amino-acid sequence, enough for him to design more than one hundred special probes that could then be tested on a vast number of gene fragments. Sensing a breakthrough, other scientists began pitching in, too. The probes consisted of short single strands of DNA that might match the sequence for EPO. When the correct probe came upon its complementary gene segment, it formed a pair, thereby providing a clue to a part of EPO's DNA sequence.

Within a few weeks, in October, Lin isolated the EPO gene, on chromosome 7. He elected to clone it using cells derived from the ovary of a Chinese hamster (CHO). One reason for this novel approach was that these CHO cells were especially responsive to treatment with the drug methotrexate, and that improved the chances that the cloned gene would successfully *express,* or switch on, its preprogrammed protein. Another reason was that Genentech had already convinced the U.S. FDA that CHO cells were suitable for manufacturing biotech drugs; this would facilitate faster government approval for EPO.

At that month's employee meeting, which by now had to be held at the nearby Holiday Inn to accommodate all 120 of them, Rathmann asked Fu-Kuen to stand up so that he could acknowledge his achievement in front of the whole company. Not surprisingly, the biologist wasn't there; he was back at the lab, engrossed in his work. It took fifteen minutes for someone to fetch him. George couldn't contain himself, though, and blurted out the extraordinary news. When Lin walked through the door, the room erupted in cheers and a standing ovation.

We were on our way . . . or so it seemed.

CHAPTER 5

EPO on Trial

BRILLIANT RESEARCH, ALTHOUGH an achievement in itself, does not necessarily lead to an effective, salable product. Given the long odds against Amgen's developing a successful medication from recombinant erythropoietin, Fu-Kuen Lin's scientific milestone could turn out to be a millstone, siphoning millions of dollars and hours from the company. That's the nature of the biotech industry.

For a 2003 study, researchers at Tufts University evaluated sixty-eight medicinal compounds that entered into human trials to see how they ultimately fared. (Six were genetically engineered; the rest, conventional pharmaceuticals.) You can see in table 5-1 that about two in three agents test well enough in phase I investigational studies to warrant proceeding with phase II, but only one-third of phase II clinical trials deliver results worthy of moving on to phase III.

To put in perspective the excruciatingly slow tempo of progress in biotechnology, Amgen was nearly four years old when it finally unlocked EPO's molecular secrets. It would take two more years before we could begin testing the hormone in patients, and then an-

TABLE 5-1

The cost of each phase of drug testing

Phase	Cost	Likelihood of moving to the next phase of clinical trials
Phase I clinical trial	$15.2 million	71 percent
Phase II clinical trial	$23.5 million	31.4 percent
Phase III clinical trial	$86.3 million	—

Source: "The price of innovation: New estimates of drug development costs," Tufts Center for the Study of Drug Development, Tufts University; William E. Simon Graduate School of Business Administration, University of Rochester; Department of Economics, Duke University, 2003.

Note: All figures represent the mean.

other three and a half years until Epogen finally reached the marketplace. This was equivalent to a new world speed record.

Knowing that we had a long way to go and that the enterprise could collapse at any point tempered some of the excitement over Lin's discovery. Don't get me wrong: the whole company was thrilled, but we were also cautious. Nor did EPO's leapfrogging to the front of the line diminish the commitment to our other prospective human therapeutics and the diagnostics program. However, the relatively poor showing of our work in specialty chemicals and animal pharmaceuticals led us to discontinue them soon thereafter so that we could concentrate our financial and human resources on therapeutics and diagnostics.

THE DRUG APPROVAL PROCESS

The United States adheres to the world's most rigorous guidelines for ensuring the safety and efficacy of medicines, but it wasn't always that way. As is true of consumer protection in general, government regulations to safeguard the American people have been fortified layer by layer over time—often in the aftermath of a tragedy.

Under the Food and Drugs Act of 1906, the first major piece of federal legislation pertaining to pharmaceuticals, manufacturers were required to demonstrate only the strength and purity of their products. In 1937 the S. E. Massengill Company of Bristol, Tennessee, marketed an elixir of its popular antibacterial medication sulfanilamide, then available in tablet and powder forms. Hundreds of men, women, and children across the country fell deathly ill after ingesting the raspberry-flavored liquid, which turned out to contain a lethal chemical solvent used in antifreeze.

All told, 107 people died. The death toll would have been significantly higher were it not for the quick action of the U.S. Food and Drug Administration (known previously as the Food, Drug, and Insecticide Administration and, before that, the Bureau of Chemistry). Two hundred forty gallons of sulfanilamide had been distributed; with remarkable speed, the FDA tracked down and recovered all except about six gallons.

S. E. Massengill denied any culpability. Legally, the company could not be held accountable, for pharmaceutical firms weren't obligated to test their products for toxicity. But chief chemist and pharmacist Harold Cole Watkins, who'd formulated the elixir, committed suicide. The tragedy prompted Congress to pass the Food, Drug, and Cosmetic Act of 1938. Among the law's provisions was a requirement that new medications be proved safe before they could be marketed.

It took a near catastrophe twenty years later to spur the next landmark drug regulation. In 1958 a nonprescription morning-sickness aid called thalidomide appeared on drugstore shelves in West Germany and eventually throughout Europe. Two years later, evidence began surfacing that thalidomide could cause severe birth defects. By the time the William S. Merrill Company withdrew the drug in 1961, thousands of so-called thalidomide babies, whose mothers had taken the drug during their pregnancies, exhibited thalidomide's disfiguring effects.

The United States was spared a similar epidemic only because Merrill's application to sell thalidomide in the United States landed on the desk of FDA scientist Frances Kelsey. Ironically, she'd been involved with the recall of liquid sulfanilamide more than twenty years earlier. While reviewing the materials submitted by Merrill, she questioned some of the findings and requested further information, postponing approval. During the delay, the story about thalidomide-induced deformities broke internationally. But as the *Washington Post* noted in an investigational report on July 15, 1962, it was only Kelsey's diligence (and perseverance in the face of criticism within the agency) that kept the drug from passing muster. Three thousand American women received thalidomide anyway, because free samples had found their way to some thirteen hundred U.S. doctors.

Congress responded swiftly by unanimously amending the Food, Drug, and Cosmetic Act. For the first time, pharmaceutical companies would have to prove to the FDA's satisfaction "through adequate and well-controlled studies" that a new product was both safe *and* effective. What's more, manufacturers were required to advise the government of all adverse reactions to a drug and to make sure its advertisements carried comprehensive information for physicians about unwanted side effects as well as benefits.

The Drug Amendments Act of 1962 was beefed up four years later. Originally, the new provisions allowed any medication introduced before 1938—when only product safety had to be established—to remain on the market as long as there was no proof that it didn't work. But in 1966 the FDA assigned the National Research Council of the National Academy of Sciences the monumental task of assessing the effectiveness of each of those roughly four thousand drugs. "The Drug Efficacy Study," as it was named, took three years.

Preclinical Studies

Before a pharmaceutical agent can be evaluated in people, it must show impressive results in the laboratory and in animals. Most folks probably aren't aware that the FDA requires animal testing for all potential medications. Because a compound's effects generally differ from one species to the next, it is typically given to more than one type of animal. For much the same reason, the results of animal studies can't necessarily be extrapolated to human beings, but they provide us with essential, if preliminary, information: how the body absorbs the drug; the types and severity of toxicity; and the time the drug takes to be excreted.

Just so you know, all animal-research facilities must adhere to stringent government standards for the ethical and humane treatment of the animals used in testing. Animals in a well-run research center live in a cleaner environment and eat healthier diets than do most people.

According to the Tufts Center for the Study of Drug Development, this preclinical phase consumes $5.2 million and three and a half years, on average. After the company has analyzed and compiled its animal test findings, it develops a plan for a clinical trial: a study incorporating human volunteers. The information is submitted, along with an investigational new drug application (IND), to the FDA. Experts there review the laboratory and animal research. Unless the FDA rejects the application within thirty days, the clinical trial may proceed.

Under certain conditions, the FDA may allow investigators to recruit patients instead of healthy subjects for a phase I trial, as in the case of Epogen. One reason was to expedite the process, because there was no existing treatment for dialysis-related anemia. The other reflected a safety concern: epoetin alfa was intended solely for people with depleted red counts. If a patient's red-cell level was normal, taking the drug could actually be harmful.

Patient Studies: Knuckle-Cracking Time

Epogen's phase I–phase II clinical trial commenced at Seattle's University of Washington Medical Center in December 1985 under the direction of Dr. David Dale, a prolific investigator in the area of anemia and other secondary blood disorders brought about by other conditions.

Large university hospitals, traditionally steeped in research, tend to be the settings for most early-stage medical studies. They're preferable to smaller nonacademic facilities for several reasons. Impeccable record keeping and patient scheduling are imperative. If the protocol calls for daily injections of the experimental compound, that's what it must be. No exceptions. Big centers have the staffs to make it happen on time. They routinely keep accurate records, and, more to the point, they consider research a priority.

They also have large patient populations. Compliance by physicians and patients is likely to be better, and costs will be lower, if a study takes place at a single institution where all the participants are treated by one doctor, or perhaps two or three, as opposed to having twenty-five subjects under the care of twenty-five doctors. (However, phase III studies, which involve hundreds more subjects—sometimes thousands more—must necessarily be carried out at multiple centers.)

Regardless of the hospital's size, it cannot administer an experimental drug to patients without the approval of an *institutional review board* (IRB), a local body appointed by the FDA to authorize clinical research. The board, composed of scientists, doctors, and nurses not affiliated with the study, critiques the trial's safety in advance and either grants approval or demands changes before giving the go-ahead. Most major university research centers have IRBs in house, but if not, they can use the services of another IRB.

During my eighteen years at Amgen, we had some drug candidates that dazzled in the lab only to fizzle in clinical trials. That's something no one can foresee. However, we never had a product re-buffed by the FDA because of questionable science, as has happened to many other companies. Probably the most memorable instance of this in recent years involved the New York biotech company Im-Clone and its highly touted colorectal cancer drug cetuximab (brand name Erbitux), a genetically engineered version of an antibody that interferes with cancer-cell growth.

In 2001, ImClone appeared to be months away from receiving a license for Erbitux, which had been featured on *60 Minutes* and graced the cover of *BusinessWeek*. Based on early-phase clinical trials, the drug looked as if it would be such a winner that pharmaceutical giant Bristol-Myers Squibb agreed to pay $1 billion for the rights to sell Erbitux domestically and in Canada while letting ImClone keep 60 percent of the profits.

But on December 28, 2001, the company sheepishly disclosed in a press release that the FDA had rejected its application, citing serious flaws in the phase III study. For one thing, the trial was supposed to demonstrate Erbitux's effectiveness against *metastatic* colorectal can-cer (denoting that the tumor has spread to another organ or organs) in patients whose disease had not responded to previous treatment with an approved chemotherapy drug. Yet half the men and women enrolled in the trial did not meet that criterion. What's more, said the agency, the data concerning safety was incomplete and riddled with discrepancies and inconsistencies. ImClone lamented publicly that its having to run more studies would delay the product's launch by months. People in the industry knew better: if Erbitux ever joined the ranks of commercially licensed anticancer agents—by no means a certainty—it would probably take a year or two. We weren't sur-prised that the drug didn't go on the market until 2004. Although it's not the landmark therapy it was hoped to be, there is no doubt that cetuximab has helped many patients.

The ImClone story is best remembered for the subsequent scan-dal, when it came to light that its chief executive, far from being "stunned" by the FDA's rejection, as he'd claimed, had apparently gotten wind of the decision days in advance and used that time to quickly unload millions of dollars' worth of company stock. Not only that, but he advised family members and friends to do the same. Martha Stewart, businesswoman and TV/magazine personality (and a former stockbroker), heard of the sales from her broker and promptly sold her ImClone stock. Both he and Stewart went to prison. Although it's seen by many as a cautionary tale of corporate greed and deception, and it is, at the root of the whole sorry saga was nothing more than inept design and execution of a clinical trial.

That never would have happened at Amgen. Our patient studies were meticulously conceived and carried out, largely because we insisted on having scientists, rather than physicians, devise the experiments. Why? With all due respect to MDs, medical schools typically do not teach students how to design an experiment or interpret its results. PhDs are thoroughly trained in both. Doctors participated in our studies, of course, but in advisory roles. For example, the physicians might review the design of an upcoming trial and point out that in the real world the patients would probably be taking a second medication in addition to the one being tested. That's something the PhDs wouldn't have known. So in some studies we'd add the other drug to the protocol for a more realistic, meaningful experiment.

Amgen's criteria for choosing principal investigators sometimes frustrated our sales and marketing staff, who tended to favor highly prestigious doctors—opinion leaders who can give speeches and get people to listen to them. My feeling, and that of R&D, was that a study's positive findings carried far more weight than the chief researcher's name recognition. As CEO I instituted what I believe was a fair rule: our people in R&D would select the physicians—after all, they were responsible for conducting clinical trials—but they had to give serious consideration to recommendations made by sales and marketing.

The fact that U.S. drug manufacturers provide nearly all the funding for such studies and therefore hire the doctors who run them touches on a bit of a systemwide dilemma. It can be argued—and plenty of people have—that this arrangement creates an inherent conflict of interest for the physicians involved and could conceivably taint the findings. The reality is that few universities are endowed with a sufficient budget to finance wholly independent drug-evaluation studies.

I can tell you, though, that fears of professional bias are largely unfounded. Confirmed cynics may sneer, but the vast majority of medical researchers are highly ethical and impervious to any implied pressure to tinker with the facts. Their allegiance is to high-quality science and to patients, and not to the company bankrolling the study. Besides, no amount of spurious interpretation can alter the data, which is scrutinized by medical science professionals at the scientific journals that publish clinical trial results, not to mention the FDA. (For the record, one of the most notorious cases of clinical trial fraud in U.S. history occurred under the direction of the federal National Institutes of Health; in 1993 a Montreal researcher participating in a large multicenter NIH study comparing two types of breast-cancer surgery was found to have falsified results.)

Is there room for improvement? Of course. A 2006 report in the American Medical Association's journal, *JAMA,* examined the findings of more than two hundred randomized patient studies of cardiovascular medicines between 2000 and 2005. Here's what the two authors, from Boston's Harvard Medical School and Brigham and Women's Hospital, found: about 40 percent of the trials financed by not-for-profit organizations favored the experimental therapy over the standard therapy. When the source of funding was a for-profit organization, such as a pharmaceutical manufacturer, the drug being tested proved superior in 66 percent of the studies; and in studies jointly underwritten by both types of organizations, the newer treatment came out on top 54.5 percent of the time. Is this proof of investigator bias? No. What I draw from these numbers is that a pharmaceutical company knows more about its drug than any outsider; therefore, it's able to design more accurate trials. Shoddy data and faulty conclusions stem mainly from incompetence and carelessness. In any event, the debate is likely to go on forever.

A SURPRISE FROM THE FDA.   Certain medicines lend themselves to testing a hypothesis more readily than others. For instance, what if you were assessing the effectiveness of a medication intended to treat pain and stiffness from rheumatoid arthritis? No diagnostic procedure can measure the degree to which an arthritis sufferer hurts or the pain's characteristics (sharp, dull, tingling, and so on). So the verdict might be based on the volunteers' oral or written responses to questions such as, "On a scale of 1 to 10, rate the intensity of your pain both before and after you took the medication."

With anemia due to kidney failure, however, the answer to whether Epogen worked could be assessed from a single number. *Hematocrit,* as it's called, expresses in percentage form the volume of red blood cells contained in blood. When you have your annual physical, the hematocrit test is routinely performed as part of the complete blood count (CBC), with the blood drawn from a vein in your arm or the back of your hand. The average range for a man is 42 percent to 54 percent; for a woman, 38 to 46 percent.

Regular kidney dialysis does a remarkable job of removing impurities from the blood in the absence of functioning kidneys. Unfortunately, the treatment has no effect on red-cell production. Until Epogen, the only therapy available to people with dialysis-related anemia was to undergo transfusions of red blood cells. This was a temporary solution and fraught with complications: repeated transfusions may bring about a potentially serious disorder known as iron overload, where too much of the mineral accumulates in the body; and they can transmit infectious diseases such as HIV and hepatitis B and C. The procedure can also mobilize the body's immune system into churning out antibodies against the foreign red blood cells. This could preclude a patient from one day receiving a kidney transplant, the one full-fledged cure for ESRD.

The average dialysis patient's hematocrit is about one-half to one-third that of a healthy adult. "Testing erythropoietin seemed as if it would be really straightforward," says Kirby Alton, then the leader of our interferon projects. "You're anemic, your hematocrit is low, you're given EPO, and your hematocrit goes up. That is a very doable, successful experiment."

He was shocked, then, when the FDA objected to using hematocrit as the study's medical end point—the general outcome that the protocol is supposed to evaluate, such as severe side effects, disease progression despite treatment, or death. "We'd gone to Washington to meet with the FDA and get approval for our study design," says Kirby. The first thing out of their mouths was, 'Improved hematocrit is not a clinical benefit. What's the clinical benefit?' John [Adamson] nearly fell out of his chair." John Adamson was to be one of the study's authors, along with his University of Washington colleague Dr. Joseph Eschbach. The two had performed important research on EPO in the late 1970s and early 1980s, working with sheep.

A higher hematocrit didn't confer a clinical benefit? Was the FDA kidding? If your percentage of red blood cells is increased, your tissues are imbued with more life-sustaining oxygen. Your energy returns. Indeed, as would be shown only months into the study, recombinant erythropoietin transformed patients' lives.

Well, prove it, said the FDA.

"So," says Alton, "we ended up having to use the subjects' dependence on blood transfusions as the study's end point." In other words, the goal was to demonstrate that raising the patients' hematocrits would reduce the number of transfusions they needed to be able to function.

OF MICE AND MEN. Although recombinant EPO had worked extremely well in mice, it could still fail in people. Many human biological systems are controlled by a feedback loop and sometimes include the equivalent of an accelerator and a brake. In mice, EPO acted as a gas pedal, stimulating the bone marrow to manufacture red blood cells. But what if ESRD sufferers became anemic not due to a defective accelerator but because they had a faulty braking mechanism that somehow interfered with red-cell production or prevented the cells from maturing normally? If that proved to be the case, flooring the gas pedal might merely prompt greater resistance from the brakes. That was one big question we needed to answer.

Another question concerned the effect of increasing the hematocrit of people on dialysis. In some medical circles, it was believed that ESRD patients were *supposed* to have abnormally low hematocrits; that the body reduced the volume of red cells for good reason, intentionally thinning the blood. No one knew for certain whether that was true. A third source of worry was whether the drug would trigger an immune response, with the body attacking the genetically engineered hormone.

Every one of those doubts was erased well before the end of the trial. Data from animal studies helps us to estimate the therapeutic dose in people: a dosage strong enough to induce a response (hopefully) but not so high that it produces bothersome side effects (again, hopefully). The twenty-five participants were injected with Epogen at their thrice-weekly hemodialysis sessions. Of the eighteen men and women administered adequate doses, eleven soon saw their hematocrit levels increase dramatically—and with that, a boost in energy—and twelve patients who had regularly required transfusions no longer needed them. These results occurred at a dosage so low that not one negative side effect was observed. In fact, we once calculated that an aspirin-sized amount of Epogen's active ingredient would be enough to treat someone with ESRD-related anemia for forty years.

We did have one scare, though, when patient number 6 arrived at the dialysis center looking as red as a beet. It so alarmed a physician associated with the trial that he immediately alerted the FDA instead of contacting us or the lead investigator. Was EPO instigating a dangerous rise in blood pressure? Was it an unanticipated inflammatory reaction? We couldn't imagine. For two days, everyone at Amgen seemed to wear the same fretful expression. Then the cause of the change in the man's complexion was revealed: he'd gone to the beach and suffered a nasty sunburn. Now it was the reporting doctor's turn to be red faced.

The study, published in the January 8, 1987, edition of the *New England Journal of Medicine,* concluded, "These results demonstrate that recombinant human erythropoietin is effective, can eliminate the need for transfusions with their risks of immunologic sensitization, infection, and iron overload, and can restore the hematocrit to normal in many patients with the anemia of end-stage renal disease."

Phase III: Prospective, Randomized, Controlled, and Double Blind

One more crucial step remained: a large-scale phase III prospective randomized controlled double-blind clinical trial, the type universally preferred by researchers and drugmakers alike because it delivers the purest, most convincing information for proving a definite link, or causal relationship, between a particular treatment and a health condition. The best way to define the lengthy term is to deconstruct it word by word:

- *Prospective:* any research project that studies one or more groups of patients from the present time until some point in the future. (A *retrospective* study analyzes data that was collected in the past.)

- *Controlled:* a comparison study in which participants are assigned to one of two or more groups. The study group receives the investigational treatment, and the control group is given a lookalike inert substance (the placebo). If merely prescribing a placebo could jeopardize the health of the volunteers, the current standard therapy is used as a control. There are even sham surgeries, simulated acupuncture treatments, and so on for evaluating the effectiveness of new procedures.

- *Randomized:* If we're comparing one treatment to another or to a placebo, we need to have some idea of their relative value. The purpose of randomization is to make sure that the control group and the treatment group are comparable. In this way, if we introduce an investigational therapy in one group and not in the other, and if the study group gets better compared with the other, there's a high probability that the effect shown is due to the therapy.

  Many factors can distort a study's outcome, beginning with the selection of patients. Employing a random process for distributing subjects to the study group and the control group precludes the possibility that someone involved in the trial will subconsciously stock the experimental arm with "ringers"—patients who, for whatever reason, would respond well, thus resulting in more favorable results.

- *Double blind:* Surely someone can tell whether she's been given a placebo, right? Not if she's part of a blind study. In a single-blind trial, the participants don't know whether they're in the control group or the study group until the experiment is completed; a double-blind trial also keeps the research staff in the dark. Why do researchers take this precaution? It's because a doctor might inadvertently reveal which protocol a patient is on, through facial expressions, body language, or tone of voice. Keeping the subjects' group allocations confidential also prevents investigators' personal biases from influencing the results.

Epogen's phase III clinical trial, carried out at the University of Alabama Medical Center, recruited 333 anemic dialysis patients. Within twelve weeks, all except 2.6 percent of the control group exhibited improved red-cell levels, and not one required a transfusion—powerful findings by any definition. The drug was so effective, in fact, that the researchers had a difficult time trying to disguise which patients were in which group. As an Amgen scientist observed pointedly to one of the frustrated doctors, "Why, I can stand here halfway across the room and tell you which patients are on EPO and which are on placebo."

"How can you do that?"

He said, "Well, *look* at 'em! Some of them are pink and some of them aren't." The men and women taking Epogen had healthy complexions and felt good, but the people in the control group were pale. Pretty soon, many of the volunteers had figured out who was receiving what. The drug was that effective.

The Internet has complicated the process of conducting blind studies, because some patients open an online chat room and tell the world how they're feeling and swap information, trying to deduce which group they're in. Usually it's only a matter of curiosity. However, at times a person will determine that he's in the placebo group and quit the trial; it's one of the unforeseeable negative aspects of access to information through the Internet. Clinical studies must enlist more people than in the past to compensate for the higher dropout rate.

Incidentally, the FDA automatically classifies dropouts as *nonresponders*—people for whom the experimental therapy did not work. Once, in a weight-loss trial that we were conducting, the volunteer who'd lost more pounds than anyone else was tragically killed in a car accident before completing the study. Under FDA rules, he was reported as having dropped out and therefore was considered a nonresponder, when in fact his response to the drug had exceeded everyone's expectations.

THE SIMI VALLEY HOSTAGES

After the third and final phase of human trials, the drug company carefully analyzes all of its scientific data and then submits it to the FDA as a new drug application (NDA) or a *biologic license application* (BLA). An average NDA or BLA runs more than 100,000 pages. Based on the spectacular results of our patient studies, there was no question that Epogen would receive the FDA's blessing and become Amgen's first commercial product, so we were understandably eager to speed the process on our end in any way we could.

In August 1987, a team of about twelve staffers began the arduous task of preparing the documentation. The job probably should have taken about 280 days; our employees resolved to get it done in only 90 days, working in shifts virtually around the clock.

One of them was Dennis Fenton. "We didn't have a lot of office space where we could work undisturbed," he recalls, "so we rented a block of ten rooms at the Posada Royale Quality Inn in Simi Valley," about ten miles away. The team became known as the Simi Valley Hostages.

By this time, we'd licensed some of the rights to Epogen to Ortho Pharmaceuticals (you'll learn more about that in chapter 6). When the people at Ortho heard that we planned to complete the BLA within ninety days, they told us it was impossible. "It was quite an inspiration to us," says Fenton. "We felt, 'We'll show those guys! We're going to get it done in ninety days, like we said we would.' And we did."

Well, almost. It took ninety-three days, to be exact, from August 3 to October 30. Mike Downing, our clinical affairs director, painted "The Simi Valley Hostages Are Free! 93 Days!" on a bedsheet and hung it over the entrance of building 1. The paperwork was compiled into 140 volumes, which formed a stack nine feet high.

"In a weird way, it was kind of fun," Dennis says. "It built a lot of close relationships among the people who were involved. For a number of years, we used to have reunions back at the same hotel." This wasn't the last time that the people who worked at Amgen displayed an extraordinary dedication and commitment to getting the job done. How do you find employees like that? And how do you keep them? In chapter 9, I tell you.

CHAPTER **6**

Partnerships Made in
Heaven—and That Other Place

ONE DAY IN THE fall of 1988, George Rathmann called me into his office and told me that he was stepping down. Before I'd even digested that news, which came as a shock, he shook my hand and said, "Congratulations, Gordon. The board has elected you CEO."

At the time, Amgen was only months away from earning FDA approval to market Epogen, and our second recombinant hematopoietic growth factor, filgrastim (Neupogen), had recently tested well in a phase I/II clinical trial for cancer patients undergoing chemotherapy. The question on many people's minds, inside and outside the company, was, "Why on earth is George retiring now?" After an arduous eight-year trek up the mountain, why not savor the view from the top, at least for a little while?

"It was a combination of things," explains George. "I'd been working extremely hard, and my wife decided that she would much rather have a poor husband than be a wealthy widow. But also, I felt it was a good time for Amgen to bring in a new CEO, so that he would have the momentum from taking Epogen across the finish line, instead of coming in afterward." He adds with a laugh, "It turned out to be a brilliant call." (It was so brilliant, in fact, that twelve years later I followed his precedent, timing my retirement just as the pipeline was about to deliver four new products. Neither of us believes in changing horses in midstream.)

Still, the announcement shook up everyone. "We all loved George," says Kirby Alton. "I spent six hours in his office one night trying to change his mind." I'm sure, too, that some folks questioned the wisdom of leaving a biotech firm in the hands of a "finance guy" instead of, say, a molecular biologist. After six years as Amgen's CFO, however, I'd become fairly fluent in the science. I didn't always have the answers, but I'd learned enough to ask our researchers most of the right questions about ongoing projects. Although we tend to think of scientists as reserved and dispassionate, nothing could be further from the truth; their eyes lit up whenever they discussed their work.

I'd always been fascinated by science, having grown up in Alamogordo, New Mexico, a major government site for testing and developing guided missiles, pilotless aircraft, and other research programs. In my home town it wasn't out of the ordinary to see a missile streak toward a radio-controlled airplane overhead and knock it out of the sky. For a teenager, this was thrilling stuff. I made up my mind then that I was going to become an engineer and, by God, help put a man on the moon. But I got sidetracked.

After graduating from Purdue University with a BS in electrical engineering in 1957, I served three years as an officer on the USS *Intrepid,* now a floating pierside museum in Manhattan. Even during peacetime, aircraft carriers spent six days a week at sea because navy pilots had to practice flight maneuvers constantly. One thing about being in the middle of the ocean is that you have plenty of time on your hands. Between reading *Fortune* magazine and a pile of books about business, I became increasingly drawn to commerce and less interested in electrical engineering. As soon as my tour of duty ended, I enrolled in the Harvard Business School MBA program.

In Amgen's early years, almost every employee held a doctorate in one science or another, and with biotechnology still in an embryonic stage, it was central to the company's success that its first chief executive happened to be a scientist himself. That was no longer true in 1988. Given the makeup of the company, Amgen would always be inextricably anchored in research no matter who sat in the CEO's chair. And by the time I handed the reins to Kevin Sharer, a background in science was even less a prerequisite for a biotech chief exec.

The board of directors could have hired a veteran CEO from outside the company, but the members knew that it would involve a great deal of change, and they wanted Amgen to continue as it was. I'll let Dennis Fenton describe the mood around Amgen after Rathmann made his decision known: "At first, there was a sense of panic over George's leaving. But then we thought, 'Wait, it's OK—it's Gordon. Always very reasonable, always willing to listen. We're going to be all right.' With an outside person, though, everyone would have worried that the whole place was going to change."

By announcing his retirement and his successor at the same time, Rathmann enabled Amgen to avoid a runoff for the job. That's one of the worst things an organization can do. It turns candidates who should be working together into competitors, and that can poison the atmosphere by forcing lower-level employees to choose sides. It all but guarantees that every one of the losing contenders will end up leaving the company.

Amgen tried a different approach: under our new structure, George would remain chairman of the board for two years, and Harry Hixon, VP of product development, was elevated to chief operating officer and president. Hixon had come to Amgen in 1985 from Abbott Laboratories, where at one time he'd reported to Rathmann.

Although this arrangement was intended to ensure a seamless transition, to some extent it strained the organization at the seams.

George Rathmann divvied up the company, starting with research and development, which had always been a single entity. Now development was handed to Hixon, along with manufacturing and marketing, and I oversaw research, finance, all staff functions—and Harry. It's hard for me to be impartial, so here are Kirby Alton's observations on this shaky period in Amgen's history: "George probably restructured the organization this way in order to give Gordon and Harry enough control that both would stay. But it created a lot of friction. As the new vice president of development, I was kind of caught in the middle, because development basically fits in between research and manufacturing."

Hixon has been quoted as saying that he and I are two very different people with dramatically different management styles, and on this point we're in full agreement. To be honest, the board of directors probably sensed from the outset that the shotgun marriage might be headed for trouble. Both of us were told bluntly that if we didn't try to make this sort of coalition government concept work, an experienced CEO would be imported from another company, and we would both have to leave. As professionals, of course we had every intention of working together. But we were like two porcupines mating: how do they do it? *Very* carefully.

Although George Rathmann had been named Gold Medalist biotechnology CEO of the Year in 1987 and 1988 by *The Wall Street Transcript,* following in his footsteps wasn't as daunting as you might think. Amgen was in great shape, with great people, great product candidates, and momentum. It also helped that with Epogen's approval drawing near, the company was changing. George had thrived on the vitality of a smaller organization, and the larger it became, the less fun it was for him. (He intended to try his hand at a life of leisure, but within a year and a half he became the chief executive officer, chairman, and president of ICOS, a biotech company in suburban Seattle. After eight years there, Rathmann quickly cut short a second retirement to assume all three positions at a California biotech firm called Hyseq.)

As for me, I couldn't wait for Amgen to grow. I'd worked for large firms before and felt that my managerial skills were even better suited to a company of that size.

One classic mistake that executives often make following a promotion or a change in companies is to try to imprint their style too soon—sometimes when no change is warranted at all. For example, Kevin Sharer freely admits to being overly aggressive when he arrived at MCI Communications Corporation from General Electric:

At GE, there was a presumption that a new general manager would make an impact on the business quickly, and that if you can run one business, you can run any business. When I went to MCI as president, I was forty years old and, in some ways, a relatively young and unsophisticated senior executive. I probably felt my oats more than was fully prudent. After just a month or two on the job, I went to the CEO and told him, "I think you've all misconceptualized this business, and we need to fundamentally reorganize." The fact that I was right didn't matter. I hadn't built sufficient internal credibility.

At the senior executive level, management is more nuanced, and you have to carefully weigh the organization's readiness for change. Obviously, if you believe it's a burning platform issue and the very existence of the organization is threatened without the change, then you're more likely to act in a somewhat unilateral way. But if it's change that could happen three months from now, or six months from now, it's a lot better to prepare the ground first than to simply exercise your power to effect change.

I realized my mistake and learned from it, so that when I came to Amgen three years later, I consciously waited to become an insider before making any dramatic moves. The changes were subtle. People would notice that things were different, but they couldn't point to any single decision that caused it.

As for me, I certainly had no intention of instituting immediate wholesale changes as chief executive officer. There was no call for it. Besides, my time was monopolized almost entirely by two crises that could have capsized the company.

PATENTLY ABSURD: THE CASE AGAINST GENETICS INSTITUTE

Only three months into my tenure as CEO, Amgen was embroiled in a pair of lawsuits with two other drug companies. The first involved a patent-infringement suit that we'd filed against Massachusetts bio-tech firm Genetics Institute (GI) and its Japanese partner, Chugai Pharmaceutical Co., in 1987.

Patent litigation is so commonplace in the biotech field that it gets factored in to the overall cost of bringing a drug to market. And what a cost. A no-stone-unturned dispute can drag on for years and easily chew through $20 million to $30 million on each side. Yet you spend it without flinching because it's your only way to protect your research and development achievements. If Amgen had owned billions of dollars in gold bars, we'd have locked them away in an underground vault and posted armed guards around the building to prevent theft. However, our assets were intellectual property—intangible human knowledge and ideas (see "What Is and Isn't Patentable"). So we hired patent attorneys to preserve the rights granted to us by the U.S. Patent and Trademark Office (USPTO).

A U.S. product patent entitles the patent holder to prevent anyone else from making, using, or selling its invention or discovery for twenty years from the date the patent application was filed. Because

What Is and Isn't Patentable

Over the years, the U.S. Patent and Trade Office has gradually clarified the ground rules for patenting genetically engineered products and processes. Here's a rundown of the key guidelines:

- A naturally occurring gene or protein *as it exists in the body* (an important distinction) is not eligible for patent protection. However, once the substance has been isolated *outside of the body*—and has been shown to have at least one credible use in therapeutics, diagnostics, or some other application—it can be patented.

- New uses for a product are also patentable, even if the gene or protein itself has been patented by someone else.

it typically takes the USPTO three years to issue a patent, in reality the protection lasts roughly seventeen years. When the patent expires, all companies are free to make, use, and sell the discovery or invention. In addition to patent protection, under the Orphan Drug Act, Epogen was already guaranteed seven years of market exclusivity, to start as soon as it received FDA approval.

Amgen submitted its patent application on December 13, 1983. As of mid-1987, we were still waiting. The patent office operates a bit like a Turkish bazaar. Invariably, it initially turns down most claims. The applicant then supplies additional documentation and restates its case. Frequently the USPTO rejects claims a second time, forcing the company to submit even more evidence. In the end, the patent office and the company may agree on a narrower patent. The haggling can go on for years.

Another problem was that the USPTO staff consisted almost entirely of engineers and chemists, and not molecular biologists. Consequently, the agency didn't really know how to process claims on genetically engineered drugs. Applications started to pile up, and it took longer and longer for patents to be issued.

Out of frustration, our trade association, the Biotechnology Industry Organization (BIO), offered to train USPTO employees in the science of biotechnology at no cost—anything to speed up the process. The patent office gratefully accepted, and the program was highly successful in helping reduce the backlog of applications.

To be fair to the USPTO, the complexities regarding ownership were far from settled. To some degree, they still aren't. What exactly are you declaring as yours? The gene sequence? The amino-acid sequence? The process for making the drug? The drug formulation? A method of using the drug? All of the above? The patent ultimately issued to Genetics Institute claimed only the purification of EPO from human urine, whereas our first patent covered the gene sequence of human EPO. We had filed for other claims as well, including one covering the amino-acid sequence and several related to manufacturing, but these were still pending.

On June 30, 1987, Genetics Institute announced that it had been awarded the first patent for EPO, completely blindsiding us. Amgen had filed its application more than a year before GI. Also, as our general counsel, Robert Weist, explains, "Usually you'll know what your competition is up to because publications in foreign countries will contain news about other companies filing patent applications there. In the case of Genetics Institute's patent on erythropoietin, there was no such early warning. For whatever reason, they hadn't filed outside the U.S., so our normal patent surveillance didn't reveal anything about what they were doing here in the States." At the time, U.S. patent applications remained confidential until the patent was assigned, whereas other countries publish patent applications a year or more after they're filed but before the patent is granted. The USPTO has since joined the rest of the world in publishing patent applications prior to granting patents.

Weist continues:

Not only that, but after we'd filed our basic patent applications, I'd written letters to all the other companies that had been trying to clone the gene for EPO and put them on notice that Amgen had no intention of licensing the patent to anyone; we were going to manufacture and distribute Epogen ourselves or with a partner. We received some interesting responses. 3M, one of the world's most ethical organizations—but also highly aggressive at filing on any and all inventions and pressuring the USPTO to issue stronger patents—sent a very gracious letter of congratulations and said that it would pursue other projects.

Genetics Institute's position was altogether different. Basically, they said that Amgen might have been first, but they were working in this area, too, and they saw no reason why the field wasn't big enough for two players. They planned to proceed with their own recombinant erythropoietin product.

Bob wasn't overly worried, though. Neither was George Rathmann, who over the years had learned to analyze patents about as well as any patent lawyer, in part because one of his brothers was a patent attorney. According to Weist, "We felt comfortable with the position that Amgen was indeed first, we'd made a significant discovery, and we'd filed the patent applications properly. We were confident that would be recognized in the courts if it came to that." But considering that the patenting of genes, proteins, and so on was unfamiliar territory, nothing was certain.

For some technical reason, our application and GI's application had been reviewed by different sections of the patent office. Apparently the section that handled its application took fewer coffee breaks; how else can we explain why GI was awarded its patent first? We perfected a slow burn throughout the summer, knowing that the moment we received our patent on the DNA used to produce Epogen, we would sue GI in federal court for patent infringement. That day came on October 27, 1987. As expected, Genetics Institute immediately countersued, claiming that our patent was invalid.

A drug company with a potential blockbuster on its hands often feels like the besieged sheriff of a dusty frontier town. One desperado after another comes gunning for him on the off chance that they might outduel him and be free to plunder the town bank. Generic-drug manufacturers often do this. Rather than wait until an existing patent expires, they try to prove it invalid. If they're successful, it's often a double victory: not only do they get to market early, but also they usually receive a head start on their generic competitors as the sole producer for six months.

Another strategy is to pressure the patent holder to enter into a settlement. Predictably, at one point GI offered to cross-license Epogen with us in exchange for dropping its suit. Under this arrangement, each company would be free to sell EPO. We refused. Genetics Institute didn't even start working in earnest on EPO until well after Fu-Kuen Lin's successful cloning of human erythropoietin, so why should we share the rewards from our groundbreaking—and immensely costly—research?

The USPTO froze all further work on applications related to Epogen until the lawsuits were settled. As a result, throughout 1988 two companies were laying claim to recombinant human erythropoietin, each with its own patent, and with still other patents pending. Wall Street investors weren't sure what or whom to believe.

Genetics Institute had a policy of licensing its drugs to large pharmaceutical firms instead of marketing them itself. Thanks to a loophole in a federal trade law, the Tokyo-based Chugai company could help GI conquer the U.S. market in a way that no company based in the United States could. Our patent prevented competitors

Two Landmark Laws That Shaped Biotech History

Nineteen eighty was a watershed year for biotechnology-related legislation. Without the Bayh-Dole Act and the Supreme Court ruling in the case of *Diamond* v. *Chakrabarty*, it's doubtful that the industry would have grown as rapidly as it did.

In the early 1970s, a General Electric biochemist named Ananda Chakrabarty genetically modified a *Pseudomonas* bacterium so that it would break down and consume crude oil; the compound was designed for use in the event of an oil spill. The patent office denied his claim, asserting that "as living things, microbes are not patentable subject matter." After eight years of legal appeals, the case landed in the U.S. Supreme Court. In June 1980 the Court narrowly upheld Chakrabarty's patent by a 5–4 vote, stating that the oil-eating bacterium was manmade and not a product of nature. With biotech companies now assured of protection for their discoveries and inventions, research surged.

Six months later Congress passed the Patent and Trademark Act Amendments of 1980, cosponsored by senators Birch Bayh (D-IN) and Bob Dole (R-KS). This law, too, stimulated research by permitting small businesses and universities to own the titles to inventions resulting from federally funded research programs.

Until then, those patents had belonged to the government, which handed out nonexclusive licenses to anyone and everyone. With no patent protection, few companies were willing to invest in and develop these discoveries; of 28,000 government-controlled patents, only about 1 in 20 were licensed to industry. Today approximately 2,000 patents are awarded to universities each year, as compared with perhaps 250 annually before the Bayh-Dole Act took effect in 1981.

from manufacturing Epogen in the United States, but it did not apply to those that produced the drug outside U.S. borders. Remarkably, this oversight—corrected many years later—created the absurd situation wherein a company such as Chugai could circumvent a U.S. patent simply by making EPO offshore, freely using the protected technology, and then exporting the product to America. For a time the U.S. patent system actually favored foreign-based businesses over their U.S.-based counterparts.

Four days after our patent was issued, Gabe Schmergel, GI's president, publicly stated that his company intended to ship Chugai the genetically engineered cells needed to make EPO. We complained vigorously to the U.S. International Trade Commission. ITC Administrative Law Judge Sydney Harris agreed with our contention that Chugai would be guilty of patent infringement. Nevertheless, she dismissed our initial complaint on the grounds that, for technical reasons, the commission lacked jurisdiction to prevent the importation of EPO. Although that decision was overturned on appeal in federal court, no action was taken; the judge concluded that the matter should be remedied by Congress in the form of new legislation, and not by the legal system.

The U.S. patent system is designed to grant patents to the first person to invent, and not the first person to file. Thus Genetics Institute could contest Amgen's patent on any of four grounds:

- *We did it first.* This was GI's contention.

- *The patent is not valid because the invention was "obvious."* The challenger must demonstrate that prior work in the field renders the invention an inevitable development rather than a true innovation. GI claimed this, too.

- *The patent is not valid because the invention was covered by "prior art."* Once something has been published or otherwise revealed publicly, it cannot be patented. Many otherwise patentable university inventions cannot be protected for this reason.

- *The patent is not enforceable because the applicant misinformed or withheld information from the patent office.* As far as I know, patent applications are the only documents submitted to the government in which the applicant is required to disclose every reason it can think of that the application should be rejected. The onus is on the patent seeker to make all relevant details known to the patent office, including information that might reflect poorly on its application. Failing to reveal the whole truth is considered "fraud on the patent office." Strangely, this action doesn't void your patent but makes it unenforceable. Of course, there's always the chance that the data you supply could derail your obtaining patent protection in the first place.

One frequent mistake that patent filers make is to pursue the broadest possible protection in the belief that casting a wide net will provide the most security. In fact, the reverse is true. I learned this little-understood principle when I was at Litton Industries in the early 1960s.

At the time, there was a British inventor who'd been awarded a patent on any and all printed circuit boards, believe it or not. He had thirty companies paying him sizable royalties. IBM and Litton, though, held out and refused to pay royalties. Litton's strategy was to stall and hope that some other company would dispute the patent, pay the necessary legal fees, and win.

Thank you, IBM. A judge threw out the patent on the grounds that it was too broad. For years, those thirty companies had been paying money for an invalid patent.

You see, patents constitute a covenant between inventors and society. Society says, "We will give you exclusivity for a period of time to produce and sell your product. In return, you will reveal to the world what you've come up with." Society does not want one person to wield too much control, though, and rightly so. At some rung on the legal system ladder, a patent that is too broad will get knocked down. The ideal patent should be broad enough to prevent other people from infringing on the claimant's innovation, and no broader.

It's wise, though, to apply for multiple patents with multiple claims; theoretically, as long as you possess one ironclad claim, you win. Adding others, even if they're weak, can help reinforce the power of the first, because judges and juries are likely to feel that a product embodying more than one invention and protected by more than one patent is more deserving of exclusivity.

AMGEN AND GENETICS INSTITUTE GO TO TRIAL

The federal district judge who was set to try *Amgen* v. *Genetics Institute* in Boston was mired in a complex, high-profile organized-crime trial with more than a dozen defendants. He indicated that, at most, he'd be able to devote one day a week to our case—and two hundred others. To expedite matters, both sides agreed with his recommendation to go before Patti Sarris, then a magistrate. (In Massachusetts, a magistrate is a local judicial official, and not an actual judge, who presides over a case under a judge's supervision. Most states do not have magistrates.)

The trial opened in January 1989. If you sit in a courtroom long enough, you'll conclude that big-time law firms, prominent attorneys, and major corporations have no compunction about putting forth the most preposterous positions imaginable. My all-time favorite was uttered in a different patent dispute involving Epogen. The opposing company had run afoul of an Amgen patent on using mammalian cells to manufacture EPO and a second Amgen patent on using vertebrate cells. Our adversary used human cells to produce EPO; Amgen, as I've mentioned, relied on Chinese hamster ovary cells.

Any high school student who stayed awake during biology class knows that humans are both vertebrates and mammals. Yet opposing counsel got up in court and with a straight face argued that, in the context of this patent, humans were neither vertebrates nor mammals. Amgen won the case.

Genetics Institute's countersuit contained several equally audacious claims, not the least of which was its allegation that one of its scientists had come up with Epogen first. During the trial, Magistrate Sarris determined the exact date on which Amgen's Fu-Kuen Lin had invented the drug. "We've won!" I thought. GI's "inventor" wasn't yet an employee of the company at that time. This seemingly insurmountable evidence did not rattle the witness in the least. "I invented EPO during my job interview at Genetics Institute," he testified under oath. Next, the person who'd allegedly conducted the interview took the stand to attest that, yes, the scientist had invented Epogen in between asking about GI's benefits package and vacation policy.

Admittedly, this account does fall within the realm of legal possibility. In patent law, the date of invention can be the date that the inventor "conceived" the idea. However, for the invention to be patentable, the inventor must exercise reasonable diligence in reducing the invention to practice.

All scientists keep hardbound laboratory notebooks in which they record each day's findings. A second staff member then countersigns the pages to prevent someone from backdating information. These notebooks are introduced as evidence in patent-infringement cases. The Genetics Institute scientist produced no such notebook dated before ours. Nor did the company document that it had met the requirement of due diligence.

I was convinced that the case would go Amgen's way and that therefore we should fight it to the end. Attorney Steve Odre, head of our patent department, agreed, but few others did. Every Wall Street analyst I knew disapproved of our aggressive position and urged us to accept GI's offer to cross-license our respective patents. Even some of our board members were leaning in that direction.

I fully understood their concern and caution. Whenever a business litigates, it assumes a degree of risk, no matter how sturdy its case. New evidence can be introduced that undermines your position. And judges are human and make mistakes. What if the magistrate declared both Amgen's and GI's patents invalid? Then any company would be free to manufacture EPO. One thing was certain: the lawsuit was depressing the price of Amgen stock.

The ongoing dispute produced our first incident of corporate espionage. An Amgen researcher secretly mailed Genetics Institute several pages of documents related to Epogen. His accompanying note said, "This is just a free sample" and promised much more important information for sale. It ended, "Where can we meet?"

To GI's credit, it alerted us. George Rathmann immediately called the Thousand Oaks police department to report the theft. He was astonished when the officer manning the desk brushed him off. "We really aren't equipped to do much about white-collar crime. If somebody robs a bank, we know what to do, but we can't help you very much. Sorry about that." Out of frustration, he called the FBI. At first, the person he spoke to was equally dismissive. "We're really busy and have limited resources. Because there's so much white-collar crime, we don't investigate any theft under one million dollars."

"Fine," snapped George. "This is worth *hundreds* of millions of dollars." With that, the bureau came on board. One of its agents spent enough time at Amgen to learn the language of biotechnology. Then he called the suspect, pretending to be from Genetics Institute, and arranged to meet him at a local restaurant. By the time the thief arrived, hidden cameras had been installed, and every waiter and patron had been replaced by a member of the FBI in disguise. It didn't take long for the cameras to capture money changing hands, and then papers. Soon the suspect was in handcuffs and hearing his Miranda rights. He went to jail for two years. Thankfully, his theft didn't harm our case at all.

The second week in January 1989, Magistrate Sarris upheld Amgen's patent but at the same time preserved GI's patent. The decision wasn't the complete victory we had hoped for; that would come two years later in federal appeals court. However, it appeared to clear the way for Epogen's coming-out party.

Any relief we felt was quickly extinguished, though. On January 23, Ortho Pharmaceuticals, a subsidiary of Johnson & Johnson, filed a court action requesting an injunction to block the launch of Epogen. At Amgen, reaction to the news was one of shock. After all, Johnson & Johnson was our business partner.

AMGEN'S SEARCH FOR PARTNERSHIPS

Amgen's original business plan had called for enlisting partners to market our first three products, an established practice that started with Humulin, the first biotech drug. Genentech produced the synthetic insulin, but it was sold by pharmaceutical heavyweight Eli Lilly and Company, which boasted major distribution capabilities and, most important, plenty of money.

We recognized that even though Amgen would probably be a decade old when its first product was ready, we still would not be large enough to market pharmaceuticals on our own. Seattle biotech firm Immunex, founded the same year as Amgen, discovered the disadvantage of being small the hard way in the late 1990s. Immunex developed the highly effective arthritis medication Enbrel, only to find that its modest production plant couldn't keep up with consumer demand. Of the more than one million Americans who suffer from severe rheumatoid arthritis, only seventy-five thousand could get their hands on the drug. Many more went onto a waiting list for Enbrel. *BusinessWeek* estimated that the production lag cost Immunex at least

$200 million in profits in 2000 alone. A year later, the company agreed to be bought by Amgen for $16 billion, in the largest biotech acquisition in history.

From the start, we were convinced that we had only a few years in which to become a full-fledged biotech pharmaceutical firm. If we failed, we'd be dog meat or, at best, somebody's acquisition (see "The Fermenta [Near] Fiasco"). Surely, we thought, the big pharma corporations would eventually catch on to the promise of biological medicines and take over the industry. Much to our surprise—and satisfaction—they waited for more than a decade before leaving the starting gate, an action that gave the biotech industry the opportunity to develop.

Amgen's strategy for geographic growth was as follows: We would license out the distribution of our first product in each of three markets—the U.S., Europe, and Japan. After that, the company was to be running at full speed and capable of doing everything itself in all major countries. Unlike many start-ups, Amgen actually adhered to its global strategy; history shows that it was a good plan.

After Fu-Kuen Lin cloned the EPO gene in late 1983, it seemed a ripe opportunity to seek out partners. For an up-and-coming company, partnerships also help establish credibility with stock investors and provide healthy infusions of cash.

Although we weren't even a year removed from our $43 million initial public offering, Amgen never stopped trying to raise money. When your future success turns on research and development, there's no such thing as enough. Many companies worry about dilution of their stock holdings and sell fewer shares than they could. Amgen didn't concern itself with dilution. The way we saw it, raising twice as much money would enable us to hire twice as many scientists, conduct twice as much research, and develop twice as many products. There really wouldn't *be* any dilution.

Furthermore, given the poor showing of our stock, along with most other biotech stocks, we couldn't be certain that Amgen would

The Fermenta (Near) Fiasco

Numerous companies launched during the first wave of biotech firms were eventually swallowed by other firms. To date, only one potential buyer has ever contacted Amgen.

In 1985, Refaat el-Sayed, a thirty-eight-year-old Egyptian business-man by way of Sweden, came calling. In only four years, the charis-matic el-Sayed had amassed the second-largest fortune in Sweden by buying up money-hemorrhaging drug companies, starting with one called Fermenta. Swedish national TV named him the country's man of the year.

George Rathmann was intrigued by Fermenta's proposition and in-vited el-Sayed to an Amgen board meeting to explain what he had in mind. The directors were almost universally turned off by the man, in part because he brought with him an executive from another Swedish company to sing his praises. It seemed odd. Neither I nor the other senior managers were in favor of collaborating with el-Sayed, so noth-ing came of it.

It was a good thing, too. A few months later, el-Sayed was exposed as having fraudulently misrepresented himself as a microbiologist holding multiple PhDs. The accusations, which he admitted were true, sank a proposed merger with Volvo, Sweden's largest company, and forced el-Sayed to resign as Fermenta president. By 1987 he had filed for bankruptcy, with debts of $60 million.

be able to conduct a second public sale very soon. Conventional wis-dom says that bankers or investors won't accept a second offering at a price below the IPO. To them, it's a bad sign, indicating that the company is heading in the wrong direction. Amgen had a long way to go to climb back to $18 per share.

We were always extremely disciplined financially. Certain things were out of our hands, such as unanticipated lawsuits from partners and competitors or an industrywide drop in stock prices. But whatever we could control, we did, like making sure that our plans for acquiring new buildings and personnel were in line with our financial capabilities. Three fiscal years in a row, Amgen showed a profit—not bad for a company without any products. Our aim was to get our stock price up and earn at least one penny per share each quarter, because there's magic in being in the black. Why one cent? We wanted to spend the extra money on R&D, and earning two or three cents per quarter wouldn't have been any more beneficial than a one-cent gain. That made sense to me then, and it makes sense now.

Our search for a corporate partner started at home. Much to our shock, not a single U.S. pharmaceutical firm showed interest. Perhaps we shouldn't have been mystified; if you'll recall, before our initial public offering, Abbott Laboratories, one of Amgen's original investors, had the opportunity to be involved in the Epogen project. CEO and chairman Bob Schoellhorn turned it down. He'd been influenced by Abbott's chief chemist, who apparently didn't think much of drugs based on large proteins. As we would discover, that bias was not unique to Abbott; in fact, it dominated traditional pharma.

One company's representative informed us that his bosses were passing on Epogen because the opportunity was too small; their market research department predicted that sales would never eclipse $50 million per year. (For the record, the drug generates $10 billion in annual revenue. Some market research!)

Next, George Rathmann and Dan Vapnek went to Japan several times to search for an overseas partner there, while Noel Stebbing and Phil Whitcome, our director of strategic planning, made multiple trips to Europe. All four came home astonished that no one else seemed to share our unshakable faith in biotechnology-based pharmaceuticals. Not one of the five products we had in the clinic or headed for the clinic elicited so much as a nibble.

"*Surprised* is an understatement," George Rathmann recalls, chuckling at the memory.

> We couldn't crack the European market, because they were all looking to buy cheap. Whatever your figure was, they wanted to pay significantly less. For instance, we met with Hoechst Marion Roussel [now part of Sanofi-Aventis Pharmaceuticals] about partnering with us on Epogen. They asked how much we wanted for it.
>
> I said, "Well, we started with the idea that we'd get $10 million plus a 10 percent royalty on all sales." They offered $6.5 million and a 6.5 percent royalty, then added that Hoechst would expect to credit the milestones that it paid against future royalties.

Then there was the fellow from a British pharmaceutical firm who flew across the pond for a meeting about the possibility of his company's licensing Amgen products. About halfway through, he grumbled, "Wait a minute! Are you telling me that all of these drugs are injectable?"

As mentioned earlier, they had to be injected, either into a vein or a muscle, or subcutaneously, just beneath the skin. As large proteins, they couldn't be administered orally, because if you swallowed them, the enzymes in your digestive tract would chop them up and digest them. Oral drugs, or small-molecule drugs, as we called them, were designed to resist the enzymes so that the stomach or intestines could absorb them and send them along to the bloodstream.

The man stood up and snapped, "Well! I wish you had told me. You could have saved me a trip across the ocean!" And with that, he stomped out of the room; he didn't even stay for the rest of the meeting. He knew that injectable medicines generally had much lower sales than those taken by mouth; therefore, his company wasn't about to license any of our offerings, including Epogen.

As for Japan, its once blossoming market for finding licensing partners had been effectively trampled by Genentech, our San Francisco rival. From 1981 through 1983, nearly twenty U.S. biotech companies had entered into collaborations with Japanese companies, Genentech being one of the most active. Rathmann explains:

> Genentech had cut several deals with Japanese companies for huge sums of money, like $20 million for one of its recombinant interferons. These large payments were just for the rights to sell its products in Japan, a market that would be hard for an American company to enter anyway.
>
> So we thought that we'd have no trouble getting $20 million, too. That was the benchmark. We met with a small Japanese pharmaceutical firm and were pitching the chief executive on making a significant equity investment, when he suddenly became highly animated and started ranting in Japanese, pounding his hand on the conference table. Afterward, we learned what he had said: "Twenty million dollars? Amgen thinks it's worth twenty million dollars for something that doesn't even resemble a product yet? It's not worth it!" Ironically, Amgen was further along with some of its programs than Genentech was when it signed that $20 million deal, but by 1984 that rose had lost its bloom.

AMGEN'S PARTNERSHIP WITH KIRIN

As it turned out, that wasn't entirely the case. Out of nowhere, we received a phone call from Japan's Kirin Brewery Co. It seemed that an employee there had the job of poring through the U.S. and German press and clipping articles of interest for her superiors. Why U.S. and German? Because those were the two foreign languages she knew. A news item about Amgen's discovery of EPO caught her attention, and she forwarded it to her boss. Kirin, looking to enter the biotech field, had been trying to develop human recombinant EPO but without any success.

Kirin faced the kind of financial problems that any business would love to have. It was highly profitable and generated cash faster than it could use it. To make things "worse," it was too successful in its primary business, which was beer. Japan's federal antitrust system is less formal than that of the United States; when Kirin's share of the nation's beer market approached 60 percent, the government, instead of filing a lawsuit, quietly discouraged the company from getting any bigger in that line of business. Brewery executives decided to funnel some of their excess cash into marketing hard liquor in a joint venture with Seagram. The new enterprise was a failure in that it became a highly profitable cash cow right away. Next, Kirin entered the soft-drink market and "failed" again. Money continued to flutter down upon Kirin like cherry blossoms in the spring.

What's a poor company to do? The answer, Kirin decided, was to start a business that would consume huge amounts of yen and take many years to creep into the black. That's how Kirin's pharmaceutical division was born. When the people there learned that Amgen scientists had discovered the elusive EPO gene, they made the fateful overseas phone call.

Soon afterward, a contingent of executives flew to Thousand Oaks to serenade us, and in no time at all, the two companies were almost falling into each other's arms. We had much in common, such as fermentation know-how. Kirin also understood the importance of R&D. It was probably the only beer maker in the world to boast a bona fide science-based R&D department. To most beer manufacturers, brewing was an art.

Before inking a deal, however, the folks from Kirin wanted to be certain that the cultures of our respective companies and countries were harmonious. None of Kirin's people knew how to play golf very well, and, probably somewhat to their surprise, neither did we.

Nevertheless, about twelve of us went out on the links together to watch one another miss easy putts and hook drives into the trees. We took a traditional communal bath together. Fortunately, Rathmann, Weist, and I all loved Japanese food and were reasonably adept with chopsticks. I did, however, draw the line at eating raw chicken.

Once we learned such arcane Japanese protocols as which person gets on the elevator first, last, and so on, we started being less formal with one another. By then, the Kirin executives had seen that the heads of Amgen had demonstrated respect for their customs. The Kirin people, in turn, showed a willingness to learn from us and respect our customs as well. As one of their executives put it succinctly, "We cannot become Americans, and you cannot become Japanese. So we both have to move toward the middle, or else this is not going to work." It seemed clear to everyone that compromise would not be a problem for this partnership.

During the subsequent negotiations, we were pleasantly surprised to discover that, as per Japanese tradition, deals are conducted with a minimum number of attorneys. Contracts are unusually short, too. The Japanese principle is that a business relationship should always be fair to both sides. Consequently, if the terms of the original agreement cease to be fair to one side, because of changing circumstances or whatever, the terms must be amended accordingly. It is not exactly a Western concept, but a wise one.

A Japanese contract contains phrases such as, "The division of the cost of the advertising program will be negotiated later."

Later?

The rationale is this: we don't know enough right now to make a fair allocation. So we'll figure it out when the time comes.

For example, one of Amgen's contractual obligations to Kirin was to manufacture EPO for all preclinical and clinical testing—as you've seen, a time-consuming process. A few years later, one of our scientists came up with a method to produce everything we needed for a fraction of the $2 million earmarked for this purpose. Thinking like true Americans, we fretted that we would have to give back the considerable difference. It seemed a bit unfair to be penalized for having made a scientific breakthrough. When we raised the issue with our partner, the head representative looked right at us and said, "You take the full $2 million." Just like that.

What he didn't say was that there was now an invisible IOU—a rather large one—sitting on the table, and at some point in the future it would have to be repaid. In other words, the reverse situation would arise eventually, and we'd be expected to reciprocate with equal generosity. The system works, but only if both parties are mutually trustworthy and flexible like Amgen and Kirin.

A joint venture was struck in May. Kirin obtained the rights to sell Epogen in Japan; we retained full control of the United States. Europe was to be shared. Our partner put up $12 million; Amgen chipped in $4 million, largely as a sign of good faith, along with $8 million in EPO-related patents and technology. The influx of licensing money helped us step up the pace of research and development on Epogen. If we'd collaborated with a U.S. company instead of Kirin, I firmly believe that Amgen would have wound up having to split the U.S. market, at the very least.

We threw a celebration dinner for both companies at the exclusive Jonathan Town Club, a century-old establishment housed in a magnificent Italian Renaissance–style building in the heart of downtown Los Angeles. I stopped in early to see how the preparations were going, as did one of Kirin's regional sales managers. To our dismay, we discovered that the club didn't have a drop of Kirin beer. Fortunately, the sales manager was able to call a nearby hotel and convince the head bartender to send over several cases right away. They arrived just before our guests did. I took it as a good omen, and to this day the collaboration between Amgen and Kirin stands as a model of cooperation.

THE AMGEN PARTNERSHIP
WITH JOHNSON & JOHNSON

The same cannot be said about our alliance with Johnson & Johnson, which soured almost from the outset. George Rathmann brokered the September 30, 1985, product licensing agreement, and by his own admission, selecting Johnson & Johnson as a partner remains the one serious blunder Amgen has made. We sold its Ortho division the rights to sell EPO everywhere in the world except Japan and China, leaving us the one hundred thousand American kidney dialysis patients suffering from chronic anemia.

On August 19, 1988, the two companies signed an agreement to work together on three major drugs, one of them EPO. We would sell Epogen; Johnson & Johnson would sell its own brand of epoetin alfa, Procrit, which Amgen would manufacture. Less than six months later, Johnson & Johnson and Ortho ambushed us with the request for an injunction in the U.S. District Court of Delaware. According to Johnson & Johnson, Procrit would suffer "irreparable harm" if Epogen hit the market first. We failed to see how, considering that our drug was intended exclusively for the dialysis market, and Procrit had a lock on every market except dialysis. Johnson & Johnson asked the court to postpone Amgen's planned launch, tentatively set for late March or early April, indefinitely. Bob Weist took the phone call from our partner informing him of its intentions:

> It was a Friday afternoon. Our good friends at Johnson & Johnson told me that if we didn't do this, that, and the other thing, they were prepared to take immediate legal action. They were basically placing a gun to our heads, especially since Gordon and George Rathmann were both out of the office. George was home recuperating from back surgery, while Gordon had just left the hospital following surgery to remove a melanoma, a life-threatening form of skin cancer.

I asked if we could have until Monday to respond, but they didn't find that satisfactory.

The lawsuit was filed the same day.

It was hard to believe that the same company whose corporate credo begins "Our first responsibility is to the doctors, nurses and patients, to mothers and fathers, and all others who use our products and services" would pursue a legal outcome that, if successful, would temporarily deny more than one hundred thousand dialysis patients the only effective treatment for their condition. To this day, contempt for Amgen's former partner runs so deep that many employees proudly proclaim their homes to be 100 percent "J&J free." Considering that Johnson & Johnson and its many businesses sell more than one thousand products, from Band-Aids to Tylenol, that's no small feat.

The hearing, in Wilmington, Delaware, was scheduled for March 17—St. Patrick's Day—giving our attorneys a scant six weeks to mount a defense, whereas Johnson & Johnson's move probably had been in the works for months, maybe even years. This opening salvo of litigation hurled so much shrapnel into the air that debris would still be crashing to the ground as recently as 2003. Let me whittle the basic complaint down to its core.

Ortho contended that Amgen had breached the recently signed agreement because we had not worked hard enough to help it get Procrit to the market. Our position was that, to the contrary, we'd met every one of our contractual obligations and then some. If anything, Ortho was delinquent in doing what it was supposed to in order to move its drug along toward licensure—a clear violation of the contract. As it turned out, Procrit did not receive FDA approval until late 1990, eighteen months after Epogen did. Even we didn't realize that Johnson & Johnson was so far behind.

Amgen submitted a counterclaim requesting that the license agreement be terminated. We'd learned that our partner's clinical trials of Procrit were recruiting patients with chronic renal failure, the one territory that we believed contractually belonged to us. We believed that Johnson & Johnson was supposed to be testing its brand of EPO only in nondialysis patients, such as people with cancer whose red-cell counts had fallen as a result of chemotherapy.

Many people were highly critical of our deal with Johnson & Johnson, though no one more so than we. What I regret aren't so much the terms but the fact that we didn't do a thorough job of researching Johnson & Johnson's history when it came to partnerships (see "20/20 Hindsight"). You could argue that we gave away too much, and maybe we did. But at the time of the joint venture, in 1985, we needed cash flow to get the necessary clinical trials of Epogen under way. Teaming up with Johnson & Johnson, a highly respected company, brought in a quick $6 million, enabling us to achieve our goal of showing a profit for the first time ($548,000 on $23.4 million in revenues), for the 1985–1986 fiscal year. Ironically, in 1986 our stock rebounded sufficiently that we were able to execute our second public offering after all, raising $35 million, and a third financing the next year brought in $120 million.

The part that rankled me most was Johnson & Johnson's dragging this matter into federal court. In negotiating the pact between our two companies, we'd agreed to take all disputes to arbitration as an alternative to expensive, protracted lawsuits with endless appeals. We'd even specified a neutral city, Chicago, where the hearings would take place.

Another advantage of arbitration is that details of the case are kept confidential. That can be crucial if one or both companies are publicly owned. Every time a document is filed with the court, it's out there for everyone to see—security analysts, business reporters, the general public, and your company's customers and vendors—and that tends to keep the litigation perpetually in the news.

Our dispute taught me a valuable lesson that most attorneys know but few business executives realize: under some circumstances,

20/20 Hindsight

One of George Rathmann's famous sayings was, "Success is the ability to survive your mistakes." Had those of us in management done a more thorough job of researching Johnson & Johnson's previous partnerships, I believe we would have uncovered enough evidence of problems that we would have chosen a different business partner.

When I speak in front of an audience of businesspeople about partnerships, I ask, "How many of you have hired a senior executive in the past year?" A bunch of hands go up. "How many of you checked references on the person you hired?" About the same number of hands go up.

"Now, how many of you have signed a major corporate partnership deal in the past year?" Lots of hands. "How many of you checked references on your corporate partner?" No hands—but a lot of sheepish expressions. You would think that all companies research prospective partners as thoroughly as they do potential new hires. But they don't. We didn't, either.

One lesson we learned from our happy experience with Kirin Breweries was that the most important factor in any partnership is ethics. If your partner is untrustworthy, there's no contract binding enough to protect you. But at the time we entered into our early partnerships, we didn't give much thought to how ethical the companies were. We were more focused on the size of their sales force, the brilliance of their marketing, and so on. We learned rather late—and the hard way—that ethics should have been at the top of the list.

an arbitration clause cannot prevent a party to a contract from by-passing arbitration and taking its case to court.

What was a skirmish for Johnson & Johnson was a life-and-death struggle for Amgen. That may have worked to our advantage. I can remember Rathmann's being contacted at one point by a business-man whose company had been burned by Johnson & Johnson in an-other partnership deal. He despised the large corporation so much that he offered to help us however he could.

"Chin up!" he said. "You're going to win." How could he be sure? "Because," he said, "when you've driving to work in the morning, this is all that's going to be on your mind. You'll think about it when you're driving home, eating dinner, and in the shower. *They won't be.* This is no big deal for them. That's why you'll find a way to win."

It sounds like a pep talk delivered by a football coach at halftime. But the fellow was right. In April 1989 the hearing judge dismissed Johnson & Johnson's lawsuit, saying that it belonged in arbitration and not in district court, just as the partnership agreement stipulated. Be-cause an arbitrator does not have the authority to issue an injunction, Ortho's bid to block Epogen's arrival dissolved like a sugar cube in the rain. Although the legal maneuvering succeeded in delaying the launch by two months, for Amgen the judge's decision removed the final obstacle to getting our first drug to patients and their doctors.

EPO GOES TO MARKET AT LONG LAST

Correction: there was still one hurdle left to clear, albeit a small one. The Food and Drug Administration notified us that it was going to license Epogen for use effective June 1, 1989, a Thursday. The FDA also must approve all patient and physician information that is to ap-pear on the box it comes in, as well as the package insert—a folded sheet of paper crammed with essential details concerning dosage, side effects, and so on.

Typically, pharmaceutical companies take about thirty days from the approval date to introduce a new product. It's a hectic four weeks, with a national sales meeting to arrange, sales training to implement, and sales aids to print, among still other preparations. Amgen couldn't afford a leisurely approach; we needed Epogen to start earning money right away.

"We are going to have this product ready to sell within twenty-four hours of approval," I told everyone. "That's the goal. Now let's figure out what we have to do to make it happen." Looking back, I have to laugh at how naive we all were. We went ahead with the plan, blissfully unaware that it bordered on the impossible.

In hopes of saving time, we asked the FDA to give us the go-ahead on the language for the box and the package insert a few days in advance. In that way, we could start printing. Sorry, came the reply, can't do it. However, the agency informed us off the record that it was going to make us change some words—although which ones, it couldn't say.

We took a chance and had the vial labels, boxes, and package inserts printed exactly as we'd submitted them, in case the FDA changed its mind and approved the wording. Then, to cover ourselves, we paid a local printer to reserve an idle press for us—with its crew standing by—so that printing could commence as soon as we knew what had to be changed. This went on for days.

Finally, the FDA revealed the required rewording responsible for all this tension and commotion: an *a* had to be changed to a *the*. Or was it a *the* to an *a?* I can't remember. At the time, though, with twenty-four hours to go before the launch of our first product, it was a critical change.

The warehouse at Thousand Oaks was piled high with tens of thousands of boxes of Epogen. Every one of them had the wrong word printed on it. Before we could ship the drug, we had to remove each vial from its box by hand and place it in the newly printed box.

Amgen scientists and laboratory personnel volunteered to stay through the night to get this done. In fact, so many of our family of 650 offered to help that we had to turn people away.

Pizza was brought in, and the partylike atmosphere continued until Thursday morning. The warehouse echoed with laughter and lots of kidding around. When the sun rose, sure enough, we were ready to ship the product. We had met our goal. Thirty days was the industry standard. But for us, even forty-eight hours would have been considered a failure. It was a matter of pride. Everyone departed into the sunlight, looking forward to a well-deserved product launch.

After eight years and $300 million, we'd done it.

7

Red Hot Summer

THE LAUNCH OF EPOGEN in the summer of 1989 changed every-thing. After three consecutive years of posting a profit, ramping up for the big debut had left Amgen $8.1 million in the red for fiscal year 1988–1989. The drug earned $20 million its first day on sale—exactly the cost of building 6, our first large-scale production facility, built expressly for producing EPO. When construction started in 1986, the $20 million expenditure had seemed like a huge gamble, especially because it represented about 80 percent of the company's liquid assets. But the plant would manufacture $8 billion worth of epoetin alfa before being mothballed in 2003.

Fortune named Epogen the number 1 product of 1989, a year in which our profits more than tripled, to $19.1 million. In 1990 they nearly doubled, to $34.3 million. Total sales for both years: $580.3 million. Quite an impact for a product targeted to a market that dozens of other companies had scorned as too small. Epogen's im-pact on the lives of chronically anemic kidney-dialysis patients, though, was incalculable.

On August 25, 1990, Amgen entered the NASDAQ exchange, which sent our stock rocketing to $149 per share following a two-for-one split. If you'd purchased one thousand shares when it had bottomed out five years before, your $3,750 investment would have grown to roughly $285,000. Meanwhile, Kirin was generating additional income, having received clearance to distribute Epogen in Japan. Then, on the first business day of 1991, our other partner, Johnson & Johnson, finally won a license from the well-established FDA to sell its Procrit brand (manufactured by Amgen) in the United States. The approved indication was for managing anemia related to the antiviral drug zidovudine (ZVD), then the first line of defense for people infected with the HIV virus.

The most dramatic developments surrounding Epogen, however, were taking place in Washington, D.C. On January 15, 1991, the FDA rejected Genetics Institute's petition that it overturn Amgen's seven years of exclusive rights to Epogen under the Orphan Drug Act and allow GI to sell its version of epoetin alfa, to be called Marogen. The decision left our foe from Massachusetts pinning its hopes on the ongoing patent-infringement case, which, after two years of split decisions, now rested in the hands of a U.S. Appeals Court.

In March the three-judge panel upheld Amgen's patent on Epogen, effectively ending GI's chances of getting Marogen on the market in the United States, at least until the last claim of the original patent expires in 2013. The *New York Times* called the decision "a stunning victory," noting that GI/Chugai had been expected to make significant inroads into Amgen's market—as much as 20 percent, according to some industry analysts. Paradoxically, GI's attempts at infringement kept Marogen out of the marketplace longer, because if not for its lawsuit, all of Amgen's patents would have expired sooner.

Naturally the news was greeted ecstatically at Amgen, which had recently undergone a radical transformation. Chairman of the Board George Rathmann no longer reported to building 10 daily as he had since resigning as CEO. In December 1990 George severed his remaining ties to the company. It marked the end of an era, and all 850 staff members attended his retirement dinner to wish their beloved leader well.

A few weeks after I assumed the chairmanship, Harry Hixon left Amgen. Our two years of working in tandem had been difficult, though by no means unbearable. It may have been a positive experience for me, giving me time to learn a lot of what a CEO needs to know. However, by 1991 it was apparent that if the dual setup continued much longer, it would start to become divisive, especially with Rathmann the peacemaker now gone. It wasn't Hixon's fault, and it wasn't my fault. We had a lot of respect for each other and still do, but the situation just wasn't workable.

I felt so strongly about it that I went to the board and told the directors that they should choose one of us to run the company, and soon. Otherwise we'd reach the point where people had to start choosing sides, and that, of course, could damage the company irreversibly. The board decided that I should be the one to stay.

My daily routine changed drastically. We decided to hold off replacing Harry for a while, so all the people who'd reported to him now reported to me in addition to those already under my supervision. I had to get more deeply involved in areas such as sales and marketing, which previously had been managed by Hixon.

The biggest change of all was that on February 21, 1991, Amgen became a two-drug company.

SOMETHING NEU: NEUPOGEN

In a sense, Amgen had been a two-drug company ever since Fu-Kuen Lin successfully cloned human erythropoietin: from then on, there was Epogen, and there was everything else. Call it classic R&D management. When you have one high-priority product, decisions regarding the allocation of resources become simple. Basically, the

Epogen team got whatever it needed, whether human resources, equipment, or Rathmann's time.

The Neupogen project, which crystallized in 1986, was spearheaded by Amgen molecular biologist Dr. Lawrence Souza. Neupogen began life known as G-CSF, which was short for granulocyte colony-stimulating factor. Like epoetin alfa, G-CSF is a naturally occurring protein. But instead of stimulating the bone marrow to churn out red blood cells, G-CSF hikes production of a type of white blood cells known as neutrophils, which are the immune system's principal defenders against bacterial infections.

One hallmark of cancer is frenzied, uncontrolled cell division. The toxic chemotherapy drugs used to treat cancer destroy many of these cells. Unfortunately, other cells in the body—healthy ones—exhibit rapid growth, too. These include the cells that make up the delicate lining of the digestive tract, from the inside of the mouth down to the intestines; hair; red blood cells; and neutrophils. Most anticancer agents cannot distinguish fast-dividing benign cells from malignant ones, and that is why chemotherapy often, although not always, gives rise to side effects such as sores in the mouth and throat, hair loss, and abnormally low levels of neutrophils, a condition called *neutropenia* (see "Different Grades of Neutropenia"). Consequently, for a week or so following drug treatment, patients may become highly susceptible to infection until the neutrophil level recovers.

The harm from neutrophil depletion is twofold: not only is an immunosuppressed person less equipped to fight bacteria, but if her absolute neutrophil count does not rebound in time for the next drug cycle, her oncologist may be alarmed enough to postpone therapy, reduce her drug dosage, or both. In a national survey of cancer patients, nearly half had at least one chemotherapy treatment delayed because of severe neutropenia. The interruption could conceivably allow the cancer to progress.

Souza, a graduate of the University of California, was collaborating with scientists at New York's Memorial Sloan-Kettering Cancer

Different Grades of Neutropenia

The blood test used to diagnose neutropenia is called an absolute neutrophil count, or ANC. Without going into detail about what the numbers mean, a normal ANC ranges from 1,800 to 8,000. A person with an ANC of 1,000 to 1,800 is said to have mild neutropenia, with low odds of developing an infection. Therefore, most patients in this range do not have their next cycle of chemotherapy delayed or their dosage lowered. Moderate neutropenia (500 to 1,000) carries a moderate risk of infection, while severe neutropenia (499 or less) places patients at high risk of infection.

Center. By the late 1990s, Amgen had about three hundred such arrangements with researchers around the country. Individual scientists initiated the process, and Larry's collaboration with MSKCC turned out to be a major part of Amgen's ultimate success. He eventually succeeded Dan Vapnek as head of research.

Memorial Sloan-Kettering possessed what I called "Mrs. Murphy's Chowder": a mixture of about two hundred proteins. But it didn't have the technology to separate them. Amgen did. The cancer center suspected that this protein hodgepodge held stem-cell growth factor. Today you hear a lot about *stem cells,* the undeveloped "seed" cells that mature into red cells, white cells, or platelets. Stem cells are found in the bone marrow as well as in the peripheral blood vessels. At that time, few people, including scientists, knew much about them.

As it happened, the sample contained not stem-cell growth factor but a much more valuable growth factor: granulocyte colony-stimulating factor. Souza and his team pursued this lead vigorously and discovered the human gene that produces G-CSF, located on chromosome 17. Once isolated, the gene was cloned using the same process as for human EPO, but with E. coli bacteria as the replicating organism instead of Chinese hamster ovary cells.

Memorial Sloan-Kettering had filed a weak patent, not knowing what it actually had. Therefore, said my general counsel, Amgen was legally free to proceed on its own, without paying a royalty to MSKCC. That didn't seem ethical to me; without Sloan-Kettering, we wouldn't have stumbled across filgrastim (Neupogen's generic name, pronounced *fill-grass-tim*). We negotiated a license with a modest royalty.

Months after Amgen's discovery, our erstwhile nemesis Chugai— which, despite everything, I considered to be Japan's best pharmaceutical company—isolated and cloned filgrastim independently. Suddenly there were three patents on file vying for the rights to the protein. Chugai indicated that it intended to litigate.

Frankly, we had Chugai over the proverbial barrel: as the licensee, Amgen held the original Sloan-Kettering patent, so if a judge or arbitrator chose the victor based on which organization had applied first, we would win. What's more, the Amgen patent, though filed after the Japanese drugmaker's, was much more complete, so if the judge based the decision on that criterion, again we would win.

During our previous legal tussle, over Epogen, I'd become friendly with Chugai's CEO, whom I admired very much. Realistically, he knew that Chugai had little chance of beating us. We reached an agreement allowing both companies to sell Neupogen in Europe, with Amgen retaining exclusive rights to the U.S. market. Negotiating instead of litigating saved both sides many millions in legal fees and resulted in a fair outcome for everyone. Without the mutual respect between the two companies, that probably wouldn't have been possible.

The initial human trials for Neupogen took place at Memorial Sloan-Kettering Cancer Center and at the Ludwig Institute for Cancer Research in Melbourne, Australia. We didn't have any employees Down Under at the time, but the world's greatest experts on colony-stimulating factors were there, so it seemed a logical choice for a science-driven organization. Typically, drug manufacturers choose one medical center over another to run their clinical trials because it is conveniently located or charges less. We wanted to work with the leading authorities wherever they might be located and whatever the cost.

Dr. George Morstyn, head of the Ludwig Institute's clinical program, stood out as exceptionally talented. He was also unusual in that he was both a PhD and an MD. We recognized right away that he would make a terrific addition to Amgen. After a year of wooing by Kirby Alton—and many thirty-hour plane trips—in 1991 George joined the company as vice president of medical and clinical affairs.

Designing the patient trials for Neupogen was trickier than it had been for Epogen. We couldn't attempt to prove that the drug would help people with cancer live longer, because that would entail a prohibitively expensive and time-consuming study. Merely demonstrating an increase in the number of circulating neutrophils—the objective of the early investigations—wouldn't be ambitious enough to satisfy the FDA when it came time for phase III.

"We had to show that Neupogen could decrease the incidence of infection associated with chemotherapy," explains Kirby. "The problem was, it can be hard to document infection in cancer patients using the standard laboratory tests. After negotiating with the FDA, we came up with an acceptable end point: febrile neutropenia." Success would be measured by a significant reduction in the number of chemo patients who developed neutropenia accompanied by fever.

In a phase III trial carried out at various centers, 210 men and women with lung cancer were randomly assigned to two groups. For ten days during each three-week chemotherapy cycle, patients received either Neupogen or a placebo. Because it was a double-blind study, neither they nor the investigators knew whether they were being injected with the active ingredient or a harmless solution. The results were impressive, as shown in table 7-1.

TABLE 7-1

Results of Neupogen tests

Result	Study group (Neupogen)	Control group (placebo)
Percentage of patients who developed at least one infection following chemotherapy	40 percent	76 percent
Percentage of patients who needed to be hospitalized due to infection	52 percent	69 percent
Percentage of patients who required treatment with intravenous antibiotics	38 percent	60 percent
Percentage of patients who developed severe neutropenia over the entire course of chemotherapy	57 percent	77 percent
Average number of days patients were neutropenic	First cycle: 2 days All cycles: 1 day	First cycle: 6 days All cycles: 3 days
For neutropenic patients, average severity of neutropenia as measured by absolute neutrophil count (ANC); the higher the number, the better	First cycle ANC: 72 All cycles ANC: 403	First cycle ANC: 38 All cycles ANC: 161

In the late 1980s, there were perhaps fifty chemotherapeutic drugs, some of them more immunosuppressive than others. Because different forms of cancer call for different agents, our Neupogen trials covered a range of malignancies, including breast, ovarian, kidney, and neuroblastoma, a type of cancer that affects the nervous system in children. What we didn't want was for the FDA to approve the use of Neupogen only for some cancers or only with certain anticancer drugs. On February 21, 1991, word came that we'd received the broader indication after all: for any chemotherapy that suppresses bone marrow, the body's blood-cell factory.

A NEW BREED WALKS THE HALLS OF AMGEN: SALES REPS

Neupogen gave Amgen its second grand slam in a row. The drug racked up $233 million in sales its first year—the fourth-highest debut in the history of the pharmaceutical industry (Epogen being second)—and was named product of the year for 1991 by *Fortune*. Our profits nearly tripled from the year before, to $97.9 million. In 1992, the year that we leaped into the *Fortune* 500 and the S&P 500, Amgen rang up $1.1 billion in total sales, for a profit of $357.6 million. We were now an international company, too, with marketing and sales operations in Europe, Australia, and China.

For the next few years, our focus shifted, as it had to, toward establishing our two products. Epogen, to an extent, sold itself. One key difference between Epogen and Neupogen was that no acceptable alternative existed for Epogen's target: managing chronic anemia in people on kidney dialysis. A low red-cell count didn't rally on its own; patients would need transfusions, which if repeated too often could trigger complications in the future.

In contrast, not all oncologists saw the urgency in reversing neutropenia in cancer patients, even though this condition could increase the chances of infection and possibly force chemotherapy to be postponed or the dose reduced. It was our sales staff's job to bring to their attention studies concluding that men and women with cancer fared better when full chemotherapy dosing was maintained consistently.

Another difference between Neupogen and Epogen was that dialysis patients could feel EPO working; the drug was infused into their dialyzing machine, or they injected it under their skin, and soon they had much more energy and were able to function again. In contrast, Neupogen didn't make patients feel better; in fact, it allowed their oncologists to hit them harder with the cancer-killing drugs.

Many chemo patients don't develop severe infections anyway. So if a physician treats a large number preventively, or *prophylactically,* some of those men and women would have done just as well without Neupogen. There's no way to know which ones stayed healthy because of the drug. It's no different from chemotherapy itself, which for many cancers is an *adjuvant,* or add-on, treatment; after surgery or radiation therapy to remove the tumor or as much of it as possible, the systemic drugs are given to hunt down rogue malignant cells that may be lurking in the body. Most patients, though, when faced with a life-threatening illness such as cancer, are willing to take advantage of any treatment that may improve their chances, no matter how small, of staying alive or beating the disease.

If you were a sales representative for Neupogen, you'd want oncologists to know that the drug halved the risk of infection associated with chemotherapy and greatly reduced the need for inpatient antibiotics. That's a substantial benefit, because the last place an immunocompromised person wants to be is in a virtual petri dish like a hospital, where every year about two million Americans acquire clinically significant infections. Also, by cutting down on hospitalizations, Neupogen more than paid for itself, a winning feature from the standpoint of health-maintenance organizations and insurance companies.

Most folks probably assume that physicians are routinely brought up to speed on the latest medicines, their side effects, the results of clinical trials, and so on. But that's not necessarily the case. Once doctors graduate from medical school, there is no formal system for continuing instruction; unlike, say, accountants or schoolteachers, physicians need not meet an educational requirement to retain their licenses. Not only do drug companies fund the bulk of medical research and development in the United States, but their sales representatives serve as most physicians' primary source of information about new products for patients.

Pharmaceutical sales is something of a misnomer, at least at a science-based company like Amgen. A sales rep isn't selling anything; it's not as though he walks out of a sales call with a purchase order. There is no purchase order. What we call *sales* mainly entails imparting information. And by that I don't mean strictly promotional literature; the sales reps give doctors information from new studies in leading medical journals that might help them better determine whether a patient could benefit from a particular drug. They also provide information about new techniques for administering medication and tips for minimizing side effects.

It is not an easy job. Much of a sales rep's time is spent behind the wheel and sitting in doctors' offices waiting for an audience, all for four or five calls a day lasting about ten minutes each. From the drug company's point of view, it couldn't be less efficient, but it has to be efficient for the doctor, who may be slotting a sales rep between appointments.

Physicians often depend on the sales rep to summarize journal articles that they don't have time to read in depth. One aspect of conventional sales applies here: the object is to solve problems, the most effective sales approach of all. You get the customer to describe the problem, and then you explain how your product or service can help solve the problem. The end.

A stereotypical "salesperson" straight out of central casting, with the quick smile and I-can-sell-snow-to-Eskimos attitude, doesn't last in this field. Many of the people who gravitate toward pharmaceutical sales took premed, biology, or chemistry in college and see themselves as part of the health-care system and contributing to improving patients' lives. Maybe not all reps feel this way, but most of them take pride in their jobs.

It's always more fun to sell a brand-new product; doctors are happier to see you and full of questions, and you often get to go to the front of the line, ahead of reps from other companies. Therefore, hiring

Amgen's sales staff, beginning in 1988, turned out to be easy. The word was out that Epogen was going to be a blockbuster medication; it didn't just pave over a symptom or two but effectively treated the problem of anemia.

Our partner Johnson & Johnson probably didn't believe that Amgen would go through with forming its own sales division. In fact, that had been a bone of contention going back to the original licensing agreement in 1985. We had to insist that our company would handle its own sales and marketing, or we'd find a different partner.

Although Johnson & Johnson went ahead with the deal, I suspect that executives there thought that when the time arrived, we'd come to our senses and hand over that responsibility, something Johnson & Johnson would have been more than happy to oversee. What it and most other members of Big Pharma may not have realized was that Amgen didn't need an army of salespeople as they did. Taking our cue from Genentech, the only other biotech firm that had assembled its own sales and marketing department, for dialysis patients we could cover Epogen's entire national territory with about forty-five people.

How? Well, we weren't pitching to every general practitioner in the United States, only to specialists in diseases of the kidneys (nephrologists) and the blood and bone marrow (hematologists). Our representatives didn't necessarily have to visit them at their offices; they called on the dialysis centers. A second burst of hirings took place before Neupogen's introduction, because our salespeople would be dividing their time between nephrologists and oncologists. But the forty-odd figure was adequate for the launch of Epogen.

Everyone in the industry agreed that we'd scored a coup by luring Paul Dawson away from pharmaceutical company G. D. Searle to head up sales and marketing. Paul's goal was to have the staff in place three to six months before FDA approval. Because of the delay created by the ongoing legal skirmish with Johnson & Johnson, it turned out to be closer to a year. So our salespeople went out into the field extraordinarily well trained to anticipate any question a physician might have. We even sent them for multiday training at Ohio's prestigious Cleveland Clinic, where they donned white coats and accompanied the doctors on their rounds.

Similarly, before the debut of Neupogen, we arranged for a similar learning opportunity at M. D. Anderson Cancer Center in Houston. No one balked at the extra education; if there's one thing that a sales representative hates, it's having to say "I don't know" to a doctor's question. They really liked being the people with the answers.

At dialysis centers, we expanded our sales calls to include the nephrology nurses, because often physicians aren't there at the facility; the nurses are tending the patients. They were full of questions about Epogen. Ultimately, we hired nurse trainers, whose sole job was to work with the nurses. It turned out to be an excellent policy, one that Amgen continues to this day. If we could get in to see the hospital pharmacist, we'd educate her, too, because she was also an important decision maker.

One of our best innovations was to establish an 800 number program for answering questions about Amgen products from doctors, nurses, and pharmacists twenty-four hours a day, in addition to an 800 number strictly for patients. Questions might be something along the lines of, "I gave Epogen to a patient of mine, and he exhibited [a certain symptom]. Could this possibly be a side effect of the drug? Was this reported in any of the clinical trials?" If it took waking up an Amgen doctor in the middle of the night to get the answer, that's what happened. Most pharmaceutical companies maintain toll-free numbers, but the folks who call them are often disappointed by the responses they receive, especially if they phone at night or over the weekend.

I went to the call center once to watch it operate, and it was really something. The person taking the call, usually a pharmacist or nurse, would prepare an e-mail to the sales rep from that territory, informing him of the doctor's questions, explaining how they were answered, and so on. Consequently, when the salesperson went to see that doctor the next day, it was as if he'd been in on the conversation.

Including nurses and pharmacists was unorthodox at the time, and very different from what many traditional pharmaceutical companies did. But our feeling was that we owed it to the patients to establish a relationship with all of their medical professionals, because they were part of the supply chain—the people who delivered Amgen products to our customers.

CHAPTER 8

Nuclear Winter

WITH EPOGEN AND NEUPOGEN solidly established, Amgen returned much of its attention and resources to developing new products. In 1993 we funneled $255 million into R&D, a fourfold increase over the budget at the time of Epogen's introduction. Another $324 million and $452 million followed in 1994 and 1995, respectively.

The world, it seemed, was waiting for Amgen to complete a hat trick of three blockbusters within only four years, the blink of an eye in the time line of biotechnology. When 1993, 1994, 1995, and then 1996 went by without a new drug approval, people began to wonder. Had Amgen merely been lucky twice? Had the company lost its golden touch? Why was the pipeline empty? The whispers were particularly loud among naysayers on Wall Street—this, even though our profits nearly doubled, from $383.3 million in 1993 to $679.8 million in 1996, the first year total revenues exceeded $2 billion.

Such expectations ignored fundamental realities of biotechnology, such as the fact that it typically takes nine to twelve years to develop a drug. Nor was it a secret that Amgen had temporarily diverted a good deal of research funding to our two big products. I didn't expect this decision to make our scientists happy, and it hadn't. The day I took over as CEO, in 1988, head of research Dan Vapnek came into my office and said intently, "Gordon, we're going to have to start spending some money again on new-product research." He was right, and his sense of urgency was understandable. But for the next few years, we simply were not able to devote much capital to that part of the company. It was time to work as hard as we could on Epogen and Neupogen. If we were successful, we reasoned, before long Amgen would have plenty of money to invest in research. That is exactly what happened.

Some observers failed to appreciate the inherent uncertainties of science. Amgen's mid-1990s pipeline, far from having dried up, brimmed with a number of promising early-stage product candidates. Following are profiles of the winners and some of the also-rans.

BIG CATCHES

That many of our potential products would not survive clinical trials was to be expected. A bigger story was that six of our potential medications did make it onto pharmacy shelves. Like a pack of presidential hopefuls at the start of primary season, only the strong survived.

Interferon Alfacon-1 (Infergen)

Infergen was one of Amgen's original five therapeutics to get as far as patient studies, and the only one (besides Epogen) to go all the way. Its FDA license came in 1997, breaking our six-year lull. Type-II gamma-interferon also belonged to that fivesome, but it did not impress as a remedy for viral infections and was the first to be abandoned.

Infergen, a genetically engineered synthetic version of type I interferon, is used to treat chronic viral hepatitis C in adults who are also suffering from other diseases of the liver. When the body's immune system detects the presence of an invading virus, it releases natural interferons into the circulation to fight the HCV infection. Infergen sold disappointingly in the United States—other interferons got there first—and its U.S. rights were peddled to another company (see "20/20 Hindsight").

But Infergen did find a welcome home at Amgen Japan. Our Japanese subsidiary had been frozen out of both Epogen and Neupogen by our preexisting licensing deal with Kirin Brewery. Meanwhile, several of the products under development for the U.S. market weren't suitable for Japan. Year after year, Amgen Japan pressed ahead with development but had nothing to sell; in my view, it was threatening to become a serious morale issue.

There are several subtypes of hepatitis C. It so happened that Infergen was most effective against the type most prevalent in Japan. Yamanouchi Pharmaceutical Company, today the country's second-largest drugmaker (under the name Astrellas Pharma, following a

20/20 Hindsight

Looking back, I can see that Infergen was a long shot that didn't pay off, in part because we had to quit working on it for several years while we were building up Epogen and Neupogen. By the time Amgen got into the market, Schering-Plough was already there with its interferon alfa-2b (brand name Intron A). It was Schering's top product, and it put its best people on it, whereas interferon would never be number 1 for us. We just couldn't compete with Schering's A team.

Yet, given the identical circumstances again, I would make the same decision to go ahead with developing Infergen. In the end, it could have turned out to be highly superior or far worse, and it wasn't overly expensive for us to find out which.

2005 merger with Fujisawa Pharmaceutical Company), was willing to partner with Amgen Japan. Several competitors had staked their claims to the market long before our arrival, but the drug has built up a 16 percent share and continues to grow.

Ancestim (Stemgen)

One aggressive approach to combating certain cancers is to administer extremely high doses of chemotherapy followed by *peripheral-blood stem-cell rescue.* It's hoped that the toxic dose will eradicate the tumor cells. But high doses inevitably kill the bone marrow. Stem-cell rescue, an alternative to bone marrow transplantation (BMT), entails using a special *apheresis* machine to "skim" stem cells (or progenitor cells) from the circulation and then return them to the patient's bloodstream to replenish the impaired marrow.

The trouble is that our bodies make few peripheral-blood stem cells (PBSCs); if a patient's supply is further depleted by harsh chemo drugs, collecting stem cells can be like panning for gold. Amgen's genetically engineered human stem-cell growth factor (Stemgen) stimulates stem-cell production. In Stemgen's phase III investigational study, the subcutaneous drug was administered in conjunction with Neupogen to roughly one hundred women with breast cancer. Another one hundred or so breast cancer patients received Neupogen alone.

The women on the combination protocol required less apheresis to accumulate the necessary volume of transfusable stem cells (four treatments compared with six). In addition, significantly more of them (63 percent versus 47 percent) reached the targeted goal, and their bodies produced two to three times as many stem cells as did the bodies of participants who'd been given Neupogen only. Therefore, more of them were able to undergo high-dose chemotherapy with PBSC, which in the United States is now performed as frequently as bone marrow transplantation. In addition to being less expensive, the newer procedure doesn't require general anesthesia. Furthermore, patients' levels of red, white, and platelet cells seem to return to normal faster than they do following BMT.

Unfortunately, in the eyes of many physicians and insurance companies, these advantages didn't justify the cost of Stemgen, which also produced some adverse side effects. Because the company had more-promising product candidates competing for limited R&D resources, we dropped the drug as a human therapeutic. However, it has found a use for growing stem cells outside the patient (in vitro) and is employed in many stem-cell research projects.

Cinacalcet (Sensipar)

Once Amgen grew large enough, we could afford to license other companies' discoveries instead of the other way around. One of those was cinacalcet, our first small-molecule drug. The significance of that probably eludes the average person suffering from secondary hyperparathyroidism; all these patients need to know is that Sensipar comes in tablet form to be taken orally.

By the mid-1990s, the biotech sector began to understand that most people's bodies contain ample amounts of most proteins. Clinically significant deficiencies, such as neutropenia and anemia, are uncommon. Given the limited number of therapeutic proteins, we realized that we needed to expand into small-molecule drugs. A number of our contemporaries had reached the same conclusion: in 1996, about half the new medications manufactured by biotech firms were derived from small molecules; today that proportion is about 70 percent.

The question was where to begin. The Big Pharma companies had been working with small molecules for decades; Amgen had a lot of catching up to do. Assessing the effectiveness of small-molecule agents tends to be trickier because they mostly inhibit, or block, processes of the body, whereas proteins promote, or stimulate, biological activities. I felt confident that our scientists' expertise in molecular biology would get Amgen off to a fast start, but our development staff's lack of experience in small-molecule drugs would probably cause mistakes and delays. Therefore, we needed to adopt a small-molecule product candidate that was already undergoing human testing; it almost didn't matter which one. "I don't care if it fails," I said. "Let's just give our development people something to work with and learn from."

Amgen's scientists went off in search of a small-molecule therapeutic, not really knowing what to look for. A New Jersey company called NPS Pharmaceuticals licensed to us a compound designed to treat the hormonal disorder secondary hyperparathyroidism, and we set to work on it.

Secondary hyperparathyroidism usually occurs as a frequent complication of chronic renal failure. The parathyroids, four pea-sized glands located in the neck, secrete parathyroid hormone (PTH). Hormones act as chemical messengers. PTH's job is to regulate the amounts of calcium and phosphorus in bones. The kidneys, too, balance calcium levels. When someone's kidneys fail, the body no longer absorbs the mineral efficiently from food. Consequently, the concentration of calcium in the bloodstream falls.

Calcium sensors on the parathyroid glands read the dropping level, become alarmed, and secrete excess PTH. To restock the circulation, calcium is leached from the bones, in what becomes an endless feedback loop. Eventually, the bones may lose too much calcium and weaken.

The drug we were working on, cinacalcet, acted directly on the parathyroids' calcium sensors to break the cycle of hyperparathyroidism. First, though, we had to correct a problem with the molecule. NPS hadn't performed metabolism studies to see how the body rid itself of the drug. If it had, it would have realized that about one in one hundred people lacks the gene to produce the enzyme primarily responsible for metabolizing cinacalcet. For those few, the medication would have cleared too slowly from their systems, causing a serious overdose. Our scientists ingeniously redesigned the molecule so that it was metabolized by a different enzyme and yet retained its therapeutic effect.

Sensipar, approved in 2004, has sold exceptionally well. Because we were already familiar with the dialysis community and its physicians, the drug turned out to be an excellent choice for Amgen's entree into small-molecule pharmaceuticals—and an unexpected success.

Anakinra (Kineret)

Licensing an outsider's discovery is one strategy for building a product portfolio; buying the company lock, stock, and high-pressure liquid chromatograph is another. In 1994, with a whopping $700 million in cash on hand, Amgen purchased twelve-year-old Synergen Inc. for $254 million. It was our first acquisition.

Only a year earlier, the Boulder, Colorado, biotech appeared to be en route to success with a recombinant drug for treating systemic bacterial infections (*sepsis*), which take one hundred thousand lives each year. The compound, Antril, performed well in early clinical trials, reducing death rates by as much as 28 percent over placebo. Two other companies—Centocor and Xoma—had recently seen their promising sepsis drugs go up in smoke. However, Synergen's employed a different mechanism of action, interfering with the body's immune response, whereas Centocor's and Xoma's agents more or less tried to apprehend toxins in the circulation like a pair of arresting police officers.

In a replay of the unpredictability of drug development, Antril faltered in phase III, testing barely better than placebo. It wasn't Synergen's first flameout; another medication, for treating the debilitating foot ulcers that diabetics frequently develop, advanced to phase III, only to flop. News of Antril's failure sent Synergen stock plummeting from $40 to $13 and change per share. By the time we stepped in to buy the company, it had laid off more than half its employees.

Probably makes you wonder why Amgen would even consider acquiring the company, doesn't it? Actually, we had been interested in some of its other projects, such as a compound for treating the painful joint inflammation associated with rheumatoid arthritis (RA). The drug, anakinra (Kineret), became Amgen's fourth approved human therapeutic in 2001.

At the time we bought Synergen, though, anakinra was performing so disappointingly in early-stage clinical trials that we stopped accepting additional patient volunteers. From a purely scientific position, we should have halted the study then and there, but for contractual reasons, and from an obligation to the patients already enrolled, we let it continue. It's a good thing we did, because the long-term data was encouraging enough to warrant further testing.

Rheumatoid arthritis, which affects more than 2.1 million men and women in the United States, descends from a dysfunction of immunity. As with other autoimmune disorders, for some reason the body's defenses mistakenly attack the person's own tissue—in this case, the joints. Anakinra controls inflammation and slows destruction by blocking the protein interleukin-1, one of the immune system's weapons against infection.

Less than a year after its approval, Kineret was eclipsed by another RA drug. Etanercept (Enbrel) was the prize of Amgen's acquisition of Immunex, the Seattle-based biotech that had introduced Enbrel in 1998. At the time, it was the first genetically engineered RA medication. Though somewhat similar to anakinra, etanercept belongs to a different family of biologic anti-inflammatories called tumor necrosis factor (TNF) inhibitors. Adding etanercept to methotrexate, the drug of choice in RA management, produces superior results (compared with the use of either drug by itself) in relieving pain, tenderness, and swelling; slowing joint erosion; and enabling patients to go about their daily activities in greater comfort. Enbrel's acquisition nudged Kineret to the sidelines, but that's the kind of "problem" most pharmaceutical companies would love to have.

THE ONES THAT GOT AWAY

As for the prospects that slipped off the hook before we could reel them in, they had looked just as promising as the big catches. But that's science and medicine. You ride the experiment as far as it will take you, and most of the time it's not far enough.

One of the disappointments, megakaryocyte growth and development factor (MGDF), would have been the third gem in Amgen's crown of hematopoietic growth factors. Epogen jump-started the marrow's production of red cells, Neupogen did the same for white cells, and MGDF was expected to stimulate production of the blood's other primary component: platelets, the disc-shaped cells that converge on wound sites and stanch bleeding. Cancer patients on heavy doses of chemotherapy may need platelet transfusions because their suppressed bone marrow makes fewer platelets. Although transfusions are generally safe, there's always a slight risk of acquiring an infectious disease.

Clinical trials got under way in 1995, but our onetime nemesis Genetics Institute beat us to the market with interleukin-11 (Neumega) two years later. However, that's not what caused us to discontinue MGDF. In 1998 a handful of the volunteers in the phase III studies developed neutralizing antibodies; their immune systems perceived the drug as an intruder and deactivated it. Worse still, the antibodies were destroying whatever platelet growth factor their bodies made. We discontinued development.

Another experimental agent identified with four letters, this one called BDNF (brain-derived neurotrophic factor), also progressed all the way to phase III studies before fizzling. Developed in collaboration with Regeneron Pharmaceuticals, BDNF was intended to slow the devastating degenerative disease amyotrophic lateral sclerosis, also known as Lou Gehrig's disease. Although BDNF had performed extremely well in the lab and in preclinical trials, it struck out when tested head-to-head against a placebo in humans.

A small protein called epidermal growth factor (EGF) was initially considered a likely godsend for people with stubborn bedsores and other skin wounds, and not only by Amgen. In the mid-1990s, more than half the R&D partnerships in the biotech industry were sold by Paine Webber. One day the firm came to us with an offer: tissue growth factors represented an untapped product opportunity. Paine Webber wanted to enter this area by creating a limited partnership for R&D with a star biotech company—Amgen was its first choice—to develop tissue-healing drugs. Its idea was that the partnership would raise so much money that no other company would want to compete in this field.

We weren't enthralled by the idea of pursuing EGF, but it wasn't unrealistic, either. There are substances that the body uses to speed tissue growth; we were working on one ourselves. Ultimately we agreed to the deal, a bit reluctantly. While finalizing the terms, Paine Webber came back and said that we'd have to chip in some royalties from Neupogen. "After all," the rep said, "that's a sure thing; the rest of this is speculative." So we agreed, *more* reluctantly this time, and the partnership was on.

As promised, money for research was lavished on Amgen. But the much-anticipated breakthroughs never came. In animals the compounds made wounds heal faster, but in human trials, the benefit wasn't substantial enough to make the drug a commercial success. To this day, no one has been able to make a wound-healing growth factor work, for various reasons.

One of the studies inadvertently pointed up the impact of substandard medical care on people's health. We conceived a clinical trial for hospital patients suffering from intractable wounds that had resisted every available treatment. The reason for the hospital setting was that the patients would receive constant attention from the nursing staff, so we could be assured that the ulcers, abscesses, and so on were being tended to properly. Remember that in an investigational study, you try to weed out all variables that could skew the findings.

All the patients in the trial were afforded first-rate wound care; additionally, half were put on our growth factor. The result? Many of the patients in *both* groups healed. This was highly embarrassing to the doctors and nurses. The trial proved that many of these patients had not been adequately cared for in the past and that the excellent nursing care required by the clinical-trial protocol was far more effective than the product under investigation.

Perhaps the biggest disappointment of all was the weight-loss biologic leptin. In 1994 researchers at Rockefeller University, in New York City, discovered and isolated the gene for a hormone that plays a major role in regulating body weight. It does this by acting on the part of the brain known as the hypothalamus to govern food intake and calorie expenditure. Rockefeller University named it leptin, a derivation of the Greek word *leptós,* meaning "thin." Mice and rats injected with the genetically engineered protein ate two-fifths less food during the experiment; they also lost 30 percent of their body weight in a matter of weeks. Given that some seven in ten Americans can be classified as overweight, this was exciting news. When Amgen licensed the research for $20 million—with the university to receive an additional $70 million if we should successfully turn the protein into a salable drug—the *New York Times* gushed, "It could turn out that Amgen has bought a license to print money." Not quite. We had bought a license to *spend* money.

In the large patient trial that we sponsored, 30 percent to 45 percent of the people who took leptin for thirty days lost a modest four and a half pounds or more. But 19 percent of the control group, given an inactive substance, achieved the same results through diet and weight counseling. This wasn't the first time that a potential medication worked well in mice but not in people.

Leptin is still being studied, but not as a cure for obesity. Based on recent patient trials, it may be applicable to two conditions that involve the hypothalamus: hypothalamic amenorrhea (the unexplained absence of menstrual periods in menstruating women) and lipodystrophy.

People with the latter disease lose their body fat and subsequently develop metabolic disorders such as insulin resistance and hyperglycemia. The hormone may also prove helpful for men and women with type 2 diabetes.

TAKING STOCK

A total of six drugs from this period would eventually win FDA approval. But as of 1995, the year that Amgen celebrated its fifteenth birthday with a party for its four thousand employees on the lawn behind building 34, we were still looking for a blockbuster product to join Epogen and Neupogen. It was a serious cause for concern, not only on Wall Street but also within the company.

At one point, the board of directors appointed what it called a strategy committee. Before each board meeting, the members met with the researchers for a few hours to try to figure out whether we knew what we were doing. They didn't say we did, but neither did they say we didn't.

I never lost confidence that Amgen was on the right path. We were simply feeling the pinch of the gap in the pipeline caused by the temporary lack of resources when everything was devoted to Epogen and Neupogen. The organization wasn't doing anything "wrong." We had our fair share of company, too. Starting in about 1992, the biotechnology sector slid into several years of doldrums. "Nuclear winter," business scribes came to call it. A number of companies had failed to come through with much-lauded technologies, and before long disenchanted investors were being seduced by promises of the untold riches to be mined in cyberspace.

It was one of those times when a CEO truly earns his pay. You become a corporate cheerleader, constantly offering encouragement within the company and correcting fallacies on the outside. I often reminded everyone that each year management carefully reviewed the portfolio of products under development, and we were convinced that our research was producing viable drug candidates. At the same time, we were actively seeking licensing opportunities. In short, Amgen was doing everything it should be doing. We just needed to stay the course and keep on believing that everything was going to work out.

The annual portfolio review was a painstaking process. For three days, top management pored over thick books of information about Amgen drugs that were either in human trials or about to be: the market, competition, patents, potential manufacturing issues and costs, the effect on the sales force—pretty much everything. We rated the projects *A, B,* or *C,* with those rated *A* (high priority) receiving the most funding and resources. Some projects moved up in ranking from one year to the next, while others were demoted or halted altogether. In addition to these yearly summits, management met less formally once a month to keep abreast of recent developments.

It's not as though there was internal dissension about the direction of R&D. However, I would occasionally be asked, "If plan A fails, what's plan B?"

I thought long and hard before answering, "There *is* no plan B."

Plan A was the right approach, and we were going to keep working it until it succeeded. If it didn't, only then would we change direction. Some folks never believed me, thinking that I secretly had a plan B up my sleeve all along but wouldn't say so.

My only fear was that the stock price would drop so low that the company might be in danger of a takeover, the fate of numerous biotech firms in the 1990s. At times, names were bandied about in the financial news. Bristol-Myers Squibb was one such party, I remember. Another was Swiss pharmaceutical giant Roche Holding Ltd., which had merged with Genentech in 1990. What if Amgen were acquired and the mother company destroyed our corporate culture? We all worried about that.

20/20 Hindsight

Here are some thoughts from Kevin Sharer about Amgen's (and my) performance during this period:

> Gordon took some unfair criticism about the productivity of Amgen's pipeline in the mid- to late nineties. We had three big drugs—GDNF, MGDF, and leptin—and if any one of them had hit, he would have looked like a genius. It wasn't that we weren't swinging for the fences; it was science. Sometimes it just doesn't work.
>
> Acquiring Synergen was a bold move, I thought. The other thing Gordon did was to scale up the company so that it was ready for its next phase when I got there, and he delivered spectacular results in terms of financials and share price. He also groomed a successor that is still in the job eight years later.
>
> In my book, that's a pretty clean sweep for a CEO.

Investment bankers often pitch takeovers. Every couple of years, Morgan Stanley, Goldman Sachs, and others probably showcased Amgen to all the pharmaceutical behemoths. But when they seriously analyzed the possibility, the conclusion was always that the stock was too expensive. We figured that as long as our price-to-earnings ratio remained high enough, no one could acquire us, because it would be too dilutive to their own earnings per share.

Simply put, the best defense against a takeover is to be successful—very successful—and to make sure that your stock price keeps pace. Not once did anyone formally approach Amgen about an acquisition or merger. It became a familiar refrain for investment bankers to say to us, "If you ever want to sell the company, let us know!" To which we'd reply, "Don't worry, we will!" Then we'd laugh. Our goal was to create the world's best biotechnology company. If Amgen had been acquired, the senior managers would have felt like failures.

"THE MEMO"

Not deviating from our game plan was one struggle. The other was maintaining the fragile dynamic between the science and sales sides of the company. Bear in mind that Amgen consisted almost exclusively of researchers for its first seven years. When Paul Dawson began assembling his sales team in 1988, it was as though an alien species had descended on the campus. Sales and marketing people are naturally extroverted; that was one difference. More significantly, our new hires came from Big Pharma, where, typically, science takes a backseat to sales and marketing.

"Culture shock" is how researcher Burt Ensley describes the reaction among the scientists at this intrusion on their domain. "There was a certain amount of animosity," he says, conceding that not all of it was fair. "But the people in marketing tended to act as though they were your boss. So the disdain was mutual. That's what made it really interesting: they thought you were a bunch of egghead jerks, and you thought they were a bunch of lowlifes."

Dennis Fenton agrees. "There was a complete lack of understanding between the two groups, which I shared, too, until I became *part* of sales and marketing." One of my reasons for shifting Dennis from vice president of operations to manager of sales and marketing was to help bridge that gap. "We scientists didn't really appreciate how difficult it was to get the products to the patients," he reflects. "Maybe it doesn't entail the same degree of difficulty as creating Epogen, but it doesn't just happen on its own. And without smart people working together to get it done, Epogen wouldn't have been the success that it became."

I'd seen this indigenous tension between the two tribes when I'd interned at Procter & Gamble while in college. Most of the time, P&G was a well-managed company. But occasionally the factory manager resembled the unfortunate kid at the end of the line in the children's game (I'm probably dating myself here) crack the whip—getting jerked around by the marketing department. Someone in marketing would decide on the spur of the moment to have a two-for-one sale on Crest toothpaste, and suddenly the factory would be bombarded with orders it couldn't meet. Manufacturing didn't know whether marketing could have hatched this plan earlier or whether a competitor's unexpected moves forced the last-minute changes. All the factory manager knew was that no one had given him sufficient notice so that an inventory could be built up. Not surprisingly, some animosity simmered between the two divisions.

At Amgen, an effort was always made to encourage our different departments to learn about one another and to try to understand how their actions would affect the rest of the organization. Some companies, though, give sales and marketing carte blanche, with R&D and manufacturing ordered to cater to marketing's every whim. They waste a lot of money that way, not to mention stir up resentment.

In part through Fenton's efforts, mutual respect was built over time. "We now have a real commercialization process," he says, "where research, development, sales, and marketing are all part of a continuum to the patient. It's like a relay race. If two of the parties don't cooperate and the baton gets dropped, it's both their fault."

Things weren't quite that civilized in 1995. As sales and marketing staffers flooded into Amgen, they started vying for the company's soul. It grew serious enough that shortly after our fifteenth birthday celebration, I drafted a strong statement for everyone. It has since entered Amgen lore as "The Memo." Essentially, it said that unlike in Big Pharma, at Amgen scientists were and would always be the kings of the hill. Furthermore, although we'd briefly considered diversifying into over-the-counter medicines—a strategy that would have transformed Amgen into more of a traditional pharmaceutical company, in which marketing often directs research—the memo offered this reassurance: "Amgen has reached a broad consensus to continue to follow our science-driven breakthrough-product strategy." Everyone should get over it and get back to work.

Soon thereafter, we formulated the Amgen values. In case anyone doubted our commitment, topping the list: "Be science based."

VARIATIONS ON A THEME: ARANESP AND NEULASTA

Amgen didn't have to look far for its next two big sellers. They were right under our noses.

In science, there's always more to learn, especially as technology advances. By the standards of the mid-1990s, the technology that existed when Fu-Kuen Lin discovered the gene for human erythropoietin was fairly primitive. A team directed by researcher Steve Elliott was delving deeper into Epogen to better understand how it worked.

Meanwhile, another team, headed by Jeff Browne, Joan Egrie, and Tom Strickland, was studying the drug's carbohydrate makeup. Let me explain.

Unbeknown to either Amgen or the FDA, the Epogen that we sold was actually a mixture of five EPOs. Each had the same amino-acid backbone but with different amounts of carbohydrate attached to it. Initially our EPO contained more than five; the outliers were cut off during the purification process. When we first discovered that we were selling a combination of EPOs, we didn't understand the significance of the differing amounts of carbohydrate.

Later it was discovered that if you separated the various versions, each one exerted the same stimulatory effect on bone marrow, but to varying degrees: the protein with the least carbohydrate was least effective, and the one with the most carbohydrate was most effective. The team wanted to explore what would happen if the epoetin alfa molecule was reengineered to contain more carbohydrates than would be produced by the human EPO gene. In other words, they wanted to improve upon nature. That was something we'd shied away from generally, because when you do that you run the risk that patients' immune systems will form antibodies against the substance. All sorts of things can go wrong, so it wasn't considered a sound investment.

Carbohydrates connect like branches of a tree at specific sites on the protein. To alter the amount of carbohydrate, therefore, you must add one or more sites, a process that entails altering the sequence of amino acids. Epogen, in its present form, was extraordinarily good; more than 99 percent of patients responded to it, with virtually no adverse side effects. The only benefit of this reconfigured epoetin alfa was that because of its increased molecular weight, it would stay in the body longer and thus a person could take it less often.

On the surface, it didn't seem worth pursuing. Men and women on a self-administered blood-cleansing therapy called peritoneal dialysis (PD) would find a longer-lasting red-cell stimulant far more convenient because they had to inject themselves with EPO every day; however, PD patients made up only one-fifth of all people with end-stage renal disease. Amgen's only other market for Epogen was hemodialysis patients in the United States, and most of them had the medication administered directly into the rubber tubing of the dialyzer during their thrice-weekly treatments, an arrangement that was fully satisfactory.

In Europe, Johnson & Johnson's territory, doctors frequently injected EPO subcutaneously during hemodialysis, believing that this procedure was more effective and economical. The drug would also be ideal for cancer patients who developed anemia due to chemotherapy. But that, too, was Johnson & Johnson's area, for which we received 10 percent in royalties.

Dan Vapnek, representing the majority of Amgen researchers, summarily dismissed the proposal of developing a more active, longer-lasting Epogen. I respected his views and understood why he might feel that way. But despite listening carefully, I didn't hear compelling reasons for Amgen not to at least explore the possibility. What I heard from several of our executives was mostly personal bias offered as science-based logic.

One unspoken explanation for the skepticism was that many researchers regarded prolonging a drug in the bloodstream as "low-grade" science. Making a wholly new discovery was "genuine" science in a real-men-don't-eat-quiche sort of way. But for patients who had to inject Epogen several times a week, being able to go a whole week without a single needle stick would improve the quality of their lives in a very real way. Some folks can't bear to inject themselves, and doctors' offices are closed on weekends. A long-lasting EPO would enable them to go on vacation without having to take along the medication, which had to be refrigerated.

Internal politics, something Amgen usually managed to sidestep, also was a factor. Members of the research division were privately miffed that the scientists responsible for these intriguing findings belonged to development. What's more, they'd "defected" from R to D.

All in all, many smart people were against long-acting Epogen for reasons that weren't very good. High science, low science—what's the difference if the drug is effective, helps patients, and makes money? I certainly wasn't concerned with who came up with the idea or which department got credit. There were only two valid reasons for not adding darbepoetin alfa to our portfolio:

- We didn't yet know how long people on dialysis would be able to go between injections; perhaps the practical benefit for most of them would turn out to be minimal.

- Antibody formation might prevent the protein from working in some patients.

If either of these issues didn't go Amgen's way, we'd have wasted millions of dollars.

One potential obstacle was crossed off the list of concerns when we considered that carbohydrate acts as a sort of shield against the immune system; the more carbohydrate you add to a protein, the lower the chances that antibodies would be mobilized against it. I also spent a lot of time discussing the merits of our legal position with the law department. Johnson & Johnson could be expected to contend that its rights to the original Epogen extended to this drug as well. We were confident that a neutral third party would agree that the licensing agreement between our two companies did not entitle Johnson & Johnson to any stake in the potential new product. To proceed with darbepoetin would cost us perhaps $5 million to $10 million in legal fees, along with many times that amount for R&D.

If we won on the legal issue, the rewards would far outweigh the expense. Even if we lost, the benefit to our dialysis patients and to Amgen would probably be great enough to justify the expenditure. However, that's something we wouldn't know until we'd spent the money and completed clinical testing.

After giving the matter much thought, I felt strongly that this was a wager the company should make. Another factor in my decision was that someday the patent on EPO was going to expire. Any superiority at all, no matter how small, can loom large in a head-to-head marketing battle. It was a long way off, but a CEO is paid to think further into the future than other members of the company. The higher you go up the organizational pyramid, the longer your time horizon should be.

All these considerations made it a fairly easy decision. Kevin Sharer, who'd joined us as president in 1992, was also 100 percent onboard. A lower-level executive probably wouldn't bet a long shot like that, but it's a CEO's privilege—unless the board of directors says otherwise. It was one of the rare times that I opted to spend some executive capital and rule against the group consensus, but I knew I was in a stronger position than Amgen's scientific leadership to judge the financial rewards and risks and assess how the arbitration was likely to turn out. In announcing that we would go ahead with darbepoetin, I made it clear that I would take full responsibility for the decision.

When early attempts to design a new red-cell stimulator failed, it added to critics' views that this was a waste of funding. About one hundred molecules with varying amounts of carbohydrate were made, and in each case, the additional carbohydrate blocked its action. It took a few years, but in the end, the scientists found one that worked. Far from being low-end science, this was pioneering work. Adding two carbohydrate chains gave darbepoetin a substantially longer half-life (the time it takes the body to eliminate half the given dose of a drug), an approach that no company had tried before. It could be manufactured fairly easily, too.

Clinical trials of the drug, called Aranesp, commenced in 1996.

Meanwhile, other Amgen scientists were perfecting a way to prolong Neupogen's effect. Unlike with Epogen, we'd always suspected that filgrastim could be spun off into a beneficial second-generation medication, but not by adding carbohydrates. Instead we used a method called pegylation.

The *peg* in pegylation stands for polyethylene glycol (PEG). Adding this chemical compound to a molecule extends the life of the drug, because the patient's kidneys must metabolize the PEG first before they start working on the protein itself. The advantage of this new version over the original Neupogen was stunning. A typical cycle of chemotherapy lasts two weeks. For people considered to be at risk for neutropenia and fever, that meant ten to fourteen days of daily subcutaneous injections. To spare patients the extra injections and reduce the cost, oncologists sometimes tried to get by with fewer doses, but that exposed patients to potential infection. Pegfilgrastim (Neulasta), we found, required only one injection per chemotherapy cycle. Patient trials also revealed a self-regulation feature that hadn't been seen in animal studies or with Neupogen: the Neulasta drug remains in the circulation during the time the person is neutropenic. But when the neutrophil level recovers, Neulasta clears rapidly from the bloodstream, so that any side effects are short-lived.

ANOTHER FACE-OFF WITH JOHNSON & JOHNSON

As in every legal dispute between companies, no one at either Amgen or Johnson & Johnson, including the lawyers, could predict how this latest chapter would turn out. The issue came down to this: was Aranesp an *improvement* on the product licensed to Johnson & Johnson, or was it a new product? If it was found to be the former, our partner would have the same rights to darbepoetin that it had to EPO. If the ruling went the other way, Johnson & Johnson would have no rights to the new drug. The contract wasn't crystal clear—as is frequently the case—but we believed that its language strongly favored our position.

Johnson & Johnson certainly couldn't claim that Amgen had deliberately intended to deceive it. Even many of our brightest scientists hadn't wanted to pursue a long-acting red-cell stimulating factor. That's how *un*obvious a step it was. Our position was that we'd invented darbepoetin. Why should Johnson & Johnson be allowed to sell it, especially considering that Amgen had funded it 100 percent? That decision had been intentional on my part, in anticipation of a possible courtroom clash. I didn't want to have the issue further complicated by our spending even one penny of Johnson & Johnson's money on our new product.

The hearings took place in Chicago, the same site as our previous encounter with Johnson & Johnson. Back then, I'd decided that we should have a local law firm fight with us. Bob Weist, our general counsel, had once practiced patent law in the Windy City. I asked him to go back there, talk to people he knew, and get a recommendation for the best litigation attorney in the city. I didn't care what firm the attorney was with.

Everyone Weist spoke to said the same thing: get William J. Harte. It turned out that Harte was a private plaintiff's-type attorney and a litigation legend. Among other cases, he'd handled a famous class-action suit against General Motors in which GM was sued for sticking Chevrolet engines into its Oldsmobiles without telling anyone. When Bob went to see him, Harte's first words were, "Mr. Weist, are you sure you're in the right place? I don't represent people like you; I *sue* people like you. There must be some mistake."

It turned out that Harte's wife had cancer, and it irked him that the world's fifth-largest pharmaceutical manufacturer would try to interfere with the availability of a beneficial drug. He agreed to join the team. Harte was an interesting study in contradictions: a pillar of the local Catholic church who possessed a vocabulary that could make a navy seaman blush. It was a lot of fun to work with him, and we became good friends.

The arbitration panel's decision, handed down just before Christmas 1998, granted Amgen exclusive rights to darbepoetin, by then in phase III clinical trials. This result blew open the U.S. market for us, in that as soon as Aranesp gained FDA approval, we could sell to Americans suffering from chronic anemia due to causes other than kidney disease. We could also enter Europe for the first time. It was the sweetest victory in our long war with Johnson & Johnson.

Here's something I didn't tell anyone until after the hearings ended. Had we lost arbitration, Aranesp would have held little value for Amgen, at least not compared with the potential income it represented to Johnson & Johnson. Under those circumstances, I'd planned to inform Johnson & Johnson that it wasn't worthwhile for Amgen to put the new drug on the market. We would tell Johnson & Johnson what we knew and teach its people how to make small quantities in the lab; we didn't have a high-volume production process, and there was no incentive for us to develop one. We would be saying, in effect, "Be our guest—go right ahead."

As I saw it, a stunned Johnson & Johnson would have replied that it didn't know how to produce the drug. Exactly. We would then offer to do it, but at a high enough price that Amgen would turn a profit. I never shared the details with anyone, for fear that somehow Johnson & Johnson might find out. That was another crucial factor in the decision to go forward with Aranesp: the knowledge that even under the worst-case scenario, the decision posed little long-term financial risk.

A few of the people who had initially opposed Aranesp conceded that they were glad I'd persisted with it. Others probably thought it but didn't say so. It was a tremendous source of pride for me, especially after Aranesp reached the market in 2001, followed only months later by Neulasta. In their first year on sale, the two medications generated a combined $715 million in the United States alone.

CHAPTER 9

How Amgen Built
a Winning Team

BACK IN THE INTRODUCTION, I posed the rhetorical question, How does an organization attract outstanding employees? Answer: by devoting time, thought, and effort to becoming the kind of place where talented and motivated men and women want to work. And how do you build and maintain that kind of company? By hiring quality people. It's simultaneously the catch-22 and yin and yang of the business world.

HIRING SMART

Like any successful organization, Amgen was fortunate to sustain an exceptional workforce. With so many scientists onboard, the staff was unusually well educated. But other biotechs and science-driven firms had just as many PhDs and MDs walking the hallways as Amgen did.

Few of them, though, matched our researchers (and our "civilian" personnel) in their willingness to go the extra mile, as exemplified by the self-proclaimed Simi Valley Hostages. Clearly there's more to building a winning team than stockpiling individuals who have glittering credentials. Here are some of the ways that we managed to hire smart.

THE 360-DEGREE JOB INTERVIEW

You hear many business leaders bemoan the supposed dearth of capable employees in the United States. It could be that many employers are casting their lines in the wrong fishing holes or using the wrong bait. The bigger problem, I'm willing to bet, is that if they actually hooked a high-achieving job applicant, they'd unwittingly toss her back. That's because many of the desirable qualities that a boss should look for—such as resourcefulness, ethics, and adaptability—aren't found on a résumé. That is why, even early on, Amgen typically conducted ten or twelve interviews by seven to ten people to get a sense of how well a candidate would fit the organization and vice versa.

I hope you didn't just spill your caffe latte. "Ten to twelve interviews? For *one* person? We don't have time for that!"

Granted, it is time-consuming to spend part of a day—in rare instances, two days—compiling detailed profiles of the finalists for a position. But it is efficient, and not a waste of time, when you compare it to the weeks or months you would squander in training a new hire (pulling other staffers away from their jobs), only to discover that he isn't going to work out. That's in addition to the time, cost, and headache of repeating the process and either retraining the person for another assignment or, regrettably, letting him go.

We usually interviewed five or six people per job opening. Then we narrowed the list to two and asked them back. Each candidate might have an audience with some of the same interviewers as before, while meeting other Amgen staffers for the first time.

Corporations such as IBM, Amazon.com, and Motorola have adopted the practice of peer interviewing, wherein the folks who would work alongside the candidate sit down with her and ask questions of their own. It's a great idea, except that it addresses only two sides of the work triangle. What if you're hiring a middle-level manager? She will not only be reporting to supervisors and interacting with other middle managers but also overseeing junior workers. At Amgen, even subordinates got face time with the candidates and weighed in with their assessments afterward. Their feedback wasn't the primary factor in our offering the job to applicant A or applicant B, but it was taken into serious consideration.

Letting folks interview their prospective boss pays a dividend: if management winds up hiring the preferred applicant, workers are obligated to try their best to make the relationship work, because they own the decision in part. They can't complain that the new superior was foisted on them. Ownership is important. During my summer job at Procter & Gamble, I observed its system of hiring factory workers. The personnel department sent candidates to be interviewed by the foremen, who ultimately did the hiring. Pretty progressive for 1956. I haven't forgotten.

From Amgen's science-based point of view, having staffers representing various tiers of the company interview job applicants was only another experiment, one intended to provide a deeper, broader, multidimensional understanding of an unanswered question: is this person compatible with our organization? In the laboratory, we might expose a chemical to various substances to gauge its reaction; in much the same way, observing how someone handles questions from a variety of perspectives can be extremely revealing. Any setting will suffice, although one advantage of convening a small panel rather than conducting a series of one-to-one interviews is that you avoid repetitive questioning.

One response always raised a red flag, at least in my eyes. That was when a candidate expressed surprise that the men and women who would be working under him were included in the interview. Some seemed deeply offended. That was good to know.

But when I explained the logic of our interview policy, even the skeptics usually came to see it in a different light. "It's so important to us to hire the right person," I would say, "that we feel this is time well spent. Plus, an interview is a two-way street. We want to give you an opportunity to make the right decision for *your* future. And the more people that you meet from Amgen, the better you'll get to know our company."

It usually left a favorable impression. What's more, interviewees almost always came away dazzled by the caliber of our staff.

BE HONEST ABOUT THE JOB

Some organizations try too hard to impress. They set their sights on a hot prospect and work overtime selling him on the organization, even if it means revealing only selective information to paint a rosy picture. That's a big mistake. A job interview should be a mutual exploration of whether the two parties would make a harmonious match, with full disclosure on both sides.

When George Rathmann interviewed me for the position of chief financial officer, he made no attempt to sugarcoat the seriousness of Amgen's looming financial crisis. Nor should he have. The company needed a CFO who would be up to the challenge of obtaining private or public funding, and I needed a vivid picture of what lay ahead so that I could hit the ground running.

Do you know the number 1 reason that people leave their jobs within six months? It's feeling blindsided by unrealistic expectations, about either the duties of the job itself, the company, or their role. To be sure, it's up to job applicants to ask questions until they're satisfied that they understand what will be expected of them. But some companies make pie-in-the-sky promises—about future promotions, improved facilities and equipment, and so on—that they know aren't likely to happen anytime soon.

Never try to snow applicants. You might succeed and be sorry you did! When the hard realization settles in that your new hire was misled, whether it was a bald-faced lie or acts of omission, you have lost her for good. The sense of betrayal burns too intensely to be extinguished.

United Parcel Service, alarmed that half of its part-time warehouse workers were quitting the company, discovered that many of its interviewers were leaving candidates with the false impression that a step up to full-time status was just around the corner. In reality, it could take years, if it happened at all. After UPS corrected the lapse in communication, its turnover rate plummeted to only 6 percent. Other techniques for giving potential employees a glimpse of what they can reasonably expect include escorting them on guided tours of the workplace or producing videotape or DVD presentations with realistic portrayals of everyday situations.

Always tell applicants the whole truth. In that way, if you should make the mistake of offering the job to someone who isn't right for the position, hopefully he'll take himself out of the running—sparing you from reaching the same conclusion after the fact. It's like self-selection, but in reverse.

VOICE YOUR VALUES DURING THE INTERVIEW

Companies, like people, have personalities. In the same way that modifying DNA changes an organism's genetic structure, whenever you add someone new to the payroll you risk altering the psychological makeup of the organization, especially if it's a small company or department. You can help ensure that the chemistry will be compatible rather than combustible by espousing your company values prominently during interviews.

Ed Garnett was Amgen's head of human resources from 1994 to 2002. He recalls, "When interviewing applicants, I used to tell them, 'If you read our list of values, and they don't match your personal values, you shouldn't work here. Because you won't be happy, and we won't be happy. The Amgen values reflect what life is like here.'" The interview report form used by our HR team required them to assess a candidate on each of the values: ethics, trust and respect, and so on. Ed continues:

> By the time the person arrived at my desk, they'd passed muster regarding their technical skills and whatnot. So our focus was on assessing how well he or she would click with our culture. One of my favorite techniques was to ask, "How do you think you would react under the following circumstances?" and present them with a situation that they might face.
>
> Their answers would tell us a lot about whether or not they were likely to blend in. I might describe a scenario where a staffer showed poor judgment. If the response was, "I would call the person in and put him on probation!" well, that wouldn't work at Amgen. For one thing, we didn't discipline people for making honest mistakes.
>
> They couldn't have known that, naturally. But it gave us a glimpse into their managing style. We would try to weed out the more parochial-type administrators and, in general, anyone who was too set in his ways. We looked for people who were collaborative and entrepreneurial, which was more the way that Amgen did business.

I used to stress to applicants that they shouldn't take the job if they were uncomfortable with change, because Amgen was moving rapidly in many different directions. It was a vital piece of information. In the past, we had unwisely hired a few scientists from conventional pharmaceutical companies, where one year is just like the last.

After a while, people can develop an almost civil service attitude. It wasn't that they were bad scientists, but they felt comfortable only in a regimented environment; they didn't want to be pushed out onto the cutting edge of science. The world of biotechnology was so new, though, that the rules hadn't been written, and this made them extremely ill at ease.

For instance, when testing drugs in clinical trials, our researchers designed their own studies. Inevitably, a recent arrival from Big Pharma would ask, "Where's the Amgen clinical trials manual?" Apparently the big drug manufacturers' product-development departments had a primer on how to formulate a one-size-fits-all investigational study.

"What are you talking about?" we would say. "We don't have one."

The scientist would chuckle nervously. "Come on, stop kidding around. Where's the manual?"

"We don't have one."

"Every company has one! You can't *not* have one!"

Our people would explain that because every product is different, every clinical trial is different and must be customized accordingly. Some newcomers were put off by this; they had forgotten how to think for themselves and were so far out of their depth that they didn't know what to do next. After all, the one thing that every bureaucracy does is to substitute rules and regulations for thinking. We wanted to substitute thinking for rules and regulations.

We learned that for the Amgen approach to succeed, we needed extremely talented, adventurous people. Fortunately, those types would be attracted to a company like ours anyway, whereas those who are afraid to go out on a limb would look for an organization that operated by the book. That was fine, because we didn't want them.

Establishing values as a centerpiece of your employment criteria may not eliminate weak hires, but it will certainly trim the number of poor picks. Think about why people get fired. It's usually not that they lack the necessary skills. More likely, they've alienated their coworkers, or they're ineffective communicators, or they're not team players. Whatever the reasons, rightly or wrongly, they're out of step with the rest of the organization. This principle cuts both ways: at a poorly managed company, really good employees tend not to last very long because their work ethic, integrity, and so on conflict with the prevailing office culture.

Occasionally you come across an exceptional talent who does not play well with others in the corporate sandbox. You're aware of this because her track record precedes her; or perhaps her combative demeanor throughout the interview makes it evident that this is a person who's probably going to step on some toes. In short, she's the reason that on the fourth or fifth day, I forget which, God created managers. Should you hire this prickly personality, or should you let her be a thorn in the side of some other organization?

It depends on your needs at that moment. In business, decisions should be weighed using the twin scales of benefit and risk. You determine which is greater. Let's say that you run a struggling opera company, and the only thing that will rescue your production of Puccini's *Tosca* is to sign up for the lead role a certain celebrated soprano with notoriously erratic behavior and a volcanic temper.

There's no question what you should do: get La Diva now. You'll enforce company rules and minimize star treatment as best you can. Often, if a prima donna's presence strengthens the organization, benefiting everyone, your other employees may be willing to accept the inevitable double standard. But if her talent fades or her conduct starts to poison the atmosphere, then everyone's tolerance, including management's, may grow thin. After all, even the great Maria Callas was fired by the Metropolitan Opera.

However, a company can abide and willingly give special treatment to only a few superstars.

Prodigious talent isn't always enough to offset poor work habits or a disagreeable personality, but I discovered the hard way that talent almost always trumps experience. It took me years to learn that experience alone isn't a reliable barometer of someone's expertise; it could mean only that he has taken a lifetime to perfect mediocrity. The more salient point is that an employer should look beyond today's need and not merely fill a slot. Companies change, and job descriptions change; a person with ability is more likely to grow and adapt.

So don't reflexively toss aside an intriguing résumé just because the candidate's previous duties may not conform exactly to your current requirements or because he's worked in a different industry. True talent often renders such arbitrary boundaries meaningless. To spot and reel in gifted employees requires probing beneath the surface of a curriculum vitae and extrapolating which past experiences are transferable. Many skills transcend job titles and can be applied in different arenas. You also need to educate yourself about industries you're not familiar with, because a practice that might be unacceptable in your organization might be the status quo elsewhere.

For example, when my jet charter business, Prime Jet, was first hiring pilots, I noticed from perusing résumés that some of the applicants had bounced around quite a bit—never an encouraging sign. Then I learned why: many companies that employ pilots are undercapitalized. All it takes is one slow month or a major repair, and they vanish like a flight entering the Bermuda triangle. In the jet charter business, it happens to a startling degree. Amgen wouldn't have even considered someone with, say, five pit stops in nine years. But this wasn't Amgen, and it wasn't the biotechnology field.

TINKER WITH THE JOB DESCRIPTION

While you're at it, you can apply the Amgen principle "The people who do the work should help plan the work" (see the Introduction) by soliciting feedback from coworkers. How can the position be tailored to best reflect the organization's needs at this time?

Perhaps the departing manager was ideal for the job when you hired her three years ago. But the company may have changed since then, or the department's role within the organization may have changed, and now the skills called for are dramatically different. Once you've hired a replacement, fine-tune the job descriptions to maximize his abilities.

HIRE PEOPLE FROM TOP COMPANIES

Why should you go after people who have worked for top companies? It's because they've been surrounded by talented colleagues—that's what makes a company great—and probably have picked up good work habits. One professional football team has stated publicly that it gives strong preference in the annual college draft to players from colleges with highly successful football programs and excellent coaches.

USE THE WORLD'S BEST RECRUITERS

Your company's most effective ambassadors of goodwill are already on your payroll. Approximately one in three hirings depends on word of mouth. If you foster an atmosphere where people generally feel productive, valued, challenged, energized, and proud of their organization, they'll tell their friends and former colleagues, "Hey, we have an opening for an accounts payable manager. This is a great place to work. Why don't you send over your résumé?"

Have you ever heard the saying "Turkeys don't fly with eagles"? We tend to associate with people who share our values, including our attitudes toward work. So when a good employee recommends your company to others, they're likely to be quality candidates with compatible values. Talent becomes self-perpetuating, because talented people want to play for a winning team alongside other accomplished men and women.

Every month I used to present "An Evening with Gordon Binder." It sounds like a cabaret act, but it was a presentation to our new employees. I would tell them, "A recent study showed that for the past one thousand jobs filled here at Amgen, we had fifty thousand applicants. Each of you is one out of fifty. On average, forty-nine people wanted your job and didn't get it; you did. So you are part of an elite group. Now that you're here, it's your job to keep this going and to keep Amgen the kind of place where the best people want to work. We expect you to recruit people just like you."

As a result, Amgen rarely had to advertise or use an outside recruitment firm—for example, when we needed a superspecialist or when our expansion was so rapid that the employee referral system couldn't keep up with the demand. You can imagine how much money that saved over the years.

I'm seeing the same pattern at Prime Jet, where we treat our pilots and other staff better than do most of our competitors. Less than two years after starting the company with one aircraft, we purchased a second Gulfstream IV. The jet became available unexpectedly when an order was canceled, so we didn't have a hiring plan in place.

I worried aloud that perhaps we wouldn't be able to hire the six pilots we needed fast enough. Then my general manager smiled and opened a desk drawer. "We can start with these," he said, pointing to more than one hundred résumés that people had sent us unsolicited. They were good people, too: we promptly interviewed the ten who looked best on paper and hired four of them. It was possible because the staff had put out the word that Prime Jet is a great place to work. Two-thirds of our new employees have come to us that way.

Some organizations, such as computer networking giant Cisco Systems, have instituted programs that give cash rewards to employees for referrals. That's not a wise idea, because it implies that helping recruit people is not part of everyone's job but is optional. Everyone in the organization should naturally consider it his responsibility to encourage people he feels would be assets to join him as coworkers.

EXPLORE UNCONVENTIONAL
TALENT POOLS

As you build your exceptional workforce, don't overlook these sources of talent.

Baby Boomers

The generation born between 1946 and 1964 will almost certainly remake retirement in its own image, either by refusing to retire at all or by choosing to work part-time between yoga classes and skydiving. Given that the subsequent generation, the so-called Generation X, is only about half the size, the United States is facing an imminent shortage of men and women in the thirty-five- to forty-five-year-old age bracket. Boomers, generally well educated and health conscious, should become increasingly attractive to business. Firms have already rolled out the welcome mat by offering benefits to part-time workers.

The Armed Services

The military might be the richest repository of reliable workers in the United States. Two of Amgen's three chief executive officers served in the U.S. Navy: my successor (Kevin Sharer) and me. One of my CFOs was a navy man, too.

Yet veterans are generally an untapped resource, to the extent that many seeking to enter the private sector face out-and-out discrimination. That's too bad but not surprising when you consider that since the draft was ended in 1973, surprisingly few civilians have much personal contact with veterans—especially women under, say, forty, who make up a sizable proportion of HR departments. As a result, misconceptions abound about former military men and women.

I have been privileged to meet many senior admirals and generals, including the second-ranking army and air force generals at a breakfast at the Pentagon. Almost without exception, they were extremely impressive people—more impressive, to tell you the truth, than the average senior business executives I encounter.

Probably the most deeply ingrained stereotype is that veterans are rigid automatons unable to think for themselves. It's true that being in the armed forces teaches you respect for authority—try finding a boss who wouldn't welcome that!—but the typical servicemember makes as many pivotal decisions daily as any company employee. The U.S. Army's longtime slogan "An army of one," recently retired, is truer than most folks realize.

Kevin and I have often talked over the years about what a valuable experience our navy service was and how it has benefited us in business. I may be guilty of generalizing here, but people who come out of the military tend to exhibit many of the traits that a manager should have: leadership, responsibility, self-sufficiency, a belief in teamwork, and a drive to get the mission done, all grounded by a moral center. I particularly like the fact that military veterans rarely make excuses.

Some of the most successful companies in the United States have made a concerted effort to recruit veterans, among them The Home Depot, Adolph Coors Company, General Motors, 7-Eleven, American Express, Hershey, and Johnson & Johnson. That's an impressive list, isn't it? Maybe you should consider following their lead.

ENSURE A SMOOTH TRANSITION

Smart hiring doesn't end with a hearty handshake and "Welcome aboard!" Far from it. Being the new person at work is no less anxiety inducing than being the new kid at school. It can take months to undo an awkward start. It is imperative that new employees not be thrown into the deep end to sink or swim while the boss turns his back. If they sink, they may carry others with them.

The damage isn't confined to staff morale and productivity. According to one estimate, a midlevel senior manager must work for roughly six months before his new employer begins recouping its financial investment, which includes salary, training, recruitment, and possibly relocation expenses. If he quits, you might have to tack on severance, too.

Increasingly, organizations are turning to a "buddy system" to help new employees navigate their unfamiliar surroundings. Naturally, this positive trend has spawned a new buzzword in HR circles: *onboarding*. (It sounds like surfer-dude speak to me, but maybe that's because I live in Southern California.) The buddy is a colleague who makes it her business to introduce the new hire, answer questions and explain the idiosyncratic protocols peculiar to all organizations, show him where to obtain supplies and equipment, and generally offer encouragement. Not insignificantly, she also asks the newcomer to join her for lunch.

Amgen never had a buddy program per se, for the same reason that we didn't go around handing out cash rewards for referrals. Our philosophy was that every member of the team should help everyone else, period, especially if someone was struggling. But any system, formal or informal, that helps folks get acclimated is a good thing.

Upper management should receive the same consideration. To stumble out of the gate at that level can have disastrous consequences, shredding credibility forever. Some executives' oversized egos may not let them accept special support from their new organization, believing that it would undermine their authority. But if it leads to improved communication and a smoother transition for everyone, why not welcome it?

In a survey of more than one hundred new senior executives, three in five claimed to be dissatisfied with their companies' efforts to help them get settled. When Amgen's partner Johnson & Johnson implemented an onboarding program for incoming corporate leaders, the response was overwhelmingly positive. Afterward, 125 of the participants were asked to put a figure on how much the extra assistance improved their performance during their initial time on the job. They pegged it at an average of 30 percent to 40 percent.

After thirty days, it's a good idea for the newbie and his superiors to sit down and review any concerns on either end. If he's working out well, tell him how pleased you are; it'll go a long way toward alleviating any uncertainty he might have. A follow-up session at sixty or ninety days—or, better still, at both landmarks—certainly couldn't hurt.

LOOK INWARD TO MOVE FORWARD

An article I read recently quoted a human resource administrator as saying that three out of five employees possess all the basic skills necessary to fill every job in a typical company. I wouldn't go that far, but I know that flashy outside applicants are often hired instead of highly competent internal candidates.

Frequently, the most qualified candidates for a position are right under your nose. And this is something that can be proved. A report published by the School of Hotel Administration at Cornell University's Center for Hospitality Research analyzed twenty studies of employee productivity covering a wide range of occupations: welders, insurance salespeople, bank tellers, teachers—even research scientists. The authors of "How to Compare Apples to Oranges" concluded that interviewing applicants from outside a company isn't nearly as reliable a predictor of future competence as performance reviews of in-house employees. Not only that, but most of the time the steady if unexciting person already in the fold is a better choice than the external candidate who wows everyone in interviews.

That shouldn't be surprising. As I've said, most terminations stem from the worker's incompatibility with the company's culture, not an inability to do assigned tasks. Someone who has worked in the same firm for a while has demonstrated that she knows how to get things done within the organization, eliminating a major concern. Increasingly, businesses seem to be recognizing this, as nearly half now let their current workers apply first for new job opportunities. Only then do they advertise the openings.

Early in Amgen's history, we did a lot of promoting internally because of financial necessity. Although we never had a single layoff during the mid-1980s, we instituted a hiring freeze once for about twelve months because we couldn't raise the necessary money at that time. This was before Epogen had entered clinical trials. Kirby Alton remembers how it was:

> When we needed something done, we'd look around the company and say, "Okay, *you* do it." That's more or less how I ended up as director of therapeutic-product development, which entailed finding doctors to run our Epogen studies and going to Washington to deal with the U.S. Food and Drug Administration—in short, getting EPO on the market. One day George Rathmann called me into his office and told me he'd like me to take on the position.
>
> I said, "Why me?" I was a molecular biologist five years out of grad school.
>
> He said, "I'll take my chances with you."
>
> I just decided, "Well, this is what we have to do." So we did it.

I mentioned earlier that the tragic death of our head of sales and marketing forced me to replace him, and the man I chose was vice president of operations Dennis Fenton. He may have been a scientist, but I had every confidence that he would excel despite having zero experience in sales and marketing. Two years later, I made our director of logistics the head of human resources. That was Ed Garnett, whom you met earlier in this chapter. Ed was smart, he had tremendous people skills, and, not coincidentally, he had trained for several years in a seminary, something that made him an extraordinarily good listener and counselor. He remembers well the day I offered him the job:

> Gordon called me into his office and said he wanted me to be his HR guy. I laughed uproariously. "What are you doing talking to me?" I asked. "I'm an operations guy!"
>
> But he insisted. He looked at me and said, "You're very good with people. You understand us and our culture. You're patient, and people respect you. You could work for me as a vice president."
>
> When I heard "vice president," I thought, "You know, I probably could learn this; I guess it wouldn't be so tough." And that's what I did.
>
> Most companies and most CEOs wouldn't do that. They would worry, "Gee, if I make this unorthodox move, and it fails, I'm really opening myself up to criticism: 'How could he be so stupid as to appoint the logistics guy to head HR?'"

The truth was, I had the advantage of having seen this kind of move work before. While at System Development Corporation, I'd watched a talented sales and marketing executive go on to become the company's head of human resources, and be highly successful. Harry Gray, my first boss, joined Litton Industries as a public relations man with a master's degree in journalism. He eventually became chief executive officer of United Technologies.

Cultivating talent from within is a major component of employee retention, a topic explored in depth in the next chapter. It's not only a matter of bold leadership; as manager, you must encourage people to step outside their comfort zones and convince them they will succeed. Just as importantly, you must reassure them that if things don't pan out, you'll absorb the blame for the decision. If management isn't willing to risk its neck, why should they?

CHAPTER 10

How Amgen Kept
Employees Committed

THE FACT THAT THE annual turnover rate in the United States approaches 40 percent should tell us that not enough employers are paying attention to the breeze being stirred by the revolving door. Nor are they in touch with their people's professional aspirations and what they look for in a job. In my experience, strong leaders are almost without exception born teachers. Throughout my career, I've had the good fortune to learn from some of the best, such as Amgen's George Rathmann, SDC's George Mueller, and Harry Gray of Litton Industries. And as an executive, I've always found mentoring younger colleagues to be one of the most rewarding aspects of running a company.

Today more than ever, a boss's ability to nurture high-caliber people is perhaps the most effective, cost-efficient way to prepare an organization for the future. In a large survey (conducted by respected consulting firm McKinsey & Company) of executives from seventy-seven companies, three in four lamented a lack of available talent. The problem seems likely to deepen in light of two trends. One is the impending shortage of workers in general. The U.S. Department of Labor predicts that by 2010 at least ten million positions will go unfilled. And that doesn't take into account the mass exodus of older workers, beginning in 2011, as the baby boomer generation reaches retirement age and starts trading in its power suits for Bermuda shorts.

At the same time, there will be fewer skilled men and women to replace them. The growth rate of the U.S. population has been declining since the 1990s and is expected to continue that way. In addition, we're entering a slowdown in the share of workers possessing at least some education and training beyond high school, further shrinking the pool of qualified managerial candidates.

The other major factor affecting staffing is the public's fractured trust in corporations following a decade of deplorable corporate scandals and rampant downsizing. Sadly, the concept of mutual loyalty between employer and employee is fading from the American picture. Every other year, Indianapolis-based research company Walker Information assesses the state of worker commitment. Its 2001 and 2003 reports are sobering. Even in the midst of an anemic job market, approximately two in three employees polled said that they planned to leave their employers within two years.

The U.S. Department of Labor has put the cost of losing a worker at one-third the annual salary of a new hire. When a management-level employee departs, an organization can expect to forfeit more than his yearly pay in recruiting and training a replacement. That's not to mention the ding to staff morale and the disruption to ongoing projects.

You've seen Amgen's financial numbers during my twelve years as CEO (see the Introduction). Also extremely satisfying to me was our 5 percent turnover rate in personnel—half the industry average and, at the time, less than one-third the median figure for U.S. companies overall. Of course, high retention can breed complacency in some people. (It may seem counterintuitive, but aggressively weeding out the least-desirable workers is one of the secrets to maintaining a low turnover rate, for reasons I discuss later.) The goal is to create an environment that encourages valuable employees not only to stay but also to stay motivated; a growing body of research substantiates something that most bosses knew intuitively long before the first management consultant came calling: an energized, committed workforce improves the bottom line. Conventional business wisdom (not always a ticket to smart business practices) decrees that the way to keep valued employees is to occasionally throw them a bone, in the form of a raise, a company car, and so forth. Certainly we all want to be compensated fairly for our skills, and a competitive salary is indeed powerful bait for luring workers *to* a company. But that's not what discourages professional wanderlust.

Likewise, no amount of perks can compensate for a company's deficiencies. I learned this from the military, of all places, when I was treasurer and vice president of finance for System Development Corporation. After the Vietnam War ended in 1973, the decision was made to discontinue the draft. The last time the country had converted to an all-volunteer military, following World War II, enlistment plunged, forcing the government to quickly reinstate selective service. A quarter-century later, the Defense Department was understandably worried that history might repeat itself. An uneasy peace may finally have been brokered in Southeastern Asia, but Cold War tensions between the United States and the Soviet Union still simmered. A way had to be found to make an all-volunteer force work.

So the army introduced a number of costly policies intended to attract and keep recruits once their hitches ended. One of them actually called for permitting *beer* in the barracks. In classic bureaucratic fashion, before long more than two hundred such benefits had been implemented. Unfortunately the military had no idea which ones, if any, truly worked.

SDC primarily designed information technology and computer systems, but we also had a psychology department. The Pentagon awarded our scientists a multimillion-dollar contract to evaluate the program's effectiveness. Thousands of servicemen and women were interviewed at length about their army experience, supplemented by questionnaires and focus groups. Interestingly, they rarely complained of wanting more this or better that. Their primary concerns had to do with negatives, especially the seemingly trifling, irritating rules and regulations that, according to the soldiers, could make military life unbearable. Ultimately, we helped the army discover that the most effective and economical way to maintain troop levels wasn't to offer one incentive after another but to eliminate the negatives as much as possible.

The same principle is just as applicable to a division of a corporation as it is to a division of soldiers. Amgen strove to be a company where the most talented scientists would want to put down roots. Many organizations unwittingly undermine their personnel by cluttering the path to progress with roadblocks, whether it's superfluous paperwork or a labyrinthian corporate structure that makes accomplishing even the simplest task an exercise in head-banging frustration. Amgen offered generous salary and benefits, but so did plenty of biotech firms. However, George Rathmann instinctively understood what the army spent millions of dollars to discover. At least once a month top management used to sit down with some of our researchers and ask them flat out, "How can we help you? Is anything getting in the way of your work?" As a rule, if any administrative red tape was found to be tying up research and development, it was unceremoniously snipped. These steps cost us little or no money, yet the scientists were as appreciative as if they'd received 10 percent raises.

Similarly, at Prime Jet, we sit around asking, "Is anything bothering the pilots?" It's usually some little thing that's dealt with easily. Here's one: we have an agency that books the hotel rooms for our pilots wherever they may be around the world. One time, according to the pilots, the hotel booked for them was so filthy that they went out and found another one and paid for it with their own money—then grumbled about it.

"Okay," we said, "new rule: if you don't like the hotel room the agency books for you, get a different one, and the company will reimburse you. But report it, so we can make sure they never book that place for us again. Pay for another room yourself or be forced to stay in a bad room? What could be more ridiculous?" The fact that somebody showed enough concern to make sure it wouldn't happen again told the pilots a lot about our company.

Now, in less enlightened sectors of the business world, where managers still bark out orders, proposing such a simple approach to lifting morale and productivity might prompt an outbreak of head scratching. *No carrot? No stick? Won't work.* Granted, it does run counter to the lessons learned in many business books and business schools. If you take into account what really drives human nature, however, the logic becomes clear.

What Do Employees Want?
Pretty Much the Same Things That You Want

That's what several large surveys of American employees have determined.[1]

The researchers may have phrased their questions differently, but basically they all asked the same thing: What do you want from your company that would make you more inclined to settle down together? Among the responses heard most frequently:

- The opportunity to contribute ideas and input on decisions

- A collaborative work environment

---

1. See "The Walker Loyalty Report: Loyalty in the Workplace," http://www.walkerinfo. com/what/loyaltyreports/studies/employee07, Walker Information, Inc., 2007; "Working Today: Exploring Employees' Emotional Connections to Their Jobs," Towers Perrin 2003 Talent Report; "Working Today: Understanding What Drives Employee Engagement," Towers Perrin 2003 Talent Report; Nancy Glube, "Retention Tools for Turbulent Times," Society for Human Resource Management, January 1998.

- Challenging work

- Feelings of accomplishment and satisfaction

- Training and career-advancement opportunities

- Equipment, information, and other resources to get work done

- Management demonstrates concern for employees' well-being

- Respect for a balance between work and home/family

- Pride in the company

- To feel appreciated, both in terms of compliments and financial compensation

Using real-life examples of our corporate values in action, this chapter presents my thinking on how we kept employees engaged and committed. I think you'll see why Amgen consistently landed on *Fortune*'s annual lists of "America's Most Admired Companies" and "The 100 Best Companies to Work For"—and how we achieved our low turnover rate.

CREATE A COLLABORATIVE WORK ENVIRONMENT

Ever been to Japan? If you walk past a Tokyo department store ten minutes after closing, through the windows you'll see the employees in each department gathered in a circle to review the day's events and prepare for the next day. They, and not the supervisors, do most of the talking. The underlying philosophy, which Amgen adopted to a greater extent than did most U.S. companies, is that the men and women who do the work should help plan the work. After all, they intimately understand the job at hand and have a realistic perspective on how much time and resources a task will take. We used to invite the future occupants of a new office or plant to give us feedback on the blueprints before we finalized the design.

Now, some would call that going overboard. I respectfully disagree, since those people were going to have to work there. After we'd built several new buildings and learned from our mistakes, we were able to go from ground breaking to occupancy in twelve months for a multistory office structure, and fifteen months for a laboratory.

Another consideration in soliciting employees' input is so that they take ownership. If you've contributed to a decision, you're probably going to try harder to make it work than if orders are handed down from on high; especially if the demands seem impractical or unreasonable.

This bottom-up style of management is gradually infiltrating American companies—startup ventures in particular. However, there's still a heavy reliance on the traditional top-down approach, where the manager sets the course for the team, who are expected to carry it out. A study by the Work in America Institute, a professional organization for human-resource managers, headquartered in Scarsdale, New York, reported that fewer than 1 in 10 U.S. employees enjoy a truly participative environment at work.

Amgen was a place where ideas flowed freely, and people were empowered to make decisions with minimal bureaucratic interference. You couldn't run a biotechnology company full of scientists any other way. Most of them came from academic laboratories, which afforded them plenty of autonomy. In contrast, commercial labs can be stifling, especially at conventional pharmaceutical firms, where marketability and profit potential often take precedence over scientific merit.

The freedom to decide how work should be done wasn't limited to R&D. I remember one time, in the 1990s, the people in our shipping department came to me with a proposal. One of Amgen's eight values was to ensure quality. With that in mind, they wanted to ship every order within twenty-four hours.

I told them I appreciated their dedication, but it just wasn't possible. The products required refrigeration, and although they were packed in reusable gel-pack ice, they couldn't be sent on a Friday and sit around over the weekend. Mondays had to be busy shipping days. "We can't afford the extra staff on Monday and have half the people in on Friday with no work to do," I explained. "It's too expensive." And distributors routinely carry plenty of inventory, so it wouldn't be important to them anyway.

The shipping department people thought about it some more, came back, and asked, "If we ship everything within twenty-four hours with no additional staff, then would it be OK?"

"I don't know how in the world you're going to do that," I said, "but sure."

On their own, they tinkered with their hours. Instead of working eight hours a day five days a week, they began to work ten hours on Mondays. Fridays, reduced to six hours, were spent getting ready for the big push on Mondays. Although you couldn't take the medications out of the refrigerators and put them in the shipping boxes on Friday, a lot of prep work could still be done.

The change in procedure benefited distributors all year but really proved its value each December. Large pharmaceutical companies often shut down for all of Christmas week, forcing their distributors to order extra product to cover patients' needs during the holidays. As you can imagine, storing all that extra inventory was expensive. Amgen, in contrast, was able to continue shipping on schedule. Our distributors loved us for it and showed their gratitude by carrying smaller inventories of our products and charging our customers a lower markup. To this day, no one else in the pharmaceutical industry does that. And the innovation can be credited to the folks in shipping. All management did was listen to them and let them implement their ideas.

Give People the Right to Be Wrong

Whenever you propose an idea, regardless of your standing in the corporate hierarchy, you're going out on a limb. People have to know they have the right to be wrong on occasion, or else they'll stop taking risks.

For that matter, how many great ideas progress from conception to implementation without a misstep or two? Very few, I imagine—especially in the uncertain world of biotechnology, where disappointments far outnumber successes. As Dennis Fenton, now Amgen's executive vice president of operations, says, "In an open environment like ours, failure is regarded as part of the process."

A company's staffers also must feel secure that their superiors aren't going to abandon them or scapegoat them if a plan fails. Otherwise, they won't volunteer ideas. Or, worse, they might try to conceal mistakes from higher-ups.

Work in Teams

Amgen's dependence on working in teams and reaching a group consensus all but eliminated that concern. I've described how our science-based culture—letting data from our experiments guide us—depersonalized decision making. Along similar lines, when everyone on a team takes responsibility for a decision, no one person can be singled out for finger-pointing if things go awry; the focus is more on problem solving than fixing blame.

A consensus-driven approach helps facilitate sound decisions by minimizing interference from clashing egos, infighting, and the like.

It isn't that it doesn't pose its own unique set of challenges, starting with the common misconception that *consensus* is synonymous with "unanimous support."

"It was never supposed to mean 'unanimous,'" says Dennis Fenton. "What it means is that you participate in the discussion and give your input, which the team leader is obligated to consider. Then the team decides what to do and is accountable for executing whatever the plan is." The first time Dennis attended a meeting at Amgen after his arrival in 1981, "it was a revelation to me that here I could actually be heard," he says. "At Pfizer the attitude was, 'Just do what you're told; we don't care what you think.'"

A team can reach a consensus even though one or two members may harbor reservations. The bottom line is, Can everybody *live* with the decision? If so, then they must all work to support it fully—because if the project fails, the excuse that "I knew this was going to fail" isn't going to fly.

The team leader's job is to guide the discussion at meetings. Not to tell members of the team what to do or to necessarily make a decision. More often than not, a clear consensus emerges from the data presented. If you de-emphasize position or level of authority, everybody in the room is just a member of the team. This encourages even the lowest-level person (who often has more detailed knowledge than anyone else in the room) to speak up, as opposed to meetings where the boss makes it clear that his view will predominate. Some attendees are going to think, "Why should I bother giving my opinion? I'll just get in trouble."

When explaining the team approach during our monthly orientations for new hires, I pointed to a chart titled "Who Manages You?" (see figure 10-1). The upper half showed the distribution of authority at most companies, and below that, at Amgen, using different-sized circles. In the typical organization, "Your boss" was the largest circle, followed by "You" and, last in significance, "Peers."

FIGURE 10-1

Employee independence at Amgen

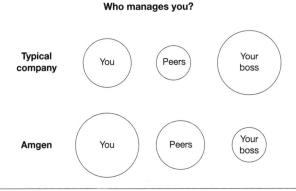

You can see from the chart that in our company, employees were granted a good deal of independence. Your peers supervised you more than the boss did. "That's what working in teams means here," I concluded, usually to a room of pleasantly surprised faces—and some skeptics. It didn't take long, though, before they discovered that the "Who Manages You?" chart accurately depicted the Amgen way of doing things. Sometimes, however, the team leader has to exercise authority, mostly in the interest of keeping the group from getting mired in interminable discussions. If we didn't come to an agreement within a reasonable amount of time, I might look at my watch and say, "Well, we've spent an hour on this and heard a lot of facts and viewpoints. We haven't agreed on either plan A or plan B. But we've got to move on, so I'll arbitrarily say that we're going to go with 'A.'"

Everybody accepted it as a boss's prerogative. I didn't do it very often, mind you; that would be dictatorial, which definitely was not the Amgen way. The decision came with a tacit caveat, too, that if time demonstrated we'd gone down the wrong road, we'd reconvene and either correct our course or change direction completely. That's another advantage of deciding by consensus: Since the action isn't associated with one person—the entire team owns it equally—it's easier for members to concede that things aren't working out. No need for saving face, an understandable human response that usually has unfortunate consequences in the workplace. Also, if the decision was science based, everyone would readily accept a change if new data happened to invalidate the previous decision.

Make Your Meetings Matter

One of the biggest complaints in most companies is that meetings eat up too much time and don't always accomplish very much. In keeping with Amgen's determination to trim red tape, we did something about that by instituting performance reviews of meetings.

First, we took a hard look at our regularly scheduled meetings, whether they were daily, weekly, or monthly. Very often those are the first meetings to outlive their usefulness, because circumstances usually change. Ask yourself, Is this meeting still constructive? Sometimes you conclude that the same information can be conveyed more efficiently via e-mail or memo, enabling you to schedule fewer meetings. If you weed out even a few sessions, you've freed up time on everyone's calendar.

We decided that we would hold only one meeting on any decision that needed to be made, with occasional exceptions. We didn't want to discuss the decision, adjourn, and then reconvene the next week. An agenda was set days in advance. The idea was that anyone with relevant information should attend. In other words, speak now or forever hold your peace. Consequently, our meetings tended to be large, a practice that violates most companies' rules. You would have key people sitting at the conference table, with junior staffers and various experts sitting behind them. They rarely spoke unless someone at the table asked them to contribute.

When you make it clear that you're hell-bent on reaching a decision before everyone files out the door, people focus. I remember one meeting that went on for about an hour without consummation. Finally, an irritated voice spoke up, "We've been here an hour. If we don't make a decision real soon, I'm leaving!" It forced everyone to get down to business.

Sometimes there isn't sufficient data on hand for making a decision, in which event you postpone it until fresh information becomes available. Otherwise, what happens? The same data gets restated, and people cling more tightly to their positions. Managers shouldn't let themselves feel pressured to go ahead with a decision they believe is reckless. Sometimes, though, "We need more information" is an excuse to delay pulling the trigger. If you wait long enough, the data will always be better. The question is, Is it reliable enough now to plunge ahead? Furthermore, no decision is irreparable; it can always be corrected. But falling into a pattern of indecision is deadly, because time truly is money.

In another break from convention, we did not defer meetings just because "Bill" or "Nancy" couldn't make it. Someone is always sick, on vacation, or at a conference. I used to encourage regular attendees at our weekly management meetings to miss a session or two. Their direct reports were to take their place, but not to merely jot down notes. In a true baptism by fire, they were expected to serve as a proxy: to have studied the agenda and to add to the discussion as if they held their boss's job. They would even take part in the decision making.

After a while, people adapted to this disciplined style of meeting. You show up prepared, bring all the experts you need, and stick to the subject at hand, and no going off on arias just to delight in the sound of your own voice. Believe it or not, it can be done, and can be done consistently.

Emphasize the Value of Collaboration

George Rathmann believed in the old saying that two heads are better than one—or, in the case of most of our teams, six to eight heads. Letting colleagues volley an idea back and forth usually improves upon the original faster than one person's ruminations. They're also quicker to recognize whether a concept is fatally flawed and should be junked.

Collaboration was so deeply ingrained in Amgen's culture that we designed our new buildings with areas that promoted employee discussions, such as clusters of seats in a sunny atriumlike setting. To me, a building should function as a piece of equipment, facilitating whatever an organization is trying to do. For instance, we put the product-development team leaders on the same floor as my office in our headquarters building. In part, the purpose was practical—close proximity fosters collaboration—but it also communicated throughout Amgen that product development was at the heart of our company and that the product team leaders were important, even though they weren't senior executives.

Product-development teams were responsible for everything related to shepherding a new product to market, and other types of teams handled other tasks. Every team had a designated leader, and every team leader had a boss, who was expected to supervise the leader with a light touch (see "Tips for Teams"). The members were given veto power over who could be on the team, a policy that few companies adopt.

Amgen, however, considered this practice essential. Let's say the team needed a statistician. It would be assigned one by the head of the statistics department. This person was under the day-to-day supervision of the team leader, although he could consult his boss for help with statistical or technical issues. If the team requested someone else, for any reason at all, the statistician returned to his "home" department, and the head of statistics had to provide a replacement.

Tips for Teams

- Groups of five to nine people tend to be most effective. Adding two or three members has been shown to aid productivity; if you go higher than that, however, scheduling conflicts and other problems begin to surface.

- They say that familiarity breeds contempt, but teams whose members stay together for a long time actually perform better. One exception, oddly enough, is teams in research and development. A study published in the journal *Administrative Science Quarterly* tracked fifty project groups at a large corporation. It showed that R&D team productivity appears to peak after about three years; therefore, it's wise to add or substitute new faces around that time.

Similarly, teams were allowed to replace members at will. Bear in mind that a project might go on for years. So "Andrea" might be a perfect fit for phase 1 but less than ideal for phase 2. It wasn't necessarily a mark against her, because a group's needs naturally evolve over time.

Encourage a Free-Ranging Perspective

You've heard of executives who say, "My door is always open." At Amgen, our meetings were always open to anyone in the company, and that helped us sidestep all sorts of petty office politics (see "Everybody Gets to Play"). If someone tried complaining to me that So-and-So hadn't invited her to a meeting, I'd reply, "Why didn't you go anyway?" End of discussion. As with any open-door policy, it was rare to find people at a meeting who really didn't belong there.

Nonteam members were encouraged to voice their opinions. If our general counsel had an idea for something that he felt R&D should consider, the research people had to listen to it. They didn't have to accept the advice or even explain the reasons for rejecting it, but they did have to listen sincerely. By the same token, if one of our researchers made a suggestion related to an ongoing lawsuit, the legal department was obligated to hear her out, because sometimes an outsider can inject a fresh perspective.

Ed Garnett, who came to Amgen as purchasing manager in 1986, remembers the first operating-committee meeting he attended after being promoted from director of logistics to head of human resources:

> It was intimidating, being surrounded by all of these ex-tremely bright scientists. I just sat there and listened. After-ward, Kirby Alton, our senior vice president of development, put a friendly arm around my shoulder and said quietly, "Ed, we have a rule that you're free to offer your opinion, even if you don't completely understand the subject. We need your input."
>
> I said, "But Kirby, you were talking about drug develop-ment. I'm the new HR guy."
>
> "Yes, but I'm sure that you have an opinion, and we want to hear the human resources department's perspective on whatever it is we're discussing."
>
> I thought, "Whoa!" That was a big shock to me.

This may sound like democracy run amok. Certainly if your peo-ple are poor listeners and undisciplined thinkers, meetings could sink beneath the weight of rambling thoughts and pointless debate.

For Amgen's policy to work, you also need a manager who is comfortable delegating to others—a skill that doesn't come naturally

Everybody Gets to Play

You know you're not distributing the workload evenly if any of the following apply:

- You always feel overwhelmed, but your team does not.

- Deadlines are missed.

- Your workers are so accustomed to your second-guessing them midway through projects and taking over that they never seem to finish anything on their own.

- Morale is low, in part because your subordinates feel that no one is helping them grow, and they resent it. How are they ever going to advance their careers?

to some people. If you're a person who thrives on the challenge of being in charge, chances are you have a talent for keeping multiple plates spinning at once, boundless enthusiasm, and the tenacity to see projects through from beginning to end. Maybe you're so good, you could practically do everything yourself.

Resist the urge. A boss who resists deputizing others for key tasks may like to rationalize that he takes on so much work out of dedication to the company. But his motivation is as much self-serving as it is altruistic. If it's really the case that "no one else can do the job as well as I can," as the nondelegator tells himself to justify hogging the spotlight, then he hasn't done a good job of hiring or of developing people.

He's letting down the organization in other ways. How will his staff ever learn to handle important projects if he doesn't give them the opportunity? What would happen if he were to miss work for a stretch due to illness or injury? The reluctant delegator should start by assigning less-skilled workers nonessential tasks. Then, as they earn your trust, reward them with more important responsibilities. A word of advice: don't let all the grunt work fall on one person—do your best to spread it around.

Fortunately, micromanagement was never an issue for me. Right, Ed Garnett?

If Gordon had one fault as an executive, it was his tendency to micromanage. I told him that as part of his 360-degree performance review. "You need to work on being more of a macromanager. Be the CEO, and hold your people accountable for results." But some of this was just part of his nature.

For instance, he had to get involved in going over the blueprints for the new buildings! I'd walk into an office, and he'd be down on the floor with the engineers, with the blueprints spread out before them. I said, "Gordon, you're just too involved with the building program."

He stopped me. "I'm not disagreeing with you, but I really like looking at the plans. Besides, if we make a mistake designing a building, it's usually irreversible." After that, if anyone complained, "Gordon's micromanaging building 32. What should I do about it?" I'd just laugh and say, "It's his hobby, he loves it, so get over it."

As should be evident, curbing the impulse to do too much may be something many managers wrestle with throughout their careers.

Save the Competition for the Competition

Some bosses, perhaps equating calm with complacency, believe in fanning the competitive flames between employees or units as a form of motivation. Ford Motor Company was like that during my five years there. In fact, it was one of the reasons I left.

I will always be grateful for the opportunity to work there; the company was a world leader in finance and control, and I learned a great deal about finance and other things that were extremely valuable later. However, I also learned some practices to avoid. Ford divisions were so cutthroat toward one another that before interdepartmental meetings, each faction plotted how to get the rest of the organization to

20/20 Hindsight

Between 1990 and 2000, Amgen's staff ballooned from fewer than one thousand to more than seven thousand. At times our policies didn't keep pace. The team system had to be tweaked, because it had become unwieldy.

According to Kirby Alton, "In the eighties, working in teams and building consensus gave us real power. The important thing was people learning and being willing to do something different. If somebody dropped the ball, you had to pick it up. But as you get bigger and more successful, it can become chaotic, especially when you have all these new people who are used to many different management styles. It ultimately led to a perception that Amgen was slow to make decisions. That's when we had to make some changes."

Dennis Fenton adds, "Our teams used to be fairly small. All of a sudden at meetings you'd have two guys from quality control, plus two guys from manufacturing, plus five guys from somewhere else, until before you knew it, there were sixty people in the room. A team of that size is going to slow down everything. So we scaled back to one representative from each department, plus a project manager, and off you went. It was like a return to the way we used to do things.

adopt its position. Compromise, even if it would benefit the company, was seen as defeat, because the objective was to "win the meeting."

At Ford, when the person representing the department came back from the meeting, his manager asked, "Did you win?" Nothing else mattered. To me, that kind of internecine battling is harmful to an organization, undermining the whole concept of teamwork. When there's a great deal of internal turmoil, too much energy gets spent licking the boss's boots or stabbing colleagues in the back—everyday occurrences at some companies. Fortunately, such behavior was rare at Amgen, especially during its first seven years, when the company consisted almost exclusively of researchers.

But when we started to build a sales force in 1987, in anticipation of Epogen's winning FDA approval, I sensed at times an almost congenital rivalry between the sales and marketing side and the science side. There are various permutations of this strained relationship in other businesses, like in the entertainment industry, where the "creative types" may be dismissive of the "suits" or "bean counters," and vice versa. You can chalk this up in part to an inherent difference in personalities. Folks who gravitate toward sales tend to be extroverted, whereas scientists are more introspective—not all of them, of course, but many of them.

Respect and Trust One Another

When employees are set against one another, they may hoard ideas and information instead of sharing them. I'll never forget the researcher who came to Amgen from another leading biotech firm. In one of his first projects for us, he was having difficulty purifying a particular molecule. Nothing seemed to work. His team was getting a little frustrated, because this was holding everybody up.

One day he came into a product-development meeting all smiles. "I did it!" he announced. "I tried another method and purified the molecule."

"How did you do it?" someone asked.

"I'm not going to tell you."

The room turned quiet. I was CFO then and happened to be at the meeting. "Oh, boy," I thought, "he's gone." Sure enough, he left Amgen only weeks later. More accurately, the company spit him out as if ridding itself of a sour taste. Refusing to reveal to your fellow workers how you did something was not the response of a team player. Later I leaned of a subplot to this story: It seems that the scientist had tried to purify the molecule using what he considered to be the superior methods of his previous employer, but nothing worked. It was only after he tried one of Amgen's purification techniques that he succeeded. I guess he was a little mortified by this and didn't want to admit it. In any event, he never would have fit in with that attitude.

It's essential for management to cultivate mutual trust and respect among the departments of the company. The best way is to make people aware of what their coworkers do and how each department supports the others. When people understand other aspects of the company, they make better, more well informed decisions. Abbott Laboratories, for example, expected every scientist to spend one day each month in the field with sales staff and customers.

Amgen encouraged our researchers to do the same thing. At first some of our R&D personnel didn't see the need for a sales and marketing department to make physicians aware of Epogen. That included Dan Vapnek, the longtime head of research. Vapnek once famously said, somewhat kiddingly, "All we need is an 800 number, and people will call in asking for EPO. It's so good, it'll sell itself."

When Epogen was launched, we hadn't yet found a salesperson for Ohio. Sales were strong everywhere except that one state. Then Paul Dawson, director of sales and marketing, expanded the surrounding territories temporarily so that Ohio was covered, and Epogen use there soared almost overnight. Dawson couldn't resist showing the sales figures to Vapnek. "I'm sure you'll agree this is pretty persuasive evidence that sales and marketing *is* useful," he said.

"Well," Dan conceded, "you've convinced me that salespeople are useful. But I still don't know what these marketing people are for." His face betrayed a faint smile. In fact, Vapnek developed a newfound respect for the sales department, a feeling that only deepened after he accompanied a salesperson on a call to a kidney specialist. He did this on his own initiative; he didn't tell me about it until afterward. Later, he organized a two-day off-site meeting for outside speakers to teach the entire research staff about finance. The scientists, much to their surprise, found it fascinating to learn about balance sheets, profit-and-loss statements, present values (compound interest in reverse), and general ledgers.

Eliminate Unnecessary Hierarchies

If I hire you and pay your salary, we're in a hierarchy. We can give it a benign-sounding name, but it is what it is. Still, a hierarchical system doesn't have to be draconian.

I can imagine first-time visitors to Amgen driving around the parking lot wondering whether perhaps they'd made a wrong turn off the Ventura Freeway, because our headquarters had no assigned parking spaces. As far as I was concerned, early arrivals deserved the closest spots. If the last car pulling into the lot happened to be mine, then I should have the longest walk to the door. This might seem to be a trivial matter, but the policy set a tone of equality and discouraged the prestige-based corporate hierarchies that can get in the way of true teamwork. As I used to stress to new employees at orientation meetings, "There's no 'us' and 'them' here; we're *all* employees." One of my favorite stories is the time that a staff member said something about working at Amgen. A colleague quickly corrected him: "We don't work *at* Amgen," he said, "we *are* Amgen."

Businesses would do well to ditch any practice that creates artificial boundaries between employees, even seemingly innocuous individual honors like "Employee of the Month." You're probably

wondering what possible harm could come from hanging one employee's picture on the wall for thirty days. Here it is: if you have one
employee of the month, you have five or fifty or five hundred "Non-
employees of the Month." Only one person benefits, at the potential
expense of many bruised egos or grumblings of unfairness. So why
do it? Furthermore, recognition of quality work shouldn't be rele-
gated to a monthly contest limited to one employee. It should be dispensed as warranted.

The military uses stripes or bars on a uniform to denote rank. In
the corporate world, distinctions in seniority may be signified with a
key to the executive washroom or some other token. This always
struck me as needlessly divisive, and it reminds me of one of my first
job interviews, with Standard Oil Company of New Jersey—later to
become Exxon—in 1957. Fresh out of Purdue University, I wanted
to investigate potential future employers before entering the navy.

The interviewer who escorted me around Standard's midtown
Manhattan headquarters told me a story about an executive there
who'd been promoted to the level just below the one where you
were rewarded with drapes for your office. His wife, an interior dec-
orator, nevertheless picked out a set of drapes for him and had them
installed.

"Now, of course," the interviewer said conspiratorially, "when he
came to work the next morning, the drapes were gone. And when he
asked what happened to the drapes, we said, 'What drapes?'"

I thought, "No way am I working for this chicken-s★★t outfit; I
don't care what they offer me." Looking back, I can't understand
why the interviewer felt compelled to share this story, and proudly,
too. Maybe he thought I aspired to have my *own* office drapes someday, and telling me this would help recruit me. All it did was convince me that Standard Oil wasn't the right company for me.

In the 1990s, Amgen bought an empty building that sat in the
middle of our campus. It had once belonged to one of the top word-
processor companies in the world back when terminals were still

dumb and computer chips were all centralized. Raytheon, the appliance-electronics-aircraft giant, bought the company, but it went out of business.

When I toured the building, it consisted mostly of drab cubicles. But then we came upon palatial executive offices with handsome wood paneling, along with a private kitchen and dining room—all for a handful of officers. "This is too nice," I said. "We'll have to bulldoze it." We did. You could have predicted the word-processor company's demise just from the glaring disparity between the extravagant executive suite and the area where everybody else worked.

Many businesspeople get caught up in trappings of success that ultimately are meaningless. "I've worked hard for a lot of years," they think, "so I deserve this." I'm not impressed with that stuff. Never have been. Maybe it's because I grew up in very modest surroundings as a child. Whatever the reason, I never cared about having a big, fancy office, or the other accouterments that seem to matter so much to many corporate leaders. Maybe a better way to say it is that other things held more importance for me. I like promotions as much as the next guy, but I knew enough not to confuse the reality with the symbol.

Executives at other companies didn't always understand or, for that matter, approve of Amgen's relative frugality and informality. Beginning in 1992, I spent eight years on the board of the Pharmaceutical Research and Manufacturers of America, including one year as chairman. After I became the first representative of the biotech industry elected to the PhRMA board, one of the members, a fellow CEO, cornered me in the hallway and said, almost angrily, "Well! I certainly hope that *now* you'll get yourself an airplane."

Far more gratifying was having an Amgen employee come up to me in the parking garage one time. The company had become too large for me to know everyone's name. He introduced himself and said, "You know one of the things I really like about Amgen? The fact that you don't have a reserved parking space." I'd wondered if anybody even noticed.

HELP EMPLOYEES EXCEL
THROUGH TRAINING

Most good workers—and that describes the majority of professionals—genuinely want to do well at their jobs and see their company prosper. In Amgen's view, the fundamental duty of management was to furnish employees with the equipment and manpower they needed and to clear away any administrative underbrush that might trip them up. If this were a football analogy, your staff would be the ball carrier, aiming for daylight, while you'd be an offensive lineman, blocking would-be tacklers.

In other words, a smart manager recognizes that he works for his employees more than they work for him. The relationship is a cycle, not a one-way street. And that should extend all the way up the corporate ladder.

High-quality equipment and facilities and the freedom to make decisions make up two sides of the employee-growth triangle (see figure 10-2). Without continued training and education, your best people will seek opportunities at firms that will invest in their future. Even more troubling, your less-talented personnel will stay—and stagnate.

Amgen did a better job of cultivating its talent after Kevin Sharer joined us as president and chief operating officer in 1992. He'd spent five years working at General Electric before becoming president of the business markets division of MCI. We more or less adapted GE's formal method of reviewing the organization's talent pool and outlining career paths for our best people. Kevin and I used to sit down with the managers and go over their rosters one by one, hour after hour.

Among the questions we hoped to answer were, Who were the most promotable candidates, and in which areas of the company? What training would they require? Which jobs would provide the

FIGURE 10-2

The employee-growth triangle

Freedom to
make decisions

Quality equipment
and facilities

Employee growth
=
Employee retention

Continued training
and educational opportunities

development opportunities they needed? These points were discussed individually with staffers as part of their performance reviews; most of them appreciated knowing exactly where they stood in the organization and what their prospects might be.

Let's say that a manager is considering a top sales rep named Frank as a future sales manager. During the performance review, the boss says, "Frank, you already have many of the skills that a sales manager needs. But there are two areas where you could benefit from more experience. We're going to give you a special assignment that will help you develop those skills." You're not promising a promotion (never promise something that you may not be able to deliver); rather, you're promising that the person will progress professionally so that he will be promotable, either at your company or elsewhere. People who know they're being trained for greater things won't be going anywhere anytime soon.

These discussions Kevin and I had with the managers often took a full day for each department in the company, but it was time well spent. Not only did it benefit our employees, but also it gave Sharer and me an overview of the people who might become Amgen's future stars.

Small businesses, which employ more than half the U.S. workforce, are often derelict in career development. Among other reasons, they often lack the necessary infrastructure and human resource personnel. Or perhaps the owners worry that their people will hone their skills only to jump to larger companies. That's a possibility, of course, but it's a shortsighted way to run a business, especially when technological advances can shake up entire industries seemingly overnight.

Prime Jet is one of those smaller businesses. We started with only three employees, and as of this writing, we're up to thirty-nine. Our retention rate rivals that of Amgen. But we recently lost two pilots, in part because of my belief and my general manager's belief that an employer has an obligation to advance workers' careers. As I see it, it's fundamental to the employer-employee contract.

Let me explain. Private copilots earn about $40,000 a year, compared with $100,000 for captains. So, obviously, there's a lot of incentive for copilots to obtain a captain's position. During interviews, we promise that if they come to work for Prime Jet, after two years we will get them certified by the Federal Aviation Administration as captains. Not only that, but if we don't have openings for captains and if they want to find positions elsewhere, we'll call around the industry to help them, even though it will lead to their departure. That's almost unheard of; in fact, in an effort to keep pilots, companies often surreptitiously try to interfere with their copilots' getting certified as captains.

Not only is Prime Jet's policy the right thing to do, but also it's good business. A report from the U.S. Department of Education found that increasing education and training improved productivity by 11 percent to 20 percent. Other studies associate education and training with higher profit margins and stock performance.

There's another benefit, too: when an organization develops a reputation as a place where people can build careers, the word spreads. You should look at training as an investment that strengthens both recruitment and retention. IBM, which spends approximately $1 billion annually on employee education, recognized this early in its history.

In 1915, only four years after incorporating, the organization established a separate education department for instructing workers on the
use of its products (such as the mechanical key punch, the vertical
sorter, and the tabulator). According to an internal study, 4 in 5 IBM
employees who are afforded learning and developmental opportunities stay with the company for at least three years.

Training used to be a headache logistically: you had to hire qualified instructors, and seminars often took place off-site, taking employees away from their work and forcing companies to incur travel
costs. Increasingly, employers are turning to e-learning, either over
the Internet or through a private computer network (intranet). One
great advantage of e-learning is that it doesn't have to disrupt the
normal workday; your people can access programs at their own pace
whenever their schedules allow. Another option popular with employees is tuition reimbursement for college courses, although only
about one-third of U.S. businesses offer it.

Amgen paid for one university course per semester for all employees, who were entitled to take one class per year unrelated to
their jobs. As is typical in Southern California, English was a second
language for many of our lowest-paid workers; all of them were eligible for free after-hours instruction in English.

HELP YOUR EMPLOYEES BALANCE THE
DEMANDS OF WORK AND FAMILY

George Rathmann and I were the "old men" of Amgen. Except for us
and a handful of others, it was a youthful organization, with most of the
researchers in their late twenties or early thirties. "Everyone in the company, it seemed, had babies within a year," Burt Ensley says, laughing.
"We used to joke that there must have been something in the water."

When I joined Amgen in 1982, many of the fifty or so employees
were new to Thousand Oaks. As often happens at start-up companies—where people work long hours in the quest of a common

goal, not to mention survival—"there was a lot of camaraderie," reflects Kirby Alton. "We all got to be really good friends."

George, himself a transplant, promoted the family atmosphere. Once a month, everyone fell out into parking lot 2 (now a volleyball court) for what became known as "fermentation seminars." It's more fun than it sounds like. Fermentation, employed to mass-produce bacteria for cloning, is also essential to processing beer and cheese. Pizza-and-beer parties is what they were; and spouses and children also attended.

Genentech, located in Sacramento, had its own version of outdoor gatherings known as *ho-hos*. I'm not sure whether the casual atmosphere at both companies was an outgrowth of the laid-back California lifestyle or of biotechnology. It was probably a bit of both. We added events such as chili cook-offs, Easter egg hunts, and Halloween haunted houses, always with families included.

In preparation for our first national sales conference, in 1989, Paul Dawson, head of sales and marketing, came into my office. "I'm going to ask you something very unusual," he said, "and if you agree to it, I promise I'll never ask you for this again. We'd like to invite the spouses and kids to the sales meeting."

No company did this, but as Paul explained, the sales staff was still new to Amgen. Most of the reps were out in the field all day, driving around and talking to doctors about Epogen. Their offices consisted of the fax machines in their homes, and that made it hard for them to truly feel a part of the company. Inviting the families, he said, would be a welcome gesture. How could I say no?

It worked out better than anyone could have imagined. My wife took it upon herself to plan day and evening events for everyone. During the afternoon, buses took all the children to Disneyland, while the spouses participated in their own activities. Everyone had a wonderful time. Pharma reps change jobs pretty often, mainly because everyone wants to be in on the launch of a great new product instead of promoting the same thing year after year. One woman was overheard saying to her sales rep husband, "You're *not* thinking about changing jobs again soon and leaving Amgen, are you?"

She may have been half-kidding. But the point is that bosses rarely consider the impact of their employees' spouses and children on the decision of whether to stay with a company. People often make these choices as a family, just as I consulted Adele before accepting George Rathmann's offer to come to work for Amgen. Not to be overlooked, the fact that my wife organized everything for the families, instead of some impersonal event-coordinating company, meant a lot to our people.

By the way, Paul didn't have to ask a second time about making our national sales meetings family affairs. It became an annual tradition—and, years later, also for our international management meetings. (Some of the kids became pen pals with children from other countries.) We wanted our employees' spouses to know that Amgen appreciated all that they did for the company; this was our way of saying thank you.

Have Fun—Most of the Time

I'm sure that this policy was a factor in Amgen's high retention rate. For instance, the entire time that I was CEO, not a single country manager left Amgen to work for a competitor, even though they were actively pursued. It wasn't cheap to fly hundreds of family members to California and arrange a weekend of fun in the sun. But if you calculated the huge cost of having to replace sales staff, I am sure that it paid for itself and then some.

The Most Coveted Commodity: Time

For a study of Americans' attitudes about work, researchers at the John J. Heldrich Center for Workforce Development at Rutgers University and the Center for Survey Research and Analysis at the

University of Connecticut surveyed one thousand employed adults. The most pressing concern, hands down, was maintaining a healthy equilibrium between career and family.

When I graduated from Harvard Business School in 1962, women made up only one-third of the U.S. workforce. Today it's about half. With increasing numbers of single parents, and with married couples sharing more family responsibilities, the worlds of work and home have come to overlap. It has become harder for people to compartmentalize their private and professional lives.

Amgen took a holistic view of its employees. Our obligation to them didn't end when they left the office; it was up to us to help people better juggle the demands at home and at work. With that in mind, the company provided conveniences right there on campus, such as a pickup-and-delivery dry-cleaning service, a film-development service, an automated teller machine, a card and gift shop, and a state-of-the-art fitness center. Employees could order take-home dinners from the cafeteria for pickup after five o'clock. We always tried to add amenities that would help ease stress and reduce the amount of time that people had to spend running errands.

"We used to have a saying: 'The worst day at Amgen is better than the best days elsewhere,'" recalls HR director Ed Garnett. "At one point, we came up with the crazy idea of having a car wash in a parking structure. The operating committee put its foot down and said absolutely not. Gordon, though, was intrigued. 'You mean I can drop off my car, and it'll be ready when I come out of work?' I said, 'Yeah, for $4.50.' He asked, 'How soon can it be finished?' The car wash was such a big hit that if you didn't get your car there by nine o'clock in the morning, sorry, you'd have to come back and try again the next day."

The centerpiece of our commitment to enhancing employees' quality of life was our child-care center, as far as I know still the largest of any corporation in the country. My wife deserves the credit. What happened was that people were beginning to ask for child care, a service provided by only one in eight employers. I dismissed the idea at first, thinking, "We all raised our kids on our own; why can't they do it?" One night I made the mistake of articulating that opinion to Adele.

"Gordon, get real!" she exclaimed, rolling her eyes. "The world has changed." Discussing it with her made me see things differently, and when I broached the possibility with Ed Garnett, he became excited. "The employees would love it if we added child care," he said. "It would help us with recruiting and retention, too."

So we looked into it. Adele toured an excellent child-care center at a government agency in Washington, D.C., reinforcing her conviction that we should start our own. "Camp Amgen," managed by a Massachusetts company called Bright Horizons Family Solutions, opened in 1992. Eight years later we doubled its size to thirty-two classrooms and sixteen playgrounds on 44,856 square feet, large enough for 432 children.

Employees paid 10 percent to 15 percent below the market rate, and Amgen provided roughly an equal amount. Having a first-class child-care center on the premises played a part in reducing turnover. According to a study conducted by Boston's Simmons College, one-third of workers have thought about changing jobs because of child-care issues. Of those, 85 percent said they would consider staying if on-site child care was made available.

Another benefit is a sizable drop in absenteeism, which has been estimated to cost employers between $650 and $1,000 per employee annually. Nearly half of all parents miss at least two days a year because of lapses in child care, such as a babysitter's illness. Child-related problems are also responsible for parents arriving late or leaving early fifteen times per year, on average. Family-friendly benefits may entitle companies to federal and state tax breaks as well, so investing in a child-care facility can actually save a business money.

There's been a lot of clamor lately for alternative work schedules: telecommuting, flextime, job sharing, and the like. These may be well suited for organizations that don't run on teamwork; nearly half of all telecommuters claim that they're more productive working from home. But none of these practices would have succeeded at Amgen, which relied heavily on teamwork and peer pressure. We explained this to our people, and, although we didn't offer these family-friendly practices, Amgen consistently made the lists of best companies to work for.

BE GENEROUS WITH COMPENSATION

A company's compensation system influences retention rates like the moon affects the tides, although it does not necessarily follow that the firm that pays the highest salaries has the lowest turnover. Employees are concerned about fairness, too, in comparison both to their colleagues and to workers in the rest of the industry.

The pay policy you choose can motivate your people to work together, or it can sow dissension. Individual incentives are appropriate for efforts that don't depend on teamwork, such as sales. On the other hand, if your business relies on collaboration, then profit-sharing plans and stock options can help encourage workers to view one another as business partners.

Amgen combined both types of compensation arrangements. I offered our senior management group two choices: all employees could receive one-size-fits-all cost-of-living increases and promotion raises, or we could award higher salaries to the highest performers and lower salaries to the poorest performers, based on the company's performance review system. The latter option is time-consuming and sometimes controversial, but it helps organizations keep their best people. The managers chose it by an overwhelming margin.

We used a matrix system, as shown in figure 10-3. (The numbers in this example are for illustration and are not the actual numbers.) One dimension was the person's salary position within the salary range for her pay grade, by quartile. The higher she rose within the range, the smaller her raise would be. The other dimension was performance.

FIGURE 10-3

Amgen salary grade performance matrix

Percent increase in salary

		4th	3rd	2nd	1st
Performance	4	4 percent	5 percent	6 percent	7 percent
	3	3 percent	5 percent	6 percent	6 percent
	2	2 percent	3 percent	4 percent	4 percent
	1	0 percent	2 percent	3 percent	3 percent
		4th	**3rd**	**2nd**	**1st**
		Quartile			

The best performers near the bottom of the salary range received the largest increases, and the raises were smallest for the poorest performers near the top of the range.

The bigger attraction, though, was stock options, which granted employees the right to buy a certain number of shares at a specified price. Options, offered by one in seven public businesses, are mutually beneficial because they allow cash-hungry start-ups to entice well-qualified people at lower salaries in exchange for the chance to make a lot of money if the company is a success. The number of options awarded to each person varied, even among those in the same pay grade. Our criteria included (1) past contributions to the company, (2) current value to the company, (3) future potential, and (4) attractiveness to competitors.

In a policy that was unorthodox for its time outside the biotech world, every Amgen employee—not only senior executives—received stock options. Ted Ledder, respected longtime CEO and chairman of

Abbott Laboratories, remembers thinking that our decision to include the rank and file was a bad idea. "I didn't see how giving stock options to the janitorial staff would help Amgen," says Ted, who joined our board of directors in 1988. "But it worked, and it's been done more and more since then."

Companywide visions of a sudden windfall, though it may never come to pass, can be a powerful agent for getting people to pull together. And your employees may be more willing to stay with the organization while keeping their fingers crossed that the stock value will appreciate. There's a good reason that options are referred to as "golden handcuffs."

If staffers aren't educated about stock options, however, their expectations may be unrealistic, and the plan could backfire. Amgen probably could have done a better job of informing our employees before the June 1983 initial public offering. People can get so swept up in the euphoria surrounding an IPO that they start thinking they will be instant millionaires. Not quite. First, the options can't be exercised for some time, perhaps years, and there's no telling what might happen to the stock between now and then. Amgen's IPO came in at $18 per share. By the third quarter of 1985, the price had plummeted to an all-time low of $3.75.

It was disappointing. But as we reassured everyone, stocks go up and stocks go down; in the long run, the best companies have the best stock prices. A business's stock price doesn't necessarily reflect its financial health. Amgen was doing fine, meeting its research targets and still flush with cash from the public offering.

"The market is cyclical," we told our people, "and the prices will come back. Don't worry."

Two years later, the price had climbed back, but only to $6 per share. As predicted, however, when we got Epogen into clinical trials, the stock stirred. By 1987, still two years before the drug received FDA approval, Amgen's price per share stood at about $40.

BE GENEROUS WITH PRAISE,
TIME, AND ATTENTION

George Rathmann and I used to joke that our researchers were so consumed by their work that all we needed to do was to stay the hell out of their way. As I pointed out earlier, this entailed doing our best to eliminate needless red tape that might impede their progress. Ultimately, no amount of stirring speeches will lift employee morale like building a winning organization. If you don't provide an efficient, energizing work environment, your words will ring hollow.

Still, even the most self-directed, independent person seeks recognition for a job well done. It's human nature. Even your suppliers appreciate recognition (see "Reach Out to Your Suppliers, Too"). It doesn't cost anything to hand out praise, and yet many managers insist on trying to prod subordinates with threats—loss of a privilege, probation, perhaps termination—if a goal is not met. This may "work" in the short term, but it does not inspire people to do their best over the long haul.

Feeling underappreciated in the workplace gnaws at people. They don't resign in a huff; instead, they sulk or simmer, which can be more

Reach Out to Your Suppliers, Too

They may not be on the payroll, but your suppliers contribute to the overall success of your company. When suppliers do a good job, tell them. Word circulates among subcontractors about which companies are a pleasure to do business with and which ones are a source of migraines. Establishing the former reputation may expand your pool of suppliers; it may even give you an edge during contract negotiations.

destructive to your organization. They're likely to grumble, "Why should I bother working hard? The boss doesn't notice anyway."

In the words of Warren Bennis, a distinguished business professor and prolific author, "Good leaders make people feel that they're at the very heart of things, not at the periphery. Everyone feels that he or she makes a difference to the success of the organization. When that happens, people feel centered, and that gives their work meaning." All it takes is for the manager to touch base regularly with workers and offer thoughtful feedback. Even a supervisor's constructive criticism is preferable to toiling in a vacuum. But try to look harder for opportunities to compliment—a 3-to-1 ratio is about right. If you can't find any, that's a different kind of problem.

I don't think I've ever seen a corporate leader more revered than George Rathmann, particularly among the Amgen scientists. Science can be lonely work, so George always made himself available, whether to offer advice or simply words of encouragement. One time, he and I were meeting with several businessmen from another company when suddenly the door to Rathmann's office flew open and two researchers burst into the room. One of them said, "We did it, George! We did it!" I can't recall exactly what it was they had done, but suffice it to say they'd solved a problem in the laboratory.

The visitors looked up, scowling, as if to say, "What the hell is going on? This is the CEO's office. Employees can't just come barging in here like that."

But Rathmann politely excused himself. "I really need to take a few minutes to hear this," he said, motioning for the two scientists to follow him into the hallway. It was obviously important to them that they have his ear right then, and George understood because he was one of them. He'd been enamored of chemistry since the age of twelve, when he traveled from Milwaukee to Indianapolis to visit an older brother-in-law who worked in medical research at Eli Lilly and Company. "Although I just got a superficial look at the labs there," Rathmann recalls, "I was absolutely dazzled." He decided almost on the spot to pursue a career in medical research.

George laughs when reminded of the interrupted meeting from nearly twenty-five years ago. "Scientists like challenges, but they need support, too. It's up to you, the supervisor, or boss, or whatever you call yourself, to fall in love with the projects that your people are working on. Otherwise, how are you going to convince them that they can conquer the world?"

LEARN FROM YOUR EMPLOYEES

I'm not suggesting that Amgen scientists were without complaint, but most were pretty content. Especially if they'd come from Big Pharma, where senior management usually treated research as a necessary evil. They didn't understand it—it wasn't sales and marketing—and didn't particularly want to. I'm sure that the scientists sensed the executives' lack of interest.

At Amgen, every Friday a different department of research held an informal poster session. The scientists stood next to poster displays and explained what they were working on to anyone who was interested. Attendance was more or less mandatory for upper research management. I went to most of them, which isn't something that a chief executive usually does. I didn't always understand the science, but it was vital for me to mill about and eat pizza with the others because it was clearly important to the researchers. It also meant a lot to them that those responsible for the project, and not only their bosses, got to talk about it.

I leaned a great deal from these informal sessions. Sometimes something that I read on one of the posters helped clarify a point under discussion at a meeting a month later. It took no more than an hour and a half per week. In twelve years as CEO, I often spent ninety minutes doing other things that weren't nearly as productive.

When supervisors fail to get out from behind their desks and interact with people from different levels of the company, the ramifications are as detrimental to them as to the rank and file. Not only do the administrators become isolated from their staff, but also their decisions suffer from the limited input they get.

One danger, particularly in upper management, is that the people reporting to you tailor the news to what they think you want to hear. Most folks want to make the boss happy, for obvious reasons, so they may gloss over troublesome details and embellish aspects that reflect favorably on the company (and maybe on themselves). The result is a distorted picture of the organization.

Once, at Amgen, we'd recently hired an influx of new sales and marketing people from Big Pharma, where this sort of thing went on all the time. Word got back to me that before our monthly marketing meetings, they were getting together to secretly "Binderize" their presentations. I suppose I should have been flattered; I was not. It was a rerun of what I'd experienced at Ford Motor Company in the 1960s. I informed them that this was not the Amgen way. "We'll have one meeting, and you'll tell me what I need to hear, not what you think I want to hear."

To help myself stay tuned in, I used to rely on the chief financial officer as my alternative channel. Typically, the CFO is involved with every part of the company and can provide an all-encompassing perspective. A talented head of human resources can be another excellent information source. People aren't always comfortable approaching the CEO, especially if they're several levels down in the corporate hierarchy. In Amgen's case, they used to tell Ed Garnett things that they wanted me to know. That was fine.

Ed, being the good guy he is, would check out the veracity of the information before passing it on to me. He might say, "I've heard this complaint from a number of people; it may be worth your looking into." Or he'd let me know that someone had come to him with a grievance, but it wasn't anything that required my attention. He was an extremely valuable third channel.

Sometimes employees are reluctant to report the truth to their supervisors because they don't want to get their heads bitten off. If you're consistently in the dark about news that's circulating on the company grapevine, ask yourself, Is it because you're frightening the messengers? A yes answer requires a change in behavior right away. You can't manage an organization based on half-truths. Says Kevin Sharer, "I always felt safe telling Gordon what I thought, even if I didn't agree with him." As far as I'm concerned, there's no other way.

Employees deserve to hear the truth from management, too—within reason, of course. In 1991, just when it seemed that things could not be going better for Amgen, a federal arbitrator in our never-ending battle with Johnson & Johnson ordered us to pay $149 million in damages. Johnson & Johnson had claimed that Amgen was delinquent in helping it to get its human erythropoietin on the market, allegedly costing the company millions in sales. We'd countered that the fifth-largest pharmaceutical outfit in the world shouldn't have needed our assistance in the first place. It wasn't our fault that Johnson & Johnson conducted business at such a leisurely pace, at least according to Amgen standards.

The day in September that the court handed down its decision was devastating. One hundred forty-nine million dollars was more money than we had! This could have conceivably spelled the end of our company. Many employees' first thought was that management must have mishandled the situation. How could Johnson & Johnson possibly deserve that much money from us? Morale was lower than hell, and I thought, "Oh, boy, how do I deal with this problem?"

The answer was to face our people and be forthright. I immediately announced that at one o'clock I would take the stage in our auditorium to explain what had happened and to field questions until

Other Ways to Build Morale

- *Help your staffers draw the connection between their duties
  and the company's success.* Twenty-five thousand men and
  women at seventeen large companies participated in a Towers
  Perrin poll about intracompany communication. The survey
  takers found that, overall, the employees were keenly interested in understanding their roles in their organizations and in
  learning how they could contribute more to helping the business grow.

- *Get into the habit of saying "we" instead of "I."* There's only so
  much credit to go around. If the big boss monopolizes the
  limelight, it is demoralizing for the other folks who work hard,
  too. As per the Chinese proverb, "The best leader, the people
  do not notice. When the best leader's work is done, the people say, 'We did it ourselves.'"

  With that in mind, share credit freely. In 1994 Amgen became the first biotech company to win the National Medal of
  Technology, the highest honor awarded by the president of
  the United States to American innovators. Usually it was given
  to individual scientists and engineers; only two corporations,
  DuPont and Bell Labs, received the award prior to Amgen. Two
  of our staff members, winners of a companywide lottery, accompanied me to a private Oval Office ceremony with President Bill Clinton and to a public-awards ceremony conducted
  by Vice President Al Gore. I accepted the award "on behalf of
  Amgen's thirty-two hundred outstanding men and women." It
  was a proud day for every member of the organization, which
  had its own celebration back in Thousand Oaks.

the last employee left. No vice presidents, no attorneys, just me, answering to the best of my abilities.

The biggest concern, not surprisingly, was that we might not be able to fund research and development. Bankruptcy, I told them candidly, was not out of the question. A few folks worried aloud whether or not Amgen knew how to wage legal warfare, and that we'd lose again on appeal. Some took it personally.

Their attitude was, "We're a great company! How dare the judge criticize us!" Still others were just plain ticked off and needed to vent.

Well, by three o'clock, the place was half empty, and by six, the last stragglers were heading out the door. Dealing honestly and openly with the crisis had healed the fractured morale in just half a day—a really *painful* half a day! Fortunately, the following year, before Amgen had to pay any of the $149 million to Johnson & Johnson, we were awarded $90 million in damages from *them*. We also had a lot more money by then.

DON'T BE AFRAID TO BE HUMAN

Counseling subordinates one-on-one is a part of leadership. Ed Garnett remembers something I said to him when he was suffering a crisis of confidence a year into his tenure as head of human resources:

> HR was a lot more difficult than I thought it would be. We were growing by leaps and bounds and hiring like crazy. One day I went into Gordon's office, and without closing the door behind me blurted out, "Gordon, I think you need to reconsider me as your HR man. I'm not sure that I'm the right guy for the job anymore."
>
> Gordon stood up, walked over and closed the door, and leaned against it. "Ed," he said, "every morning when I'm

shaving, I look in the mirror and think, 'They got the wrong guy for the CEO job.'"

I was stunned, because he always seemed so confident. "You're serious?"

"Every morning." Then he went on to reassure me that I had his complete confidence. It was probably the biggest morale booster I could have received, and I went back to work feeling much better.

To be honest, I don't remember that exchange. It goes to show the weight that a supervisor's words can carry, so be sure to speak thoughtfully, never glibly.

Let People Know Where They Stand

George Bernard Shaw, the always quotable Irish playwright, once said famously, "The greatest problem with communication is the assumption that it has taken place." In many organizations, it's not just the quality of communication that's lacking, but the quantity.

Communication between a supervisor and the supervised should be a continuous process, culminating in the annual review. At some firms, employees may go the whole year without meaningful feedback about their performance or concerns they might have until the formal sit-down with management. That's simply inadequate. For a worker, few things stir up anxiety more than not knowing where he stands. And if he's fallen into some poor work habits, a boss's failure to address them promptly is only going to make them harder to correct.

There are various forums for conveying information to your staff. Surveys find that employees generally prefer print material and e-mails to voice mail and Web casts, probably because they can read the former at their leisure. Such methods should be regarded as complementary to, not a substitute for, checking in personally with your people. The higher your perch on the corporate ladder, the more imperative it is to regularly touch back down and get a feel for what's going on. A lesson I learned in Harvard Business School—"You have to roll up your sleeves and get dirty"—still holds true.

INCLUDE VALUES IN
THE PERFORMANCE REVIEW

If you've been engaged in an ongoing dialogue with your employees, their year-end performance evaluations should be anticlimactic. No one should be surprised by the results.

Often, though, formal employee evaluations are thought of in the same terms as a grade school report card. Instead of your mother or father yelling at you, your boss does the honors. I view the evaluation more as an opportunity for education. Only after praising the employee's strengths and highlighting the ways in which she's helped the company do I discuss areas that can stand improvement. Then together we brainstorm ways that management can do a better job of helping her do a better job. Perhaps we need to provide additional training, juggle her responsibilities, or maybe transfer her to a different department. The review isn't the end product, it's the first step toward a solution and a milestone in the person's development.

Over the years, we tried various methods of employee evaluation and were never completely satisfied with any of them. There are, however, two suggestions I recommend highly. The first is to incorporate your company's values prominently in the review. As I've mentioned, when people get fired it's usually because they're out of step with the organization's culture. Amgen employees received constructive feedback if there was a value that they needed to work on. Rarely was it more than one or two. This helped make the performance review more concrete. Do you work well in a team or not? Maybe "Joe's" immediate supervisor feels that he has a bad habit of steamrolling colleagues during meetings, even though the company credo plainly states that people must "collaborate, communicate, and build consensus." What can be done about that?

Instead of Joe's boss stating bluntly, "You talk too much at meetings," she might frame it this way: "Joe, you could be a more effective participant in meetings if you made fewer points but made each one more strongly. Because by bringing up so many issues, you're diluting the impact of everything you say. Now, the next two or three meetings that you go to, I want you to listen very carefully and observe somebody who offers only one or two points, and how closely people pay attention to that person. Then take note of someone who's always talking, and you'll see it for yourself; you don't have to take my word for it."

How well a manager's comments are received often lies in the presentation. Most folks will listen to advice like that—delivered firmly but clearly intended to help, without subjecting them to ridicule or embarrassment.

And don't forget to have your own performance reviewed (see "A Review for You, Too").

DEAL WITH HABITUAL UNDERACHIEVERS

One thing that you'll never find anywhere in the business world is a boss who fires an employee and then says, "I'm really glad I didn't let him go sooner!" We always wait too long. Getting rid of a chronically poor performer is the only fair thing to do for your hardworking employees. Otherwise, not only are they forced to pick up the slack, but also the deadwood is blocking someone's opportunity for advancement.

What's more, a single employee's feeble effort can subvert productivity across the board. The rest of the staff sees what's going on. If management turns a blind eye, maybe it's not paying attention to the people who excel at their jobs. Therefore, why bother trying? Failure to take action may ultimately drive model employees, those with

A Review for You, Too

A manager who always deflects criticism from himself does not command respect. Without feedback on your performance, how are you going to grow in the job? Senior executives can easily lose perspective on themselves—it's not as though lower-level employees often collar them in the hallway and tactfully suggest ways for them to become better bosses.

Amgen offers all supervisory-level managers a voluntary 360-degree review, arranged through the human resources department. As the name implies, colleagues on all sides—subordinates, peers, superiors—fill out an anonymous performance survey. Another way is for HR personnel to interview people throughout the company.

Perhaps I have an unusually thick skin, but I volunteered for a 360-degree review every year. What's especially valuable is the three tiers of input. Some people deal effectively with their peers but come on too strong with subordinates, or vice versa. In my experience, those doing the critiquing took it seriously; no one was looking to knife the boss in the back.

The job of conducting my review fell to Ed Garnett. When I asked to hear the first critique, he didn't know how to react. "I said to Gordon, 'This is very scary for me,'" he recalls. "Most CEOs don't ask for performance reviews. They measure their performance by their salary increases and the proxy statement. Gordon said, 'I understand that, but I really want some honest feedback.' So I interviewed people around him, the board members, people below him. Then I summarized it in my words—for instance, 'Three people at the senior-management level thought this . . . ' so that none of the sources was revealed."

pride and ambition, from the company in search of an organization that values hard work and diligence.

Studies suggest that in the average company about one in seven workers can be considered complacent. The signs are usually transparent: a noticeable change in attitude and behavior, an uptick in absences and lateness, and so on. The solution may be less obvious. Termination is always an option. But unless the person is hopelessly inept or his infractions egregious, it's best to consider the less drastic route of a transfer within the company.

When a staff member wasn't meeting expectations, I had one question for him. "Are you having fun?" If you hate your job, I can guarantee that you're not performing well. I'd go on to explain that just because you don't like your current position, it doesn't mean that you have to leave Amgen. There are many jobs in various parts of the company—and even in other locations. "So how about going to human resources and seeing about a possible transfer?"

We weren't looking to reshuffle a poor employee like a bad card so that he merely became some other supervisor's problem. With file cabinets full of résumés, Amgen had no need to do that. Still, transferring a worker is less expensive than recruiting someone new; it may be worthwhile to see whether a change in duties—or scenery—can rejuvenate him.

I didn't keep score, but over the years I'd say our success rate following transfers was about fifty-fifty. It usually took no more than six months to determine whether the person was taking advantage of his second chance. If he couldn't be fired up, then unfortunately, firing was the inevitable next step.

Handling Resignations

A staff member's resignation might come as a disappointment, but it shouldn't come as a surprise. When it does, observes Ed Garnett, "that's a sign of poor management, because it indicates the supervisor was not in tune with his people." If you can learn the reasons a person is leaving, through a confidential exit survey or an exit interview, it can only be beneficial, although employees are not required to oblige.

Some human resource professionals favor taking a survey, contending that because it is confidential, it's more likely to yield honest answers. One advantage of the exit interview, however, is that you may be able to salvage the situation (assuming that you want to retain the person). She might raise issues that management wasn't aware of; perhaps they can be redressed to everyone's satisfaction, and the employee can be persuaded to stay. If that's your preferred outcome, hold the exit interview as soon as possible after notice has been given. Don't wait until the person has grown completely comfortable with the decision and colleagues are busy planning the menu for the farewell party.

BE A COMPANY YOUR PEOPLE CAN BE PROUD OF

A worthwhile mission helps a company retain employees. We'd all like to believe that our lives have meaning, and what we do for a living constitutes a large part of who we are. Amgen was extremely fortunate in this regard. As Kevin Sharer, who succeeded me as CEO in 2000, puts it, "We really *are* trying to cure cancer."

Working at Amgen was a source of pride for our people. We had a tradition that any noteworthy achievement by a team or group entitled the members to announce it on a T-shirt. It became a joke that employees would never have to buy another T-shirt, even well into retirement.

The staff members liked to wear their Amgen T-shirts around Thousand Oaks, because strangers often came up to them and said, "I just want to thank you. Your product did so much for my aunt." Or uncle. Or brother. Who wouldn't like to hear that about her company?

Employees also felt good because Amgen behaved like a model corporate citizen. In addition to bringing thousands of employees and visitors to Thousand Oaks, the company pitched in however it could. One time we bought a building that we were eventually going to tear down. An employee, on his own initiative, got the idea to contact the local fire department and invite its personnel to use the structure for practice, an offer that was gladly accepted. They could spray all the water they wanted and chop holes in the walls to their hearts' content. When the firemen pulled up outside the building for the first drill, they were as giddy as kids on Christmas morning.

A similar offer was made to the Thousand Oaks police department regarding a small bank that we'd purchased for the property. Until the building was to be demolished, someone figured that perhaps the department's SWAT team would like to use it to simulate bank robberies. They were thrilled. Nearby residents were less than thrilled, however, when they were jolted awake at two o'clock in the morning by the sounds of explosives detonating and gunfire. I'll bet the police never received an offer like that again, certainly not from Amgen.

In 1991, the city planned a huge parade to honor the men and women veterans of Operation Desert Storm. On the eve of the event, someone came into my office and said that Thousand Oaks was going to have to cancel its plans, because the city council hadn't raised enough money to cover the cost of cleanup. Seventy-five thousand spectators were expected to attend.

"How much do they need?" I asked.

"Seven thousand dollars."

"You know what to do," I said. "Take care of it." The tribute to our soldiers went on as scheduled. "Amgen Saves Parade," trumpeted the local newspaper's eight-column headline. How much money would a company have to spend to win the immeasurable goodwill that this small gesture brought us? A lot more than seven thousand dollars, that's for sure. And not that we did it for this reason, but not long afterward Amgen went before the city council to seek approval for its master building plan. A public hearing was to be held at which townspeople were invited to have their say. To ensure a balance of viewpoints, residents would fill out cards stating their position, and five or six names on either side would be called to the microphone.

At the hearing, the mayor of Thousand Oaks thumbed through the cards and started to laugh. "I guess there's probably no point in anybody speaking today," he said. "Every single card is for approval; there aren't any against."

Spread the Good News

If your business makes, say, wheelbarrows and not life-enhancing drugs, the level of corporate esteem might not be as great, but there can still be considerable pride in being a manufacturer of quality wheelbarrows sold at fair prices. Or maybe you manage an excellent division within a weak company; that too can be a source of pride. No matter what products or services you provide, your organization should take advantage of opportunities to remind employees of the good it does.

For example, we used to have patients who'd benefited from Amgen medications come to speak to our staff. Public relations isn't only external; you can use your company newsletter to relay important developments. Increasingly, companies use electronic newsletters, which can be timely, have no space limitations, and eliminate the cost of printing and distributing. Remember, though, that there's a fine line between instilling pride and making empty boasts.

EMBRACE CHANGE TO KEEP
YOUR COMPANY VIBRANT

I've mentioned that I spent a summer interning at Procter & Gamble's corporate office in Cincinnati. One aspect of the company has stayed with me: its emphasis on making change the status quo. "There's always a better way" was the Procter & Gamble philosophy, and it backed it up with action. Senior managers were expected to spend three-fourths of their time working on keeping things running as usual. But the other one-fourth was to be devoted to new ideas. It was made very clear, even to us summer interns, that innovative managers were the ones who got promoted.

I saw the virtue of this system. Incremental improvements added up to making a product cheaper, easier to use, more effective, *better.* At Amgen, we always looked for ways to refine existing products. By trying to gain a better understanding of Epogen and Neupogen, we learned things that let us develop their cousins Aranesp and Neulasta. For another example, we later changed Epogen's packaging for reasons of patient safety. The drug vials are all the same size, with the same amount of liquid; only the concentration is different. To help ensure that a care provider didn't accidentally administer the wrong dose, we instituted a color-coded system with a different-colored stopper for the 5,000-unit vial, the 10,000-unit vial, and so on.

It's more fun to work in an atmosphere where change is embraced and creativity encouraged (except when it comes to accounting; excessive creativity there can create problems). At most companies, people are conditioned to fear change. If the new approach fails, someone's head will land on the chopping block. Management must accept that innovation involves an element of risk, or else its employees will approach their jobs like an athlete playing defensively—afraid to make a mistake—instead of making things happen. Teams that play not to lose usually lose, and those that play to win are more likely to win.

George Mueller, president of System Development Corporation, where I served as CFO from 1971 to 1981, taught me a lot about the importance of taking calculated risks. Before I tell you about George, whose last name is pronounced "Miller," let me give you a little background on this fascinating nonprofit company.

SDC evolved out of RAND Corporation, a think tank that's had a hand in furthering such revolutionary technologies as computing, missiles, and space satellites. SDC consulted for the navy and the army, but its number 1 customer was the U.S. Air Force. Competitors began complaining bitterly to Congress that SDC held an unfair advantage. The company, worried that steps might be taken to put it out of business, converted to a for-profit enterprise in 1969. Under California law, this is no simple process. Legally, a nonprofit corporation belongs to the state's citizens. Therefore, you must first form a foundation, which then owns the new company and its stock.

Maybe because SDC had spent twelve years as a nonprofit, the people at the top did not know how to turn a profit. That's when they brought aboard George Mueller, who'd headed the National Aeronautics and Space Administration's manned spaceflight program from 1963 to 1969. If not for Mueller, a narrow-shouldered, bespectacled man with a PhD in physics, the United States would not have met President John F. Kennedy's 1961 pledge to put a man on the moon by the end of the decade.

Throughout his distinguished career, Mueller had consistently followed his natural impulse to achieve goals that conventional wisdom dismissed as impossible. For example, only weeks into his tenure as NASA administrator, Mueller instituted tighter controls, beginning with a landmark decision to implement "all-up" testing of the Saturn V rocket that would propel U.S. astronauts beyond the bonds of gravity.

The Saturn V consisted of three rocket-powered motors stacked one on top of the other. Under existing NASA protocols, each stage was to be tested independently. Only after the stage 1 rocket proved itself airworthy would a live second stage be added, and then a live third stage. To George, this plan seemed needlessly time-consuming and costly and, what's more, stemmed from a presumption of failure. He proposed road-testing the fully assembled rocket with the complete *Apollo* spacecraft on top. The first full-scale Saturn V lifted off from Cape Kennedy on November 9, 1967, and all three stages performed flawlessly.

Similarly, the Apollo program's original itinerary called for sixteen manned or unmanned trial flights before the first moon landing was attempted. Mueller considered this plan overly cautious and telescoped it by more than half. The streamlined plan enabled *Apollo 11* astronauts Neil Armstrong and Buzz Aldrin to plant the U.S. flag in the moon's powdery surface on July 20, 1969, months ahead of schedule.

Mission accomplished, George left NASA to become a vice president at defense contractor General Dynamics Corporation. Then, at age fifty-three, he moved on to System Development Corporation, where I watched him exhibit the same bold yet steadfast leadership. Mueller didn't merely think "out of the box," as per the latest bromide; his worldview dismissed the very idea of boxes. There was only the correct answer to whatever problem he was trying to solve.

Mueller philosophized that in business, as in life, many folks fall into the habit of saying that something can't be done, when what they really mean is only that it hasn't been done before. That alone justifies trying it. On numerous occasions, I came to him with elaborate explanations of why something the company wanted to do wasn't feasible—say, because of state regulations.

What I saw as legitimate reasons were merely excuses to George. "Well," he'd say thoughtfully, "I'd like for you to go back and see if there isn't room within those regulations to support what we want to do. If there isn't, then find a way to get the regulations changed."

Sometimes I used to leave his office thinking, "What the hell is wrong with this guy? I gave him a clear explanation of why this can't be done, and he's telling me to do it anyway." During the ten years that we worked together, I kept a mental scorecard, and you know what? At least 50 percent of the time, he was right. I'd given up too quickly. Most people do.

MAINTAIN THE ENERGY OF A START-UP
LONG AFTER YOU'VE STARTED

There's something special about the energy and passion of a start-up company. George Rathmann describes it as a place where most of the people "demonstrate exuberance. In many cases, though, businesses emphasize rigidity and structure more than they inspire new ideas." George worked at 3M for more than twenty years. There, he says, "it was a risk to be exuberant. There were behavioral restraints that advised you to be cautious and not get too excited about plans that you might not be able to deliver. But at Amgen, there was no doubt that the sky was the limit. That kind of atmosphere is very attractive."

Dennis Fenton thought so, too. When he came to interview at the small company in 1981, he notes, "the energy level was indescribably different from my experience at Pfizer. Everyone I encountered had the belief that you could do something profound with science and move knowledge forward, which was why I decided to throw my lot in with George and these scientists and see what happened."

The trick is to not lose that entrepreneurial spirit as your business grows. We were very conscious of this and spent a great deal of time working on preserving our culture. One way is to work in teams, to mimic the dynamics of a lean company. All the Amgen values and principles that I've described here—allowing employees to help plan their work, encouraging collaboration, and so on—are just as essential. They're part of a larger whole, with each one reinforcing the others.

CHAPTER **11**

The Value of Ethics in Business

IN 2000, MY FINAL year as CEO of Amgen, *Business Week* named me one of its top twenty-five managers in the world. Within a year or two, several of my fellow honorees resigned in disgrace from companies such as Enron, MCI WorldCom, Inc., and Martha Stewart Omnimedia. A few wound up trading their pinstripes for prison stripes.

The ethics scandals of the past few years have undermined public confidence in U.S. business and have helped fuel the undercurrent of cynicism that pervades our culture. I've heard some of my contemporaries remark ruefully that they're almost ashamed to admit they're senior executives. What disillusions us most is that the actions of a corrupt few tarnish the image of corporate leaders, the vast majority of whom are hard working and abide by the law.

PRESSURES ON BUSINESS

As for what can be done to prevent such abuses of power and the public trust, we need to rethink the current system. Of course individuals are responsible for their own conduct. However, three fundamental pressures have contributed to destabilizing the ethical foundation of corporate America.

Changes in Compensation Practices

Over the past two decades, changes in executive compensation practices helped spawn the corporate obsession with puffing up stock prices, a strategy that may have helped bring about some unfortunate actions in the executive suites of Global Crossing, Tyco Industries, and others. Ironically, some of the blame rests with shareholders, who complained that many executives accomplished little but were paid as generously as if they accomplished a lot. Congress agreed and passed a law eliminating the tax deductibility of executive compensation in excess of $1 million that was not "performance based."

Business responded by instituting incentive pay programs heavily weighted toward stock options and "performance" bonuses as a way to hold managers more accountable. The trend grew throughout the 1980s and 1990s. According to consulting firm Towers Perrin, base pay for a CEO at a mid-sized U.S. company currently averages 27 percent of total compensation. Compare this to similarly sized businesses in England and France, where base pay makes up 43 percent and 40 percent, respectively, of a CEO's total income, and incentives, only 35 percent and 41 percent. Companies might not have granted so many stock options if the new tax laws hadn't given them a deduction every time an option was exercised.

Having more than two-thirds of an executive's remuneration hinge on the company's reported financial results seems to invite trouble. I'm referring not only to the flagrant offenses that made the evening news—wherein some corporations spun the illusion of great profitability through accounting sleights of hand—but also to business decisions that, though legal, pumped up the stock price in the short term at the expense of long-term growth. Given the inherent conflict of interest between what is good for the company and what is good for the executive, none of this should have come as a surprise. Most executives were steadfast enough ethically to resist temptation, but many weren't.

Similarly, when directors' compensation is heavily option oriented, it can compromise their effectiveness in policing the executive leadership. Think about it: they're supposed to prevent mismanagement, but when fraud is committed on their watch, they're essentially being paid a percentage of the take. Accordingly, some companies have done away with incentives for directors and now pay them straight salaries. More businesses should follow their example.

Analysts' Conflicting Interests

Fortune magazine estimated the cost of a Wall Street soothsayer at $1 million a year, for which he brings in $500 million in investment banking business and trading revenues. If those figures are to be believed, we have had another inherently perilous set of circumstances. Analysts understood that the more business they procured for their firms, the bigger their bonuses; that undercut their ability and incentive to make sound recommendations with investors' interests in mind.

Unfortunately, the cure for this problem has substantially reduced analysts' compensation, because they aren't worth as much to their firms if they're not permitted to generate business. The result has been an overall decline in the quality of analysts, as many of Wall Street's best have moved on to other, better-paying lines of work.

The Credibility GAAP

The U.S. Securities and Exchange Commission has had a hand in this misadventure as well. Formerly, a company could publicize only one type of earnings per share, which its auditors would approve. The

SEC did not allow proforma earnings, operating earnings, or recurrent earnings, for which some of the costs are left out.

Then the SEC began allowing businesses not only to report financial statements based on the set of standards known as generally accepted accounting principles (GAAP) but also to declare an additional set of numbers. In theory, these other numbers represent the business more accurately than GAAP numbers, which often obscure more than they reveal. An auditor's job went from helping turn out accurate financial statements to determining whether the company was in compliance with GAAP. Fortunately, the two goals are not mutually exclusive. An unscrupulous but creative business executive can write a misleading financial statement that nevertheless receives the auditor's statement of approval. From what I've read about MCI WorldCom, one year senior management simply took the number it needed to meet analysts' expectations and worked backward, transferring the exact amount from expenses to capital for each quarter. I never imagined that large, publicly held companies would dare to be so blatant about it.

Maybe we should add a provision that if a financial statement is found to be false or misleading, the auditor should refuse to certify it, whether or not it meets GAAP criteria. The Universal Code of Military Justice, the legal system of the U.S. armed forces, has an article that has worked well for many years: "conduct unbecoming an officer and a gentleman." There's no definition for this charge—it's often explained as "You'll know it when you see it"—but a violation is grounds for a dishonorable discharge.

A Perfect Storm

The combined effect of these oversights created a situation wherein the natural forces would inevitably lead to disaster. It was only a matter of time. I'm a big believer in natural forces. If they align to facilitate unethical behavior, we'll see more unethical behavior; if they align to discourage dishonest behavior, we'll see more honorable conduct. How many executives would have sanctioned phony accounting if none of their income was tied to the stock price? How many auditors would have looked the other way if they made their money primarily on auditing fees and not on consulting, as was generally the case?

Maybe the tragic sight of formerly powerful corporate leaders being escorted out of their grand buildings in handcuffs and paraded before the media will prove to have a sobering effect on those who might otherwise be tempted to cheat the system.

CREATING A CULTURE OF ETHICS AND HONESTY: IT ALL STARTS WITH YOU

I've never understood people who think they must lie, cheat, and steal to get ahead; I guess that comes from the example set for me by my father, who was probably the most honorable person I've ever known.

Charles Binder was a schoolteacher and later a school principal and superintendent. He hadn't planned on teaching for a living. My dad graduated from the University of Illinois with a master's degree in chemistry. In the early 1930s, most folks didn't seek opportunities very far from home, even if they were well educated. But not long before graduation, he spotted a notice on a bulletin board: "Teach Science for a Year in New Mexico." The idea of living in the Wild West had a lot of appeal for a young single fellow. Not that New Mexico was exactly the Wild West, but to someone who grew up in Waterloo, Illinois, outside St. Louis, it must have seemed close enough.

In those days, you didn't need a teaching degree, only a thorough knowledge of the subject matter. Off went my father, figuring he would spend a year in New Mexico and then return home to marry his high school sweetheart, Rodella—or Rody, as everyone called her. But my father loved New Mexico. He also discovered that he loved teaching and loved kids. He was still fascinated by science, but here was a way to do both. He and Rody, my mother, also a teacher, married and moved permanently to Alamogordo.

My father was extraordinarily principled. I'm not sure how he got that way, but he set an example for other people, especially me. It wasn't something that we talked about much; he lived it, and that was far more eloquent. He was a phenomenal teacher. This I know, because he was my chemistry and physics teacher. In a town the size of Alamogordo—with perhaps twenty thousand people when I was in high school—there was only one chemistry and physics teacher.

He put in many extra hours to help students. One young man was a gifted athlete. He remarked to my dad that he wanted to become a javelin thrower. My father found a book about the sport and worked one-on-one with the boy after school so that he could enter the state track meet. Later, Dad became principal of a school in nearby Cloudcroft, an even smaller town. The school, which taught grades 1 through 12, didn't have a formal library or a librarian, only a bunch of books piled haphazardly in a room. Principal Binder took it upon himself to organize all the books, apply the Dewey Decimal System numbers on their spines, and create a comprehensive card catalog—all on weekends. My father provided a shining example of how an authority figure's good deeds can set a positive tone that permeates an organization.

His influence has guided me throughout my career, even when I was starting out. I'll tell you a story. Almost every job I've ever had has come through word of mouth, as when Amgen counsel Ed Huddleson recommended me to George Rathmann because he was familiar with my work at System Development Corporation. Not one help-wanted ad that I answered ever turned up a damn thing. In 1962, with graduation from Harvard Business School looming, I sought one of my professors, Myles Mace, for career advice. My dream job, I explained, was to become right-hand man to an executive at a company involved in mergers and acquisitions. It seemed extremely exciting to me. Where would he recommend I apply?

"There's only one company," he replied. "Litton Industries." Mace had firsthand knowledge of the famously successful conglomerate, having been an original board member. In 1955 the company's co-founder and chairman, the colorful Charles B. "Tex" Thornton, offered him a position as vice president and general manager of the electronics equipment division. Harvard gave its blessing; the school typically encouraged faculty members to immerse themselves in the real world every few years. Mace spent three years at Litton, increasing annual sales from $3 million to more than $80 million. Then he returned to teaching and sitting on Litton's board.

Now he called out to his secretary, "Suzi, get me Tex Thornton on the phone!" As it happened, the husky, ruddy-faced Litton chairman was in his Beverly Hills office and took the call. I heard only the professor's side of the conversation. He told Thornton, who had been the leader of Ford Motor Company's storied "Whiz Kids" in the late 1940s, that he had this bright young guy sitting across from him, an electrical engineering undergrad, and that Thornton should hire him.

"Okay," said Thornton, "have him come out for an interview."

Litton's highly decentralized corporate structure, so familiar today, was novel for its time. There were five senior vice presidents, each of whom was allotted one finance person, one secretary, and one assistant fresh out of business school. I wound up being interviewed by Harry J. Gray, a World War II army hero who'd been with Litton since 1954. He was vice president of the components group. Ultimately Gray left Litton to become chairman, president, and chief executive officer of United Technologies, another multibillion-dollar company, in the 1970s and 1980s.

"If I offer you this assistant's job and you take it," he said, "how long do you think you should keep it?"

I thought, "I don't know. What an odd question." For some reason, my mind settled on two years. We shook hands, and that was that.

Harry Gray had the best people skills of anyone I've ever met, in or out of business. Because he was a born salesman, and I am not—I tend to be introspective and am not a natural glad-hander, even now—I spent a lot of time studying his interactions with his staff and asking him questions. The Georgia native, who was forty-three when I met him, was the kind of forward-thinking executive who hired good people and then invested in them by grooming them for expanding responsibilities. He believed that a senior manager's job was to help his subordinates do their work, and not the other way around, a philosophy I carried with me after leaving Litton.

In 1964, right around my two-year anniversary as his assistant, Harry called me into his office and reminded me of our very first conversation. "Do you still think two years is a sufficient amount of time in this job?" he asked. I said I did, and he agreed with me. After investigating other opportunities within Litton, I decided to move on to Ford, where I'd served an internship.

Gray lived next door to Keenan Wynn, versatile character actor and son of vaudeville and film clown Ed Wynn. The younger Wynn was an avid motorcyclist—he raced anything that moved, on land or water—and had been after Gray to go riding with him. Harry had never been on a motorcycle and didn't want to start now, but he allowed the actor to talk him into it.

The bike skidded on an icy patch, and slammed into a guard rail. One of Harry's legs was wedged between the ground and the cycle; the other between the cycle and the rail. He wound up with compound fractures of both legs and faced several months in traction in a hospital.

Arrangements were made for another Litton executive to take Gray's place while he recuperated. However, his division managers complained that bringing in someone else wasn't going to work. "Gordon," he said to me one day, "I know you're about to leave us for Ford. But it looks like I'm going to have to keep running my part of the company from my hospital bed. If you could possibly stay until I get out of here, I would really appreciate that."

Despite the fifteen-year difference in our ages, Harry had become a close friend as well as a great teacher and an inspiration. I felt that I owed it to him to help him through this crisis. So I called my future boss at Ford and told him I wouldn't be able to start for three months. Although my new employer objected, I held firm. "I'm sorry," I said. "I promised my boss I would do this. If that doesn't work for you and you need to get someone else for the job, then so be it." They backed down and said they'd wait for me.

Conveniently, Tex Thornton's partner in Litton, Roy L. Ash, had donated the wing of the hospital where Gray was staying. We commandeered the room next door, replaced the bed with a desk, moved his secretary in there, and conducted business as usual, despite Harry's being in traction. Even if my staying on had cost me the position with Ford, it was the right thing to do. I strongly believe that doing the right thing, in addition to being its own reward, frequently pays dividends. That was certainly true in this instance.

In contrast, the unethical business executive usually considers only the external effect of her misdeeds—in other words, how her deceptions benefit her company. What she usually overlooks is that corruption at the top seeds a culture of dishonesty that extends throughout an organization until it rots from within.

When employees work at a company where crooked practices are not only tolerated but tacitly sanctioned—or flagrantly encouraged— do you think they trust management not to turn on *them* at some point? By the same token, when management encourages its people to cheat customers, suppliers, and others, doesn't it stand to reason that some of them are going to scam the company, too, whether it's pocketing office supplies, filing false expense reports, or embezzling large sums? According to a survey of 12,750 U.S. workers at all job levels and in all major industries, fewer than half the men and women polled said that they trusted their senior managers. In such an environment, the rank and file often develop a do-it-to-management-before-management-does-it-to-you attitude. The study, conducted by global consulting firm Watson Wyatt Worldwide, also showed that companies with high levels of trust outperformed companies with low trust levels by 186 percent.

Over time, self-selection comes into play. Ethical people don't want to remain at a place where lying, cheating, and stealing are commonplace, whereas those whose consciences don't nag them will fare just fine—and stay a long time.

In that same Watson Wyatt survey, one in four people claimed to have known of or suspected an ethical violation in the past two years; however, only about half reported the breach. The reasons usually given for failing to notify supervisors of misconduct are a fear of retaliation as well as a lack of faith that the organization will respond.

Now hold up a mirror to the same scene. In a company where ethics are entrenched in the culture and practiced consistently, with no double standards based on hierarchy, staff members are more likely to expose unethical practices. First, they do so because they know that management will support them; second, they take pride in their company and therefore have a personal stake in protecting its reputation; and third, they're probably the kind of men and women who genuinely resent dishonest dealings. Shady characters, on the other hand, usually get weeded out quickly at good organizations; sometimes they voluntarily prune themselves from the payroll because they can see that their "skills," such as they are, won't benefit them there.

When folks have worked for you long enough, they come to understand instinctively what's acceptable and what isn't. The organization's ethical guidelines inform their decision making, and they don't always need a supervisor to clarify it for them. One time Amgen hired a senior executive. A few weeks later, I ran into Ed Garnett, head of human resources, who told me that he'd had to fire the man.

"Fire him? He hadn't even been here for a month. What happened?"

Ed said, "We discovered that he'd falsified his résumé in a major way, so I knew I didn't need to check with you first. I went ahead and let him go."

We'd already informed the other candidates that the position had been filled, and to be honest, the abrupt departure created a mess for a while. Ed was right, though; he didn't need to check with me first. The misrepresentation almost certainly wasn't an isolated incident but indicative of the character of the employee-turned-ex-employee. It would have revealed itself again in the future, perhaps with far more serious consequences. What if he made false statements to the IRS or the FDA? There was no question about it; he was out.

Sometimes it took a while for new hires who'd come from other companies to realize that Amgen was serious about its commitment to ethics. If you follow professional bicycle racing at all, you probably know that there have been reports of cyclists injecting themselves with EPO to improve their endurance. The increase in red blood cells brings extra oxygen to the body's cells, including muscle tissue. A doping scandal marred the 1998 Tour de France, when teams from the Netherlands and Spain had to drop out because some of their members were abusing EPO. The practice is not only illegal but also dangerous: when a person who is not anemic takes Epogen, the influx of red cells thickens the blood, and that could heighten the risk of suffering a heart attack or stroke.

I believe that companies have an ethical obligation to do the right thing. An awful lot of people in the pharmaceutical business would probably disagree; in their view, it's up to somebody else to regulate abuses of medications. Amgen did whatever it could to discourage athletes from misusing Epogen. We worked with the National Collegiate Athletic Association, the National Olympic Committee, and the International Olympic Committee. At our expense, we had an educational booklet written and sent to high school coaches. To help get the word out, we invited the media to an all-day information seminar in New York City, with gold-medal winners as some of the presenters.

In addition, during my talk to new salespeople on their first day of training, I always stressed that Amgen actively worked to prevent EPO abuse. We didn't want those sales. And I could see from the smirks on some of the faces that not everyone believed me. "Oh, I get it; this is for public consumption, right? Maybe you don't want me selling like that as long as I'm making my quota, but just take a month where we're coming up short, and I'll bet you . . . " I had to drive the point home more forcefully, warning, "I am not kidding. If we catch anyone encouraging illegal use, they'll be fired. Don't think we're not serious; we're deadly serious." By the end of my chat, most of the skepticism in the room had been expunged.

I also told each class to always tell doctors the truth about each product, warts and all, even if it meant we sold less. The truth was, we'd sell more. A salesperson is nothing if he loses credibility with a doctor. Goodwill is vital for any business, but particularly a company selling health-care products.

Researcher Burt Ensley, who left Amgen in 1989 after eight years, went on to found several companies of his own. Amgen, he says, "had a higher level of integrity than anything I've seen before or since. I really learned that there and use it. Contracts were to be honored. You kept your word. That is an unusually high standard, as I discovered after leaving."

PLAYING POLITICS BUT PLAYING FAIR

At some point during your career, it may fall to you to do business with local, state, or federal legislators in order to have a say in public policy. It might be an issue close to home, such as appearing before the city planning board to seek a change in zoning restrictions. Or you might find yourself addressing Congress as it deliberates a bill that would affect your industry.

Because the biotech and pharmaceutical industries are subject to much federal legislation, Amgen felt that it needed to establish a presence in Washington, D.C. In 1993 we hired Peter B. Teeley, former U.S. ambassador to Canada, as vice president of government and public relations. Most of Pete's long political career had been spent as press secretary to Republican lawmakers—Sen. Robert Griffin (R-MI), Sen. Jacob Javits (R-NY), and Vice President George H. W. Bush—as well as communications director and chief spokesman for the National Republican Committee. He was highly respected on Capitol Hill and gained us entree to many key legislators.

When Amgen started, we knew next to nothing about lobbying. Because of a corrupt minority, the practice has been maligned as unsavory, and that is unfortunate. At its core, lobbying enables industries as well as groups of concerned citizens who come together in special interest groups to educate lawmakers about various issues. In a democracy, they're free to advocate a position; the government officials they approach are free to listen to them or disregard them, find value in their viewpoint or reject it.

Circumstances forced us to set up the Washington office. You'll recall Amgen's patent dispute with Massachusetts biotech firm Genetics Institute and its Japanese partner Chugai over Epogen, dating back to 1987. There was no dispute that we held exclusive rights to the CHO cells used for cloning the human erythropoietin gene. Amazingly, a gap in patent law made it possible for Chugai/GI to duplicate the process that we'd spent years and millions of dollars developing, manufacture its own epoetin alfa overseas, and export it to the United States. When we filed a complaint with the International Trade Commission, an ITC judge ruled that the matter fell outside its jurisdiction. The dispute called for a legislative solution, she said.

In 1995 Sen. Orrin Hatch (R-UT) and Sen. Edward Kennedy (D-MA) cosponsored the Biotechnology Patient Protection Act, which finally closed the loophole. Steven Odre, Amgen vice president and associate general counsel, appeared before the House Judiciary Committee to explain that under the existing patent and trademark laws—drafted long before the inception of biotechnology—any foreign competitor was free to trample all over U.S. companies' patent protection. Congress approved the measure in the fall.

That same year, I spoke before the House Commerce Committee about the need for reforming the U.S. Food and Drug Administration. I was representing Amgen, of course, but primarily the Biotechnology Industry Organization. At the time, I chaired BIO's Committee on FDA Reform, in addition to serving as a board member. We were there to lend support to the Food and Drug Administration Modernization Act, a bill introduced by Sen. Jim Jeffords (R-VT). Its seven cosponsors came from both sides of the aisle.

This legislation was to extend an earlier measure, the Prescription Drug User Fee Act of 1992, which had been enacted out of hair-pulling frustration with the amount of time it took the understaffed FDA to evaluate the findings of drug trials. When a manufacturer believes that its patient studies have yielded sufficient evidence of safety and efficacy, it submits either a new drug application (NDA) or a biological license application (BLA) for consideration.

By law, the agency is allowed ten to twelve months to review the results and judge whether or not the product should be licensed for commercial use, or six months if it looks to be of significant benefit and is therefore designated a priority. But as of 1986, it was taking an average of thirty months—twice as long as the FDA's European counterparts. Amgen once had to wait nearly three years for clearance to add a new use to Neupogen's list of indications. What's more, during that time we were prohibited from telling physicians how this new application could help some of their patients.

In 1992 the pharmaceutical industry took the unusual step of lobbying Congress for legislation that would impose a user's fee upon the companies themselves to help underwrite the cost of FDA reviews. Over the next five years, this brought an additional $329 million to the agency, which hired seven hundred new employees and streamlined its operations. By 1997 the NDA and BLA review time had been slashed to about thirteen months, a blessing particularly for people with incurable diseases such as AIDS. As for the drug companies, the $329 million in user fees amounted to a fraction of the sales revenue that they had been losing because of the delay in getting products approved. Talk about a win-win-*win* outcome.

Now the Prescription Drug User Fee Act was about to expire. The FDA Modernization Act would not only reauthorize the previous bill for another five years but also make further improvements, such as increasing patient access to experimental drugs and accelerating review of important new medications. Congress approved U.S. Public Law 105-115 by a nearly unanimous vote, and when President Clinton signed it into law on November 21, 1997, I was present, proud to have spearheaded the effort on behalf of both the biotechnology and pharmaceutical trade associations.

The lessons we learned in Washington also apply to dealing with local government. Lesson number 1 is to not be greedy. Ask for too much, and you're likely to end up with nothing. PhRMA, the Pharmaceutical Research and Manufacturers of America trade association, had joined BIO in making suggestions for speeding the drug review process. Some of its members were pushing for a time frame that was unreasonably short, to the extent that it could compromise patient safety. My concern was that if we made outrageous demands, the FDA wouldn't join hands with us. We needed to present a united front; otherwise, the modernization act stood little chance of passing. I imposed a rule that our recommendations had to be good for patients and the country, and not beneficial only for our industry. Anything that failed to meet these criteria was to be tossed overboard.

I said to Pete Teeley, "We've got to find some senior person at the Food and Drug Administration who could go through our proposals and tell us if there's anything goofy in here, so we can omit it before it goes before Congress." A certain person came to mind. I made the call and explained why we'd like to meet with her.

"It's a good idea," she agreed. "But I can't do it, because they keep logs of everybody we meet with in our offices, and I'm not authorized to have this kind of meeting."

"It really would make for a better bill," I countered. "Isn't there some way that we could get together?"

We agreed to meet for a drink in a hotel cocktail lounge. Pete and I went over the entire proposal with her. By the time we finished, she said approvingly, "I think everything in here makes sense."

Among the legislators present at the Congressional hearing into the proposed law were two perennial opponents of the drug industry: Rep. Henry Waxman (D-CA) and Rep. Pete Stark (D-CA). An administrator from the FDA was on the stand.

Rep. Waxman, aware that the pharmaceutical and biotechnology companies (and not the FDA) had been first to sound the call for the new law, asked him somewhat skeptically, "Does the FDA believe that the new legislation is really needed?"

"Yes, Congressman," he replied, "we do."

Waxman's face registered surprise. He asked no further questions and raised no objection to the bill. In the past, even presidential commissions hadn't been able to get FDA reform legislation through Congress. But this bill passed easily. Not only were industry and its regulatory agency both in agreement about what needed to be done, but also the measure lent itself to bipartisan support. Who could be against improving the FDA? I have been involved in countless legislative battles, and it is not unusual for members of Congress to oppose biotech on one issue and support it on another.

Lesson number 2 is to always tell the truth, no matter what, even if the facts might undermine what you're trying to accomplish. After several years of sticking steadfastly to that policy, Amgen's Washington office started receiving calls from congressional staffers asking us to verify the accuracy of information they'd received from other pharmaceutical companies. That's how much they trusted us by then.

Lesson number 3: meet with any member of a lawmaker's office. Typically, if a company expects to set up a meeting with a member of Congress, it must send its CEO. But things happen in Washington, and sometimes the congressman or senator must cancel at the last minute. The CEO is already in Washington anyway, but often he'll refuse to talk with the legislator's chief of staff, as if dealing with a staff person was beneath him. This stuff goes on all the time.

In many cases, it's more important to talk to the chief of staff than to the congressman or senator. Amgen made a rule that we would take whatever appointment we could get with whomever we could get. The more junior the person was, the more she appreciated our willingness to go ahead with the meeting, and that often worked to our advantage in the future. It's no different from the age-old advice of befriending the front-desk receptionist when you're trying to set up a job interview with the boss.

After the FDA Modernization Act passed, Amgen decided that we should thank the many unelected folks on Capitol Hill who'd had a hand in it. So we invited more than one hundred congressional staffers to a celebration dinner—no senior people, only staffers. At first, some of them thought that the invitation was intended for their bosses and had landed on their desks by mistake. No one invites D.C. staffers to a dinner out of appreciation for their hard work. But it struck us as the right thing to do. And what did it cost us? It was a drop in the bucket compared to the goodwill it generated. More importantly, many unsung heroes finally received some much-deserved recognition.

The overall experience left me with an unfashionably positive feeling about Washington, and not only because the bill passed. Despite what many folks probably think, if you have the right cause and go about advocating it in the proper way, you don't need to reach into your pocket for a large political campaign contribution. In fact, when Amgen was small, we succeeded without making any at all.

Until I started meeting legislators, I never appreciated how conscientious most of them are. They work extraordinarily long hours for not very much money. Cynics may scoff, but, by and large, most politicians do their best to make the country better in the face of many constraints, such as having to raise money for campaigns, pressure to toe the party line, and so on.

I even found myself admiring Henry Waxman, the bane of the pharmaceutical industry—proof that politics does indeed make strange bedfellows. And although I rarely agreed with Sen. Edward Kennedy, one of the industry's most outspoken critics, there's no question that he genuinely has patients' interests at heart. Whenever we requested a meeting, the senator sat down with us and listened carefully. Two years later, in 1999, he and Amgen worked closely on trying to drum up support for providing prescription drug benefits to Medicare recipients. The federal health-care program, established in 1965, had not kept pace with advances in medicine. All manner of costly surgeries remained covered, but no medications, even though prescription drugs had become the primary remedy for many health problems.

Kennedy proposed that the additional funds could be siphoned from the Taxpayer Refund and Relief Act of 1999. For a while, it looked as if we might have enough Senate votes. But ultimately, the amendment went down to defeat, 45 to 55. All except two of the nays came from the Republican side, and the yeas were exclusively Democrat, with one exception.

The loss, though disappointing, did not dampen my faith in the system. (Several years later, a Medicare drug benefit became law.) With cynicism toward politicians rampant these days, most folks probably think that the only way to get anything done in Washington is through Public Action Committees (PACs) making large campaign contributions to mercenary representatives more interested in getting reelected than on doing something good for the country. I'm not naive; I know that it happens.

It's not the only way, however. You can take the high road and succeed, as Amgen did. Our success is proof that there are still honest, conscientious people in our government. If they were as incompetent or corrupt as skeptics would have you believe, Amgen's serve-the-country-first, tell-the-truth position would not have worked to our advantage.

"WE HAVE TO DO THIS TRIAL"

"When in doubt, do the right thing"—so maintained Roy Ash, co-founder and president of Litton Industries. That was Amgen's philosophy, too. My favorite story about Amgen best encapsulates its view of itself and its place in the world.

One time in the 1990s, a bunch of us were discussing the possibility of testing Epogen in infants. Pediatricians had been using the drug for a rare type of anemia seen exclusively in babies, even though it had been tested only in adults. Conducting clinical trials with infants might yield more specific information that could be highly useful to physicians, particularly in terms of dosages and schedules.

However, every logical argument pointed to not going ahead with the study. It was not required by the FDA, it would be costly, and it could be risky.

"No mother is going to give us permission to enroll her baby in a clinical trial."

"Hardly any children have this form of anemia anyway."

"They're already getting Epogen, and it's helping."

"To do a clinical trial isn't going to help sales."

Finally, Dan Vapnek, the head of research, spoke up. "We *have* to do this trial," he said intensely. Everybody else looked at him as if to say, *Haven't you been listening?* "It's our product. Those infants need this product. And their pediatricians need to have the information to use our product properly in those infants. So we have to do this trial."

I looked around the room. No one said a word. Decision made, meeting over. Everyone stood up and filed out. From a commercial standpoint, it was not the wisest choice. But we had an ethical obligation, we were in the business of health care, and therefore we should just do it.

I was never prouder of Amgen than at that moment.

12

My Failed Retirement

THE FINAL CHAPTER OF an executive's tour of duty can't be written until after he's moved on, because one of his hardest jobs—particularly if he's the chief executive officer—is to select and install a successor.

When Kevin Sharer joined Amgen as chief operating officer and president in 1992, retirement wasn't even on the horizon for me. Our instructions to the executive search firm we hired were to find someone who could eventually be a candidate for the CEO position. It wasn't preordained that the new COO *would* ascend to the top, but he or she should at least be capable of being considered for the job.

Some chief execs handpick a virtual clone of themselves as their number two. Although that might seem appropriate for a biotechnology firm, I believe it's a mistake for any company in any field. One of the things I liked best about Kevin was that although we shared a common background—both engineers, both naval officers (Sharer aboard a nuclear submarine)—he was different from me. I liked the science side best, whereas he gravitated toward sales and marketing. That made for a good fit.

Not long after Kevin's arrival, there was little doubt that someday the board would approve him as my successor. The only question was when. I'll be perfectly honest: I loved running Amgen and wasn't in any hurry to retire. However, when word gets out that someone is in line for the number 1 job, he becomes fair game for other companies on the hunt for a CEO.

By 1999, Kevin was probably getting the proverbial seven-year itch, and I knew it. One day Ed Garnett walked into my office and tossed his keys onto my desk.

"What's this?" I said.

"Are you going to walk in here one day and just throw your keys on the desk and say 'I'm leaving today—good luck'?"

"Of course not."

"Well," he said, "don't you think you ought to talk to people you really trust about working out a transition program?"

"Yeah, probably," I said. "But I'm dreading it."

I decided to announce my retirement plans publicly on December 7, 1999—that it happened to be Pearl Harbor Day was purely coincidental. The coming year seemed ideal for the transfer of leadership. I'd be turning sixty-five in September, but more significantly, Amgen's pipeline would be turning out three new drugs in the near future: anakinra (Kineret) for rheumatoid arthritis, along with our second-generation colony-stimulating factors darbepoetin alfa (Aranesp) and pegfilgrastim (Neulasta). My stepping down as CEO on May 11, 2000, at our annual shareholders' meeting, would get the Sharer era off to a brisk start, just as George Rathmann had done to my benefit. Since my leaving Amgen, launches of new medications have become even more involved and expensive, so today you might initiate the changing of the guard at least two years in advance.

I chose to do one thing very differently than George had: to limit my service as chairman of the board to six months after my retirement as CEO, and part-time at that. A new CEO can benefit greatly from the previous chief executive's experience during the first few months. But over time, the predecessor becomes less informed, and his usefulness fades rather quickly.

Moreover, I knew that I would be uncomfortable continuing to stay at Amgen for too long. You come to work, but you almost hope that no one knocks on your door, because if they do you're afraid you'll be tempted to meddle. And if no one asks for your advice, you're not contributing, so why are you there? Six months seemed right; whatever hadn't transitioned by then probably wasn't going to transition successfully anyway.

"There is a time for everyone to retire," I told Amgen's employees in my farewell speech, as Adele, along with my sons Todd and Brant, looked on from the audience. "My time is now." The smile on my face, I said, could be explained by everything we had accomplished together over the past twelve years. Kevin was inheriting a company with a market value of more than $60 billion; nearly seven thousand employees in eighteen countries; a campus of more than thirty buildings; and a research and development budget of $845 million, or 27 percent of its sales revenue—almost twice the average percentage for the top ten pharmaceutical companies in the United States. And for the third year in a row, Amgen had just been named one of the one hundred best companies to work for by *Fortune*.

At the same time, I added, my heart was heavy "because I will miss Amgen so much and miss all of you in so many ways.

"So long, good-bye, and God bless you all."

ONE FINAL BATTLE

Days later I was sitting in Boston's magnificent ten-story brick-and-granite U.S. courthouse, perched on the city's historic harbor.

Our latest patient-infringement lawsuit revolved again around Epogen. The offender this time was a small biotech firm from Cambridge, Massachusetts, called Transkaryotic Therapies (TKT). Also named in the suit was its partner, European pharmaceutical behemoth

Aventis, formerly known as Hoechst Marion Roussel. It was our contention that TKT, founded by a Harvard researcher who specialized in gene therapy, had violated eighteen claims spread across five patents on EPO and the process for manufacturing it.

Briefly, the company used a different method called gene activation (GA) to manufacture its own EPO. Gene activation doesn't rely on genetic engineering, in that none of the DNA used by a cell to make EPO has been inserted into the cell; it simply rearranges the existing DNA. Although TKT could be congratulated on a clever scientific achievement, it didn't mark an advance over recombinant engineering, only a different route to the same destination. Even if it had been superior, that didn't entitle the company to profit from Amgen's patented product.

Having the trial set in Boston was inconvenient but necessary. We wanted this nuisance over with. If you sue a company outside its hometown, it might request a change of venue. By suing in Boston, we had precluded that action. A second consideration was that we hoped the case would be tried by Judge William Young. He'd presided over our legal clash versus Genetics Institute/Chugai years before and had impressed us with his fairness and discipline. In addition, his familiarity with Epogen and Amgen's patents could be expected to bring about a speedier decision. Indeed, he was appointed to hear the case.

A month before the trial commenced, Judge Young granted a summary judgment in our favor, contending that TKT/Aventis's EPO infringed patent number 5,955,422: "a pharmaceutical composition comprising a therapeutically effective amount of human erythropoietin and a pharmaceutically acceptable diluent, adjuvant, or carrier, wherein said erythropoietin is purified from mammalian cells grown in culture." The other claims would be decided in court.

For TKT to win the case, it would have to convince the judge that for each of our other four patents, the patent was either (1) not valid, (2) not infringed, or (3) unenforceable. In every patent case, there is a legal presumption that the U.S. Patent and Trademark Office is competent, and that places a heavy burden on proving invalidity.

Almost every stock analyst gave TKT little to no chance of pulling off a sweep. Yet during the twenty-three-day trial, stretched over four months, more than one hundred business reporters, Wall Streeters, and patent attorneys packed the courtroom—including patent counsels for other biotech firms—because of the case's far-reaching implications. If TKT triumphed, it might open the floodgates for any company to copy and market virtually any genetically engineered medication; one that another firm had spent hundreds of millions of dollars and many years to develop.

We considered TKT's stand laughable. Nevertheless, we took it seriously, thanks in part to a valuable lesson I had learned while at Harvard Business School: even if an opponent's actions make no sense to you, they apparently make sense *to him*. Therefore, you must consider the other party's thought process. Does he know something you don't? Why weren't the people at TKT saying to themselves, "We don't have a prayer of winning this lawsuit."

Here's my guess as to what was going through the minds of TKT officials: if you estimate that defending yourself in a lawsuit like this would cost about $20 million to $25 million but a win would net you more than $1 billion, it's worth doing even if the likelihood of prevailing is only 5 percent. Think about it: If money weren't an object, wouldn't you bet $20 million for a possible payout of $1 billion, with your chances being 1 in 20? In fact, it wouldn't be farfetched to say that successfully capsizing Amgen's Epogen patents could be worth as much as $5 billion to TKT. So even at 1-in-100 odds, it's a reasonable gamble.

Other factors probably contributed to TKT's decision to forge ahead: money wasn't an object, because wealthy partner Aventis was footing the legal bill. And in the short term, at least, the publicity from the trial coverage would undoubtedly boost the firm's stock. That is exactly what happened in June, when Judge Young let TKT/Aventis off the hook on patent number 5,618,698, probably the weakest of the four. In essence, he'd been persuaded that TKT's technique for producing EPO was sufficiently different from Amgen's. At the same time, he denied the defendant's motion for noninfringement of patent number 5,547,933. Transkaryotic Therapies had hinted to Wall Street that a win over Amgen would free it to produce knock-offs of nearly every genetically engineered medication. So the victory, though slight, sent tremors through the stock exchange. Our price dipped by roughly 5 percent, and our adversary's leaped 35 percent.

The mood of this trial contrasted sharply with the atmosphere at the Genetics Institute/Chugai arbitration hearing. At that one, GI's president, Gabe Schmergel, and I frequently walked to and from the courthouse together, chatting amiably. Although each of us disagreed with the other's legal position, we remained friends and continued to have great respect for each other's company.

However, we had nothing but contempt for Transkaryotic Therapies, and the animosity pervaded the courtroom. During this time, my TKT counterpart and I both testified at a congressional hearing. At the end, as everyone was gathering papers and other belongings, I said icily to him, "I don't understand why you would want to be the CEO of a company whose entire research effort is devoted to knocking off other companies' patents." I'm not proud of the remark, which was out of character for me, but that's how irritated I was by the whole business. He angrily denied that was the case, and we both stalked away.

The Amgen-TKT trial concluded on September 8, four days after my sixty-fifth birthday. Judge Young had advised both sides that his decision would take several months. Shortly after I left Amgen for good on the first of the year, the court handed down a 244-page ruling. Transkaryotic Therapies, which needed to bat 1,000, lost two of the three remaining patent disputes. The court found the company guilty of infringing all three claims related to patent number 5,621,080 and four out of five claims of patent number 5,756,349.

"In order to avoid infringing a product claim," the judge wrote, "a competitor must not make that product regardless of whether the process used to do so differs in some way from the process or processes described in the patent. If indeed the same product is ultimately obtained, it matters not that in order to do so the competitor tweaked the process in some matter." In other words, you cannot skirt a product patent simply by using a different method to make it. The ruling, later upheld on appeal, was widely regarded as good not only for Amgen but also for the biotech industry at large.

MY LEGACY

When assessing the legacy of any business leader and assigning credit or blame, you must take into account the company he took over as well as the one he left behind. That's especially true in the biotechnology field, with its lead time of many years. I'm proud of everything that Amgen accomplished under my stewardship—and of my earlier contributions as CFO—but as for summing up my twelve years as chief executive officer, I prefer to let some of the people who worked under me have a crack at it.

> *Dennis Fenton (at Amgen from 1981 to present):* To follow the founder is incredibly hard, no matter where you are. George Rathmann was beloved. Gordon stepped into the CEO job and did it right. He didn't declare wholesale changes. He's a very patient and thoughtful person. He knew where he wanted to go, and he didn't mind taking his time to get there. So you've got to give Gordon a lot of credit for that. His personality was really what the company needed at the time, too.

> *Kevin Sharer (at Amgen from 1992 to present):* Although I got to Amgen a few years after Gordon become CEO, he encountered three gigantic obstacles that he very skillfully overcame. First of all, he was put in a shotgun marriage with Harry

Hixon. Number two, he followed George Rathmann, this legendary guy who everybody loves. And third, it couldn't have been easy having George hanging around as company chairman. That's a tough situation for anybody. To Gordon's enormous credit, he won over the company, he worked with Hixon long enough to become the unquestioned number one, and he delivered the results. He did a magnificent job. Just magnificent.

Let me tell you what Gordon is really good at: He's a good decision maker, deliberate and thoughtful, never rash. There was no question that as the leader of Amgen, he was fully invested in the mission of the company. It was always about Amgen, not Gordon as some kind of personality.

He was willing to take risks. He would bet the company if he had to and was enormously courageous in doing that.

Finally, he was probably at his best when things were at their worst. He was a leader who, when things got difficult, he would get constructive, not destructive. That's hard to do.

Ed Garnett (at Amgen from 1986 to 2002): Gordon had huge shoes to fill, because George Rathmann is a legend. But so is Gordon, although in his typically humble way he'd be the first to deny it. If you look at the history of any organization, there's usually the founder, followed by the builder, and then the changer. That certainly is true of Amgen, with George being the founder, Gordon the builder, and Kevin the changer. Enormous growth took place on his watch. Would it have happened under someone else? Probably, but not to the same extent, and it wouldn't have been the same organization.

MY FAILED RETIREMENT

My wife, who has been a crucial source of encouragement throughout my career, and whom I can always count on for a frank opinion, told me flat out that I would flunk retirement. My sons seconded their mother's prediction. I knew it myself but wasn't sure what my next step should be.

Adele and I attended Amgen's annual meeting and then took a long vacation aboard a private boat that sailed around Majorca and Menorca, a pair of enchanting islands off the southeastern coast of Spain in the deep-blue waters of the Mediterranean, another of Adele's great ideas. For three weeks, we did absolutely nothing, and it was marvelous and strange at the same time. (Let me qualify that: every morning the boat's three-man crew deposited me ashore so that I could go jogging.)

Other than that, we just sailed around. Sometimes we'd fire up the engines, depending on the wind. It was relaxing, a perfect way to unwind after many years of hard work. I'd never taken a vacation that long in my life, and I highly recommend it to all retirees. The trip also gave me time to think about what I might want to do next.

After eighteen years, it seemed sensible to remain in biotechnology in some form and not have to learn a new industry at age sixty-five. However, becoming chief executive of another biotech firm—or any company—was definitely not on my list.

To get a biotech firm off the ground requires a triumvirate of entrepreneurs, private investors, and venture capitalists. I liked the idea of moving to the venture capital side. Joining an existing VC firm wasn't an option: none of any significance as far as biotechnology was concerned existed in the Los Angeles area, which had perennially trailed Boston, San Francisco, and San Diego as a hub of biomedical activity. The answer, therefore, was to start one in this under-served part of the country. In 2001, the year I founded Coastview Capital, L.A. County start-ups in the fields of biotechnology, medical devices, and health services took in $65 million in venture capital funding, compared with $681 million for new firms in San Diego.

Coastview invested in biotechnology firms at all stages of development. What we looked for in a prospective start-up calls to mind

Amgen in its early years: innovative, groundbreaking research; well-qualified management, skilled both in business and in science; and ambitions for products or technologies that could be expected to affect patients' lives significantly.

Given those criteria, most business proposals fall short, especially on the science end. Sometimes a field just isn't ready. For example, gene therapy is an exciting concept, but it is so far from becoming a reality commercially that I don't think venture capitalists should invest in it now. Other liabilities, from a VC perspective, include the following:

- The science is too old or has been attempted without success in the past.

- A comparable existing therapy is so effective that it probably couldn't be improved to any meaningful degree.

- The potential product's market is too limited to justify the expense of research and development.

- The idea is off-the-wall crazy.

Examples of each have crossed my desk at one time or another. Sometimes you can judge the caliber of the science by the credentials of the people involved. The likelihood that third-rate scientists will produce something of significance wasn't something we were willing to bet on. Similarly, we scrutinized the track records of a new company's managers. Where did they go to school? Who was their thesis adviser, and how well respected? How successful were their previous business ventures? And so on.

In 2002, in the aftermath of the 9/11 terrorist attacks, I started my jet aircraft charter company, Prime Jet. It is extremely successful. One reason is that it operates on the same values and principles that underpinned Amgen's success, demonstrating their universality. They worked at Amgen. They are working at Prime Jet. And they can work for you and your company too, no matter what business you're in.

Acknowledgments

Gordon Binder: Thanks to my wife, Adele, for your love and for making our marriage such a happy one. Thanks also for your wise counsel and unwavering support throughout my business life. Without you, this book wouldn't exist.

Thanks also to my sons, Brant and Todd, who are a great source of pride to me and my wife. Both have MBAs from leading universities, and I am proud to say that our relationship has reached the crossover point, with my sons now providing more counsel and advice to me than I am able to give them.

Thanks, too, to my invaluable assistant Lorraine Shulman.

Finally, I am grateful to Adele, Brant, and Todd for accepting without complaint the long hours, extensive travel, and disruptive job changes that a successful business career requires.

Philip Bashe: Thanks to Robert and Rachelle Bashe, the late Evelyn Bashe, Justin Bashe, and, as always, Patty Romanowski Bashe, for everything.

Together we'd like to thank our talented editor at Harvard Business School Press, Jacqueline Murphy, for her expert guidance and support; editorial director Hollis Heimbouch; associate editor Astrid Sandoval;

copy editor Betsy Hardinger; senior production editor Marcy Barnes-Henrie; jacket designer Stephani Finks; jacket copy writer Laurie Ardito; and literary agent James Levine and everyone else at Levine-Greenberg Literary Agency, Inc.

Thanks also go to the following, at Amgen, Inc., and elsewhere, for sharing their memories and insights: alphabetically, they are Kirby Alton, Burt D. Ensley, Dennis Fenton, Frederick Frank, Edward F. Garnett, Ted Ledder, George Rathmann, Kevin Sharer, Daniel Vapnek, and Bob Weist.

Finally, very special thanks to Peter Teeley for suggesting that the two of us collaborate on a book. Good advice!

A NOTE ON QUOTED MATERIAL

Most of the people quoted in *Science Lessons* kindly agreed to share their perspectives in interviews that were conducted in California or over the telephone in late 2004 and early 2005. Thanks again to my fellow Amgen CEOs George Rathmann and Kevin Sharer, as well as Dennis Fenton, Kirby Alton, Ed Garnett, Burt Ensley, Ted Ledder, Bob Weist, and Fred Frank.

Other quotations have been reconstructed as faithfully as possible from memory: things that were either said directly to me or recounted to me by another source. Any errors contained in these quotes are my own.

Index

About the Authors

GORDON M. BINDER is the managing director of Coastview Capital, LLC, a Los Angeles venture capital firm he founded in 2001. From 1982 to 1988, he served as chief financial officer of Amgen, the world's largest and most successful biotechnology company, and then became its chief executive officer (1988 through 2000) and chairman of the board (1990 through 2000) until his retirement. He is also the founder of Prime Jet, a jet-charter company.

Binder earned a bachelor's degree in electrical engineering from Purdue University in 1957 and an MBA from Harvard Business School in 1962, where he was a Baker Scholar. From 1957 to 1960, he served aboard the USS *Intrepid* as a U.S. Navy officer. He and his wife Adele reside in the Holmby Hills section of Los Angeles. They are the parents of two grown sons, Brant and Todd.

PHILIP BASHE has written or cowritten seventeen titles, spanning several genres, including health and self-help, parenting, sports, biography, autobiography, and popular culture. He lives in Baldwin, New York, with his wife author Patricia Romanowski Bashe and their son Justin.